Afterlife of the Theatre of the Absurd

The Avant-garde, Spectatorship, and Psychoanalysis

P.I.E. Peter Lang

Bruxelles · Bern · Berlin · New York · Oxford · Wien

Lara Cox

Afterlife of the Theatre of the Absurd

The Avant-garde, Spectatorship, and Psychoanalysis

Dramaturgies
Vol. 37

I would like to thank Lisa Downing, David Jones, and Fiona Cox for their invaluable advice. I also gratefully acknowledge the help and support of my parents, Natasha Alperowicz and Tony Cox, the Arts and Humanities Research Council, and the Entente Cordiale initiative at the French Embassy in London.
© Luigi Ciminaghi/Piccolo Teatro di Milano.
© Lucie Jansch.

Cover picture: The entrance doors to the Théâtre de la Huchette (Paris), showing the first actors of the theatre's production of The Bald Soprano (La Cantatrice chauve). Ionesco's play has been performed uninterruptedly in this theatre since 1957. Graphic design by Massin based on a photograph by Henry Cohen, 1964.

The book was subject to a double blind refereeing process.

© P.I.E. PETER LANG s.a.
   Éditions scientifiques internationales
   Brussels, 2018
   1 avenue Maurice, B-1050 Brussels, Belgium
   brussels@peterlang.com; www.peterlang.com

ISSN 1376-3199
ISBN 978-2-8076-0191-8
ePDF 978-2-8076-0354-7
ePub 978-2-8076-0355-4
Mobi 978-2-8076-0356-1
DOI 10.3726/b13521
D/2018/5678/32

CIP available from the British Library and from the Library of Congress, USA.

Bibliographic information published by "Die Deutsche Nationalbibliothek".

"Die Deutsche Nationalbibliothek" lists this publication in the "Deutsche National-bibliografie"; detailed bibliographic data is available on the Internet at <http://dnb.de>.

"There is scarcely any passion without struggle."
Albert Camus (*The Myth of Sisyphus* 73).

Table of Contents

Introduction

This book is about the social subversions that are lost when a past experimental theatre movement – the Theatre of the Absurd in this case – becomes stamped with the seal of the "avant-garde". More particularly, it is about the contemporary form of these lost social subversions and the present-day possibilities for resistant viewing of an avant-garde from the past. I take the Theatre of the Absurd, which hails from a period of post-World War II France, to contest the broader idea that past vanguard movements' capacity to subvert social norms are eroded with time. The Theatre of the Absurd, "an immensely successful avant-garde" (7) as drama critic Tom Bishop describes, is taken as a case study that is reflective of broader trends about vanguard movements.

Before considering the Theatre of the Absurd further, it is useful to consult a definition of the avant-garde. The Oxford English dictionary defines the avant-garde as "new and experimental ideas and methods in art, music, or literature". When the term "avant-garde" is employed in conversation, it is usually synonymous with the notion of pushing artistic boundaries, whether in fashion, theatre, dance or poetry or elsewhere. This OED definition usefully indicates that to be vanguard is not just to push boundaries; it is also to center on the idea of creative youth – "*new* and experimental ideas" (my emphasis). Another synonym for avant-garde is "cutting-edge", the idea of being at the forefront of artistic norms and patterns. The pursuit of the avant-garde is to push the boundaries of what art is presently capable of. Vanguard movements pose this challenge to artistic norms. However, they also tend to become artistic norms in their own right, when public tastes have adapted to them, in what vanguard theorist Paul Mann describes as "a theory-death of the avant-garde" (15). Any single avant-garde movement, in other words, never lasts for long. It becomes the artistic norm and is constantly replaced by new and improved avant-gardes. A quick look at the long succession of some of the "isms" in European art during the twentieth century elucidates this: Expressionism, Dadaism, and Futurism in the early twentieth century, Surrealism (during the interwar years), and Minimalism and Situationism in the post-war years and the latter half of the century. While no single avant-garde lasts for long, the vanguard pulse of perpetually defying what art is capable of is one that remains locked in the present.

What gets left behind in this formulation is how avant-gardes of the past, once themselves new and present, might *still* be capable of subversion and pushing boundaries today. By pushing boundaries, I do not mean challenging current artistic parameters. Each avant-garde of the past fits into the history of an art medium and contributes to aesthetic trends today. It would be impossible to claim that past avant-gardes defy present-day aesthetic patterns. Rather, I mean to signal the capacity of past avant-gardes to spread "experimental ideas", to recall the first half of the OED's definition of the vanguard, in our contemporary moment. The avant-garde has never just been about experimentation in form; the capacity to shake up social norms has always been soldered to a definition of the avant-garde too. This is implicit in the OED's reference to "*experimental ideas* and methods in art, music, or literature" (my emphasis). Indeed, as prominent critic in vanguard studies Mike Sell observes, in *Avant-Garde Performance and the Limits of Criticism* (2005), social "antagonism" is always coupled with the idea of aesthetic "innovation" (46) in a notion of the avant-garde.

The central idea of this book picks up on this idea of the vanguard as socially antagonistic. It suggests that simply because an avant-garde hailing from the past can no longer be branded experimental in formal method, it does not follow that the avant-garde's capacity to spread socially subversive ideas has been erased too. As will be examined shortly, too many critics assume that past avant-gardes have lost their ability to challenge social norms. Aesthetic innovation tends to dominate definitions of a vanguard movement to the extent that once an avant-garde is no longer deemed "new", it is presumed to have lost the ability to antagonize social norms.

Let us take the case study of this book, the theatrical movement of the "Theatre of the Absurd", to consider this point more closely. The Theatre of the Absurd was composed of a heterogeneous body of plays by Eugène Ionesco, Arthur Adamov, Samuel Beckett, Jean Genet, and Fernando Arrabal among others, which were staged in experimental settings in Paris in the wake of World War II. Martin Esslin, the man who coined the label "The Theatre of the Absurd" in his book of the same name published in 1961, asserted that these playwrights' work attempted to come to terms with the senselessness of the horrifically bloody war that had finished and left Europe in a state of devastation in the years following 1945. To convey such senselessness, the Theatre of the Absurd reduced plot and character details to a bare minimum. The Theatre of the Absurd diverged from the classic Aristotelian model of theatre, where a complication (the central "knot" or "nœud") that would drive the plot would be resolved in the ending or *dénouement*.

For its never-before-seen minimalism, the Theatre of the Absurd was swiftly stamped as "avant-garde". Yet the Theatre of the Absurd was also the victim of the highly temporary state of newness that dominates definitions of the avant-garde. Less than a decade after the entry of Ionesco's and Beckett's plotless dramas, *The Bald Soprano* and *Waiting for Godot* (both 1950), into Parisian theatres, the Theatre of the Absurd's ability to spread disruptive ideas about society and social norms was considered moribund. In 1956, semiologist Roland Barthes prophesied the "slow death" of Absurdism, "because the bourgeoisie will recuperate it altogether, ultimately putting on splendid evenings of Beckett [...] and tomorrow Ionesco" (Barthes 69). For Barthes, the avant-garde may at first be "the parasite" of the bourgeoisie, challenging dominant ideas and attitudes in this privileged social class, but it eventually becomes its "property" (69). Once disruptive of the tastes of the middle classes and the wealthy, the Theatre of the Absurd would be put on for the pleasure of this social group.

Barthes frames the Theatre of the Absurd as a once-destabilizing force on social class that had run out of subversive steam just six short years after Beckett's *Waiting for Godot* and Ionesco's *The Bald Soprano* – two plays where nothing much happens – rocked Parisian theatregoing audiences. Yet simply because a movement has been recuperated or popularized, this does not mean that theatre cannot continue to disrupt social norms from *within* its site of its social containment. As proponents of the "cultural turn" from the Birmingham School (Hal Foster, Raymond Williams, etc.) recount, popular art can be subversive despite its function in the marketplace as a commodity of the leisure-pursuing public.[1] Indeed, our era of advanced capitalism more or less dictates that no artwork can withstand the pressures of commercialization for long. Art almost always has a market value too, which means that we need to look for the social

---

[1] For instance: Hal, Foster (ed.). *The Anti-Aesthetic: Essays on Postmodern Culture*. Port Townsend: Washington Bay Press, 1983.

politics of art elsewhere than in its ability to stand outside of economic exchange.

Past avant-gardes may thus still be subversive of social norms even if they have become eminently marketable. But we cannot expect an Absurdist play's disruptions to social patterns to look the same today as in the past. Times change and so too do social norms; vanguard subversions of historically contingent norms will mutate too. An adequate critical tool is required to draw out contemporary social politics from past vanguard work.

Psychoanalysis, the school of thought first pioneered by Sigmund Freud at the turn of the twentieth century, is fruitful here. Freud focused on the idea of the unconscious, the psychical underside that was opposed to conscious, rational life. The unconscious may emerge in dreams, fantasies, slips of the tongue, or other arenas such as contemplating art or watching theatre. Post-Freudian philosopher Michel de Certeau, in *The Writing of History* (1975), argued that psychoanalysis "locates its veritable meaning not in the elucidations with which it replaces former representations, but in the ever-unfinished *act* of elucidation" (303). Explorations of the unconscious can keep rewriting our understanding of the past, challenging our assumptions of what we thought history or in this case historicized theatre movements were. The concept of psychoanalytic heuristic interminability, "the ever-unfinished *act* of elucidation", may renew our apprehension of past avant-garde movements whose meaning was considered settled long ago. I perform psychoanalytic readings of Absurdist plays to seek out new meaning from them. By placing these readings into dialogue with thought about current social, sexual, gendered and racial norms, I determine how the psychoanalytic "ever-unfinished *act* of elucidation" may reveal unconscious reactions to the Theatre of the Absurd in the present and in turn how these plays may subvert some of the dominant ideologies that define our present era. In so doing, I anticipate some of the politicizing effects that the Theatre of the Absurd produces in spectators today.

With all this in mind, let me state the mission of this book: five plays by five different writers of the Theatre of the Absurd are examined for their potential to spark subversions in the contemporary moment. Psychoanalysis, a tool that permits the exploration of new life in past work via the unconscious, is applied to each play to theorize how contemporary spectators might view it today. These plays have been chosen doubly for the unconscious form that they evoke and their content. Indeed, each play's content evinces a temporal plasticity allowing it to adapt to the current moment. In chapter one, Eugène Ionesco's *The Bald Soprano* is deemed to challenge the contemporary spectator's ideas about gender and sexuality. In chapter two, it is the notion of "docile patriotism", contemporary society's lack of protest about waging war in Islamic countries, that is disturbed in the spectator's mind when watching Arthur Adamov's *Off Limits*. In chapter three, Samuel Beckett's *Not I* entreats present-day viewers to reconsider a current norm of "gender exceptionalism", which deems that it is up to the Western world and mainstream Western feminism to rescue Muslim women from Islamic patriarchy. In chapter four, Jean Genet's *The Blacks* subverts gendered racism, the double form of discrimination that women of color face owing to their gender and their race, which absents black women from the social conversation about US state and police violence against black communities (as seen in the Black Lives Matter movement). In chapter five, spectators of Fernando Arrabal's *And They Put Handcuffs on the Flowers*, are persuaded to review their unquestioning faith in the present American Prison Industrial Complex (PIC), a for-profit system of incarceration that disproportionately targets people of color and the LGBT community.

It is to be noted that this book is about theoretical possibilities for subversive viewing of the Theatre of the Absurd in the present moment and not about empirical reality. I do not propose that the arguments set out in the chapters that follow are certain to occur in real-life spectatorship, but I hold fast to the capacity of theory to revive texts long ago considered devoid of subversive clout because newer avant-gardes came to replace historical ones.

The Theatre of the Absurd has become critically ossified as will be explored later in the introduction. The movement was assumed to convey messages of existential anguish, which were heavily anchored in the post-war European context. Critical stagnation is symptomatic of a broader issue in avant-garde studies: that is, historical avant-gardes are not generally thought capable of current-day subversions. Since the Theatre of the Absurd is a case in point of a general critical trend surrounding vanguards, the first part of this introduction goes into patterns in avant-garde studies to demonstrate how our exploration of Absurdism will make an intervention in this field. We then move onto the history of the Theatre of the Absurd more specifically to show how this book will enrich critical trends on this theatrical movement. The final part of the introduction delves into a fuller explanation of my chosen methodology, which combines a psychoanalytic conceptual toolkit with feminism and queer theory in order to revive Absurdist plays.

Avant-Garde Exhaustion: An Exhausted Theory

The term "avant-garde" is a military denomination by origin, referring to the front-rows of troops in battle, in contradistinction to the "rear-guard". In the early nineteenth century, however, "avant-garde" began to refer to the most voracious part of the modernist drive for innovation in technology. The avant-garde's first appearances in language were not cultural, as we may think now whenever the term is evoked, but first military and then social. The French socio-political movement of Saint-Simonianism considered evolutions in technology and industry to be the main source of social progress. With projects such as the Suez Canal, the Saint-Simonians bridged the divide between the term's militaristic origins and its social extension, preceding in the same gesture the "cultural turn" of the avant-garde, as Mike Sell terms the vanguard's cultural application, a few decades on (*The Avant-Garde: Race, Religion, War* 92-98). By the last quarter of the nineteenth century, the term "avant-garde" started to be used for cultural products that fused the aesthetically innovative with the politically radical. The Decadent journal *La Revue Indépendante*, spawned in the wake of the 1871 Paris Commune, and Russian revolutionary Mikhail Bakunin's review *L'Avant-garde* of 1878 constitute two of the earliest (albeit short-lived) sources that used the "avant-garde" as an artistic designation (Innes 1; Poggioli 11).

A foremost proponent of the artistic-cultural turn of the avant-garde is neo-Hegelian critic Peter Bürger, who exemplified Marcel Duchamp's 1917 work *Fountain* in his seminal *The Theory of the Avant-Garde* (1974). This work would define understandings in the field of avant-garde studies for years to come. Bürger propounded that early artistic avant-garde movements – Surrealism, Dadaism, Futurism, and Expressionism, and so on – overturned the high modernist mantra of art for art's sake (*l'art pour l'art*). Duchamp's signed urinal, brazenly claiming the status of art, provided a critique of what institutions and their norms held "good art" to be. Bürger translated the vanguard assault on good or respectable art into Hegelian terminology. A synthesis or "sublation" of the oppositional artwork with the "praxis of life" (54) took place in the avant-garde gesture in opposition to high modernism's isolationism of separating art from life, as its mantra "art for art's sake" demonstrated.

This synthesis of radical aesthetics and radical politics continues to underwrite theories of the avant-garde today. As Mike Sell describes, the following that Bürger has garnered has been so legion that he has his own "Eulogist School" of critics who have followed in his wake (*Avant-garde Performance and the Limits of Criticism* 197). This school reduced heterogeneous avant-gardes to one theory about the fusion of aesthetics and radical politics.

That being said, a number of other assertions lurking behind Bürger's, and his followers', arguments have been unpicked and problematized in recent years – the first being that "radical aesthetics" should necessarily have a left wing, progressive, or anarchic flavor. This is what Kimberly Jannarone's *Artaud and His Doubles* demonstrates with reference to avant-garde darling Antonin Artaud. "'Revolution', after all, does not always represent a progressive move – many right-wing movements and indeed fascisms have called themselves 'revolutions'", cautions this critic (Jannarone 15). By turning to the archive, Jannarone illustrates that Artaud's model of a "theatre of cruelty", which aimed to stir spectators' pursuit of emancipation via the creation of a chaos akin to that created in the great plagues of history, cannot be separated from a historical backdrop of a rising tide of European Fascism, and the crowd-controlling techniques (so deftly parodied by Charlie Chaplin's pop cultural, non-vanguard, rendition of Hitler) that developed during this period. Similarly, Mike Sell's (2005, 2012) and James Harding's works (2010, 2013) have laid bare the European imperialism, misogyny, racism, and religious fanaticism underlying some of the most commonly accepted histories of the avant-garde. Their books point to new counter-colonialist, feminist, and religious vanguard energies in the past that the official stories have eclipsed. Included in the tally of forgotten vanguards are feminist radical Valerie Solanas and performance artist Yoko Ono whom Harding analyzes in his book *Cutting Performances: Collage Events, Feminist Artists, and the American Avant-garde* (2013). This book argues that feminist avant-garde performance artists of the twentieth century enlisted collage technique and practices. Contesting the white hegemony of the best-known avant-gardes, Sell's works unearth among other examples the Black Arts Movement (BAM) (2005) and the Southern Christian Leadership Conference that birthed the Civil Rights speeches of Martin Luther King Jr (2012).

What these and various other collections have signaled is that a nuanced, case-by-case reassessment of avant-garde manifestations and their politics is required. More specifically, Sell's and Harding's revisionist accounts indicate a sociological turn in avant-garde studies that the current book sympathizes with. Let us turn to Sell's work in particular to contextualize this maneuver. In *Avant-Garde Performance and the Limits of Criticism* (2005), Sell identifies the twin pillars of "innovation" and "antagonism" supporting the theory of avant-garde politics as mentioned earlier. He advocates considering the category of "antagonism" (46) in terms of social context in particular. This redefinition affords Sell a departure point for an analysis of the forgotten American counterculture, namely, the Fluxus and Happening events, the BAM, and The Living Theatre's production of Jack Gelber's *The Connection*. Sell problematizes the fact that avant-garde theorists have not sufficiently separated a vanguard work's aesthetic "innovation" from its capacity for social "antagonism". The social politics of avant-garde works has too frequently been measured in terms of a work's being ahead of its time aesthetically or artistically. This is a modernist tenet that needs updating, insists Sell. The modernists aimed to create social progress via aesthetic innovation.

Aesthetic innovation has been collapsed into social politics, or better put, social politics is only judged according to what the work does to subvert artistic norms. The problem with the collapsing of social antagonism or politics into a notion of aesthetic progress is that a work becomes divorced from the ideas of political principal and conviction. Both leftist-socialist and extreme right-wing-totalitarian movements may be defined as radically vanguard when their politics are framed entirely in terms of an ideal of progress. Sell demonstrates this in *The Avant-Garde: Race, Religion, War* (2011). This book exposes both socialist/anarchist and totalitarian vanguard manifestations throughout modernity. For instance, Martin Luther King Jr.'s leadership of the Civil Rights movement and the Ku Klux Klan can both be defined as avant-garde. To distinguish what makes certain vanguards favorable to promoting egalitarian politics, Sell performs a case-by-case reassessment of how each radical movement derives from, interacts with, and/or contests microcosmic manifestations of power. This critic's revision of a notion of vanguard politics is Foucauldian in inflection.

I favor Sell's rejection of monolithic notions of vanguard social progress and his commitment to analyzing various cultural artifacts' interconnections with "power's expansion and insinuation, centralization and fracturing, reformation and radical revisioning" (48) at the microcosmic level. Rather than focusing on historical context as this critic does, however, the chapters that follow concern themselves with how each avant-garde play sits in tension with quotidian ideologies that inform our *current-day* viewing experiences.

Sell's Foucauldian model in fact responds to a different need from my own. My task is not to elucidate forgotten historiographies of the avant-garde, whether feminist, Fascist, religious in flavor. Foucault's archival and genealogical projects and conception of power are particularly apposite in this endeavor. Instead, my corpus – the Theatre of the Absurd – belongs to a commercially and critically successful and famous avant-garde. It was "an immensely successful avant-garde" (Bishop 7) to recall Bishop's words from earlier.

It is what happened to this same avant-garde following its critical success that this book aims to look at. Named variously "the Theatre of the Absurd" (by far its most famous and temporally robust nomenclature), the "new theatre", "metaphysical theatre", "meta-theatre", "the School of Paris", and the "theatre of derision", this "immensely successful avant-garde" became critically dated very quickly in its assigned outfit of "edginess", which was defined relative to mid-twentieth-century European-philosophical terms and concerns. Notably, the post-war existentialism propounded by Jean-Paul Sartre and Albert Camus framed the public's understandings of the plays belonging to the Absurdist movement. As we will see in detail later, existentialism is of its time, and radically at odds with contemporary social justice movements based on combatting inequalities relating to differences of race, gender, sexuality and other factors.

What concerns me, in brief, are not Foucauldian-inflected forgotten luminaries or historical influences of the same epoch in which the Theatre of the Absurd flourished, although a study of the movement's relationship with feminist and other contemporaneous ideologies is surely overdue and bound to yield rich results when it is finally realized in full.[2] My book does not concentrate on history but on subversive

---

2   Work on a "Feminist Theatre of the Absurd" has already begun in this respect, if only cursorily. In the North American context, Beth Henley and Margaret Hollingsworth have been located in an Absurdist genealogy, and in a British context, Sarah Kane and Caryl Churchill. I will return to the feminist post-Absurdist body of theatre in the conclusion of this book. See Michael Y. Bennett's concluding chapter of *Reassessing the Theatre of the Absurd: Camus, Beckett, Ionesco, Genet and Pinter*. New York: Palgrave

futures enabled by theoretical possibility. Just over five decades on from Esslin's *The Theatre of the Absurd*, how might plays such as *Waiting for Godot* signify subversively for spectators today? How can we conceive of its antagonistic gesture in terms of the ideologies that form us and shape our current *Zeitgeist*?

To respond to these questions, let us turn to another significant strand in avant-garde studies that has problematized the field's foremost luminary, Peter Bürger, from a different standpoint. This trend, not wholly differently from my own focus on the present, argues that vanguard gestures exist today. The progressive development of advanced capitalism in the post-war era did not sound the death knell of the avant-garde, contrary to Bürger's claims. In other words, the avant-garde never "died" and it never became an "inauthentic" "neo-avant-garde" (Bürger 54).

In a non-theatrical arena, perhaps Paul Mann's 1991 account was the first, sustained critique of this aspect of Bürger's explanatory framework, delineating "a theory-death of the avant-garde" that "takes on an especially fatalistic tone, as if the absorption of any given movement were driven by natural forces" (15).[3] Performance studies has similarly been vocal in dismissing claims of the vanguard's disappearance: from Günter Berghaus's analysis of Stelarc's "aesthetics of prosthetics" as a "latter-day Futurism" (257), to edited volumes such as *Avant-Garde Performance and Material Exchange*, which expose non-European vanguards of the current age (the Hit and Run Theatre group in Zimbabwe, for instance).[4] These works have also troubled the European imperialist, anti-performative, textual focus, and anti-capitalist biases of Bürger's *The Theory of the Avant-garde* and its "Eulogist school" (Sell) of followers. However, despite their

---

Macmillan, 2011, 101-09. Also: Celeste, Derksen. "A Feminist Absurd: Margaret Hollingsworth's *The House that Jack Built*," *Modern Drama* 45 (2002), 209-30; David, Lane. *Contemporary British Drama*. Edinburgh: Edinburgh University Press, 2010, 9. Less has been said of various women's part in the mid-twentieth-century heyday of Absurdism. This is not to say that the latter line of inquiry is an impossibility. For one thing, Fernando Arrabal's wife Luce Moreau played a pivotal role in translating the playwright's work into French, and the role of translation, as theory informs us, can never be assumed to be a passive act.

[3]   For a critique of Bürger's theory in other arenas, such as the plastic arts, see Henry, Sayre. *The Object of Performance: The American Avant-garde since 1970*. Chicago: University of Chicago Press, 1989.

[4]   Also, see Arnold, Aronson. *American Avant-garde Theatre: A History*. London: Routledge, 2000.

consideration of current-day avant-gardes, these accounts do little to tell us how past vanguards might operate with a subversive edge today.

While volumes may have investigated forgotten avant-garde histories or demonstrated the continuation of the vanguard in the now, none have explored in sustained detail the diachronic potential of a past avant-garde and its political potential today. The closest we come to this is an indication, made by James Harding in the closing pages of his book *The Ghosts of the Avant-Garde(s): Exorcising Experimental Theatre and Performance* (2013), that the field is ripe for a move in this direction. Like Sell and my current book, Harding prefers to place primary importance on vanguard gestures as "socio-political formulations" that respond to the cultural contexts in which they crystallize. Choosing to see Bürger's lament of the death of the avant-garde as the site of possibility, Harding advises us to recover the "vanquished" or vanished "vanguards" of history. This critic argues that we cannot fully comprehend post-millennial avant-gardes without a retrospective look at "ghosts" (14) from throughout the history of the avant-garde.

To demonstrate his point, Harding analyzes famed New York theatrical troupe of the avant-garde The Living Theatre and its two productions of *The Brig* in 1963 and 2007. *The Brig* depicts the pitiable conditions for inmates of a Marine prison, and it, as with much of Living Theatre's output, was inspired by a model of French dramaturge Antonin Artaud's "Theatre of Cruelty". Artaud applied the public frenzy occasioned by the plague in the French city of Marseille in 1722 onto a paradigm of theatre in *The Theatre and its Double* (1938). Artaud insisted that theatre, in order to be revolutionary, must spread a general panic in audiences similar to the 1720 plague. The Living Theatre's co-founder Julian Beck espied similar "specter[s] of the suffering" (Harding 191) in the twentieth century, most notably in the victims of the Holocaust. These trans-historical ghosts foreshadow and influenced Living Theatre's production of *The Brig*, argues Harding, in 1963. According to Beck, "Artaud believed that if we could only be made to feel, really feel anything, then we might find all this suffering intolerable [...and] put an end to it" (191). The 2007 production of *The Brig* came in the wake of another scandalous event in American military history as the tortured Iraqi prisoners of Abu Ghraib hit television screens all over the world in 2004. Harding subsequently unites three historical moments, by dint of their common affective dimensions, in the crucible of the Living Theatre's production of *The Brig*: "one might call [these] ghosts by association [...] the uncanny momentary correspondences of history, such as the haunting parallels between Artuad's [*sic*] account of Marseille of 1720, Beck's knowledge of Buchenwald in 1945, and the leaked photographs from Bagdad in 2004" (205).

This association perhaps reveals a depressing circularity to history and, equally disturbingly, an ominous dimension of what we deem to be "avant-garde". But Harding's experimental reading also enables us to understand the avant-garde in terms of trans-historical continuity and common form, one far from on the brink of extinction, *pace* Bürger, today. It is a similar "strategy for seeing beyond the death of the avant-garde" (Harding 206) that I propound in these pages – a similar quest "to discover the meanings that linger like ghosts in avant-garde gestures because they have been left unexplored or because new historical contexts bring them into play" (Harding 206). Just as the atrocities at Abu Ghraib (2004) imbued *The Brig* with new meaning in 2007, I contemplate how the contemporary moment gives Absurdist plays significance today. Indeed, Harding's framing of this trans-historical reading as an "afterlife" of an avant-garde – "a historiography open to the stealing of one historical moment for the purposes of another" (26) – inspires the title of this book.

All of the following chapters combine theorizations of spectator interpretation in the modern-day setting with a consideration of how these theoretical viewing experiences may be hindered and helped by performance and production technique. However, I also dwell on the kind of trans-historical affective energies conceptualized by Harding from Absurdist *texts* too. I am well aware of the accusations of a "retrograde methodology" that I will potentially incur in this textual move. The field of avant-garde studies has worked hard to counter the anti-performative bias of Peter Bürger's 1972 theory and the Eulogist School of the Avant-Garde over the past decades. But critics of the last decade have also sought to problematize moral judgments in avant-garde studies that assume that forward-thinking is always, necessarily "good" or desirable. We saw this earlier in a discussion of Mike Sell's critique in *The Avant-garde: Race, Religion, War* of the vanguardists' ideal of forward-looking "progress", which may be linked to Fascist movements like the Ku Klux Klan just as much as it may radical leftist movements. In this sense, any "return" to textual analysis – in quote marks since I am not proposing a naïve or nostalgic maneuver that relies wholly on the text – should not be rejected outright as a "backward-looking", therefore "bad", maneuver. My view is more broadly sympathetic with accounts by theatre critics Michael Vanden Heuvel (1991) and W.B. Worthen (1995). These critics consider that an attack *ad nauseam* on "the Text" may result in a self-defeating denial of performance-based analyses' own methodological limitations. I broach the latter topic presently in a fuller contextualization of the critical literature surrounding this rich, yet curiously overdetermined, body of theatre. In this way, I demonstrate how this book promises to be of interest to scholars, students, practitioners, and perennial devotees of the Theatre of the Absurd.

The Theatre of the Absurd

The previous section of this introduction centered on a critical pattern that pre-assumes any given avant-garde's rapid extinction. The Theatre of the Absurd is a particularly salient example of this trend. The reason for this relates in large part, I will argue here, to the universalist assumptions that inhere within the kind of rhetoric of deployed by critics, which this body of theatre has tended to invite ever since BBC critic Martin Esslin's first edition of *The Theatre of the Absurd* and the existentialist reading of the movement that this canonical tome contained.

The narrative propounded by Esslin is worth rehearsing in detail here. Paris had been a stronghold of experimental theatre throughout the twentieth century, ever since the anti-realist tide began there half a century earlier by André Antoine's *théâtre libre* (c. 1890) and Alfred Jarry's *Ubu Roi* (1896). In the mid-twentieth century, however, anti-realism took a minimalist turn. Paris saw the birth of a new theatrical trend where tenuous plotlines, inconsistent characterizations, and "incoherent babblings" (Esslin 22), as Esslin put it, were the order of the day. Samuel Beckett's *Waiting for Godot* (1950), a play in which two characters wait for the eponymous figure who never appears, and Eugène Ionesco's *The Bald Soprano* (1950), where two couples converse on banal matters to the point of repetitive frenzy and the total collapse of meaning, typify the movement that Esslin named and understood to be "absurd". Theatre, he insisted, had been stripped to its bare necessity.

This minimalism had not mushroomed in a historical vacuum, insisted Esslin. After the ravages of two world wars and the atrocities committed in the name of Communism and Fascism, Absurd theatre exemplified a troubled spirit of the age. Europe was in a state of ideological exhaustion. Why, as Albert Camus wrote in *The Myth of Sisyphus* in 1942, does human life continue in the face of such meaninglessness? Why do humans not abandon ship and commit suicide? Esslin's label was inspired by Camus's tome and his identification of the absurdity of the human condition. Jean-Paul Sartre had also philosophized about the absurd condition, leading Esslin to connect the mid-century theatre that he had identified with the existentialism proffered by both Camus and Sartre. However, for Esslin, Camus' and Sartre's plays (*Caligula* (1938) and *No Exit* (1944) for instance) constituted poorly conceived theatricalizations of absurdity. What the Theatre of the Absurd had managed to do was buck the dominant trend of naturalism, which Camus and Sartre still clung to. In short, the Theatre of the Absurd had "renounced arguing *about* the absurdity of the human condition" to "merely *presen[t]* it in being – that is, in terms of concrete stage images" (Esslin 25).

Esslin's adoption of the existentialist critical lens inaugurated a pattern that defines Absurdist theatre according to a lexicon of abstractionisms. Esslin talked of "metaphysical anguish at the absurdity of the human condition" (23-24) as the preoccupation of these mid-century plays. Following his lead are critical accounts that extend across the fifty-year period since the first edition of *The Theatre of the Absurd*: from Rosette Lamont's (1964) argument that this theatre is "*divested itself of all particulars* in order to reach concrete essences" (my emphasis) (385); to Michel Prüner's (2005) assessment that "the theatre of the absurd liberates unknown or inaudible truths, reminding us of the inhumanity that is *inside us all*" (my emphasis) (148).[5] We may in fact assign Esslin his own "Eulogist Micro-School" of followers to borrow and adapt Mike Sell's term describing Peter Bürger's ubiquitous grasp on theories of the avant-garde. Esslin's eulogists have held onto an outdated terminological framework. References to an abstract "inhumanity" (Pruner) within us all, for instance, would seem of little relevance for the twenty-first century perspective informed by the investigations of acts of inhumanity stemming from gender-, race-, class-, and sexuality-based oppression. The social movements of the twentieth century – second-wave feminism, Civil Rights, queer liberation, among them – have de-legitimized discussions of individual suffering, such as that put on display in the Theatre of the Absurd, as divorced from considerations of gender, class, race, religion, and sexuality.

---

[5] Pruner's translation is my own. Original: "les auteurs de l'absurde nous livrent des vérités inouïes, ou inaudibles, rappelant seulement la part d'inhumanité qui est en chacun de nous".

The Theatre of the Absurd was flanked critically on the one side by a social politics defined in strictly universalist terms. "Man" was in crisis on the Absurdist stage, according to Esslin. On the other side, it was held to be at the forefront of aesthetic innovation or ahead of the times, corresponding to the avant-garde label under which it was classified. The Theatre of the Absurd had advanced for the first time a series of plays without plots, resolved endings, and psychologically complex characters.

The movement's social politics, the "man in crisis" that it staged, was overdetermined by a yardstick of aesthetic innovation corresponding to the general critical trend surrounding avant-gardes. As such, the Theatre of the Absurd's ability to subvert social norms was deemed ephemeral, extinguished as soon as theatrical minimalism was no longer a novelty. Barthes bemoaned by 1956 the avant-garde's "slow death" since "the bourgeoisie will recuperate it altogether, ultimately putting on splendid evenings of Beckett [...] and tomorrow Ionesco" or "because the avant-garde playwright, acceding to a political consciousness of the theatre, will renounce pure ethical protest (indubitably Adamov's case) for a new realism" (69).[6] With considerably more optimism, Sartre, in a 1966 paper "Myth and Reality of the Theatre", understood the extinction of an Absurdist spirit on the stage as illustrative of the dialectical materialist forces of history: a forward-motion toward social progress, a striving for a "future unity" (*unité future*) (Sartre 206) of humanity, dispensed of the need for the anguish aestheticized by the Theatre of the Absurd.

By 1972, Esslin himself lamented a *critical* death of the Theatre of the Absurd that his volume had paved the way for: "what I intended as a generic concept, a working hypothesis for the understanding of a large number of extremely varied and elusive phenomena, has assumed for many people, *including some drama critics*, a reality as concrete and specific as a branded product of the detergent industry" (my emphasis) ("The Theatre of the Absurd Reconsidered," 179). Absurdism had been recuperated as popular art, and Esslin laid the blame for this on his Eulogist Micro-School of critics who followed him in proliferating

---

[6]   Similarly, Arnold Hinchliffe despaired that "Absurd fiction ha[d] lost its anguish, and the term ha[d] become historical" (99) by 1969. Arnold, Hinchliffe. *The Absurd*. London: Methuen & Co., 1969. Additionally, the putative extinction of this avant-garde led Tom Bishop to mythologize it as a lost moment in time to be longed-for anew. This critic was convinced that no other movement had taken Beckett's, Genet's, or Ionesco's place since the 1950s. "So whatever *did* happen to the avant-garde?" (7) began his lament in 2007.

theories of existential anguish as the main message of what was in fact "a large number of extremely varied and elusive phenomena" (179).

The case of Absurdism exemplifies the often-unacknowledged part that higher education has played in peddling and popularizing vanguard movements.[7] It is certainly true that the Theatre of the Absurd has been made palatable for a large proportion of Anglophone and Francophone audiences via the academy, and the subject remains a staple of a number of disciplinary curricula. This is most notably so in French Studies but also Theatre and Performance Studies, and, given the movement's association with existentialism, college courses in philosophy and intellectual history. We find ourselves teaching a subject in which, as Loren Glass encapsulates wryly, "[t]he student is effortlessly comfortable with both the formal and philosophical difficulties of the avant-garde, even to the point of indicating the ironies of this uneasiness" (559).

Yet Esslin's own words hint at a new lease of critical life for the Theatre of the Absurd. The movement's liberation from critical overdetermination – from the "reality as concrete and specific as a branded product of the detergent industry" defined by drama commentators among others as he described – will reignite our understanding of the movement as "a large number of extremely varied and elusive phenomena" ("The Theatre of the Absurd Reconsidered," 179). It is my conviction that wresting the Theatre of the Absurd from the existentialist framework will aid in this endeavor. Esslin in fact mapped existentialism onto the Theatre of the Absurd; existentialism was not something that the playwrights of Absurdism explicitly took up or wished to demonstrate with their theatre.

A divorce between existentialism and the Theatre of the Absurd will enable the student, teacher, and practitioner of Absurdism to glimpse its subversive dimensions anew in an age where movements such as feminism, queer liberation, and civil rights have made facile universalist pronouncements of a "metaphysical" or "existential anguish" no longer a legitimate activity. The kind of approach that I am proposing has taken protean form in recent scholarship on the movement, which we may define as having entered a revisionist period in light of the thirty-, forty-, and fifty-year anniversaries of the publication of *The Theatre of the Absurd*. This body of literature has sought to disrupt various received

---

[7]   The determining role of the academy in promoting and "selling" the avant-garde is also one of the broad arguments in Sell's *Avant-garde Performance* (2005).

notions, including the movement's confinement to France or the mid-century period.

Loren Glass's article in 2011 uncovered the role played by Grove Press in popularizing and democratizing this avant-garde via the publication of a wide range of translated Absurdist texts in affordable paperback format – a history that disturbs both idealists' pronouncements that Esslin has cultural authority over the movement and attackers' claims that textual bias always-already connotes elitist exclusionism. In terms, more specifically, of a new look at the movement in light of contemporary identity politics that I am suggesting, dissertations by Hillary Ione LaMont (2012) and Andrew Woodruff Anderson (2011), two books by Michael Bennett (2011, 2015), and an edited collection directed by Carl Lavery and Clare Finburgh (2015) consider Absurdism's relationship with and legacy for queer, postcolonial, postmodern-feminist politics, and contemporary Environmentalism studies respectively.

Barring Finburgh and Lavery's *Rethinking the Theatre of the Absurd: Ecology, the Environment and the Greening of the Modern Stage* (2015), which I describe in fuller detail shortly, these revisionist works have avoided a wholesale separation of analysis from the philosophical framework provided by Esslin. I want to turn in detail to Bennett's *Reassessing The Theatre of the Absurd*, published to commemorate the half-century anniversary of Esslin's canonical text, to point out the problems of this. Bennett's is, in many ways, a much-needed rewrite of Esslin's account. He unites this body of non-didactic theatre with the Foucauldian concept of heterotopia and Derridean deconstruction to suggest a powerful "postmodern parable" in which "the possibility for multiple truths" (Bennett 22) presents itself. He finally proposes a new ethical valence that "orients, disorients, and reorients the audience" (Bennett 22). The chapter on the question of a "feminist absurd" (in the theatre of North American playwrights Beth Henley and Margaret Hollingsworth) in the conclusion of his book is an especially exciting one for a field dominated by pronouncements on this body of theatre's expression of the profound anguish of a gender-normative "Man".

Bennett insists that Albert Camus, whose *Myth of Sisyphus* (1942) inspired Esslin's take on Absurd theatre, was no pessimistic existentialist; rather Camus, according to Bennett, determined "Absurdism" as a fact of living in a contradictory world that one has to accept in order to surmount. Yet, in propounding a more optimistic version of Camus, Bennett's re-readings of the canonized plays of the movement (Ionesco's

Rhinoceros, Genet's *The Blacks*, Beckett's *Waiting for Godot*, Pinter's *The Birthday Party*) rebound upon many of the fraught universalisms discussed earlier. At best, these new universalisms are allusive, harnessing these plays' determination as "descriptive, never prescriptive" (Bennett 21). At worst, however, misogyny, racism, and other discursive prejudices of the avant-garde continue uninterrupted and return us to the old universalisms of a Eulogist yesteryear of Absurdism. For instance, the characters of Meg in Pinter's *The Birthday Party* (1957) and Martha in Albee's *Who's Afraid of Virginia Woolf?* (1962) are, in Bennett's view, the embodiment of the "*archetypal childless-wife*" (Bennett 66) who will not accept their contradictory situations and accept the motherless fate that has been doled out to them, and as a corollary they torture their hapless male partners with their neuroticisms.

Another example of freighted universalist pronouncements returns us to Beckett's *Waiting for Godot*. Bennett understands this play as "a mini-parable" about hope in the face of despair. The characters Vladimir, Estragon, Lucky and Pozzo wait for "Godot" who might grant them reprieve from the interminable grind of life, but are famously left frustrated as the title character never appears. Hope in the face of despair is a fresh optimistic take on this play in which nothing much of consequence happens. However, the theatrical production of *Waiting for Godot* that Bennett studies, Paul Chan's *mise-en-scène* in New Orleans in 2007, throws up considerably more urgent, and politically speaking more concrete, questions. Chan's production came in the wake of Hurricane Katrina. Lines from Beckett's play were posted all over the city in the month prior to the staging. While Bennett concentrates on the sense of hope out of bleakness that a production like this privileges, Camusian statements such as "life is made meaningful by 'biding one's time' with friends, rather than *hoping* for an outside savior" (Bennett 31) seem paltry consolation when reckoning in the structural iniquities that a Katrina-ravaged, black-majority population of New Orleans was left to deal with. The tendency toward abstractionism despite intersectional questions of class and race signal that new universalisms flourish under the premise of adhering to Camus' version of absurdity. This is even in the more hopeful guise that Bennett presents.

Indeed, Paul Chan's New Orleans production of *Waiting for Godot* would seem to chime readily with Clare Finburgh and Carl Lavery's view, in their collection *Re-thinking the Theatre of the Absurd: Ecology, the Environment and the Greening of the Modern Stage* (2015). They argue that the Theatre of the Absurd may be re-interpreted as a representation of the decentered anthropomorphic self, particular to our current epoch of climate change. As Lavery and Finburgh state,

> [T]he mysterious, depopulated landscapes of Beckett's early plays, and Ionesco's obsession with stagnant water, airborne infection and genetic mutation are no longer simple metaphors for the human condition. Rather, they communicate a decidedly literalist vision of the world that is haunted by the spectre of imminent ecological catastrophe, a biosphere that has been rendered toxic. (32)

In the context of a Hurricane Katrina-ravaged New Orleans in 2007, *Godot*'s display of two wandering individuals in a wasteland of bleakness and boredom would have readily conjured an "ecological catastrophe" that was not so much "imminent", as Finburgh and Lavery describe, as it had just come to pass.

Finburgh and Lavery's collection covers Absurdism in France, Britain, Eastern Europe, and the United States to argue, compellingly, that the Theatre of the Absurd resonates with an era of current climate change. I build on this contemporary recuperation of Absurdism, turning my attention not to the ecological concerns of our twenty-first century but to the sociological concerns of our day and age, such as post-9/11 Islamophobia (chapters 2 and 3) and the ubiquitous Prison Industrial Complex which incarcerates in disproportionate numbers gender, racial, and sexual minorities (chapter five). In this sociological focus, and in particular the ways in which racial, gender, and sexual minorities may find a space for their causes in the Theatre of the Absurd, one of Bennett's comments at the end of his book *Re-assessing the Theatre of the Absurd* inspires me. As he remarks suggestively, universalism – a project that privileged white, middle-class men – is something that the Theatre of the Absurd cast into doubt: "There is something so unsure about so many of the men [in these plays] [...] One only has to look at some of the male protagonists in plays like *Waiting for Godot*, *The Birthday Party*, and *Rhinoceros*" (107). With this in mind, what I propose in the chapters that follow is a methodology that displaces the universal. I shift attention to Absurdism's interaction with the particular and the material (raced, classed, gendered, sexual) ideologies of our era. The chapters consider the ways in which plays from the Absurdist canon sit in tension with and subvert racial, classed, gender-based, and sexual inequalities that shape our present day.

Before outlining how the chapters demonstrate a displacement of the universal, it is important to introduce the methodology that enables contemporary revisions of the Theatre of the Absurd. Lacanian psychoanalysis and the concept of the "theoretical spectator" are central to this methodology, as is queer theory, as we shall see presently.

Methodological Toolkit

The psychoanalytic notion of the unconscious enables us to revive texts as it presents us with "the ever-unfinished *act* of elucidation" (de Certeau 303). Considering how the modern-day spectator's unconscious interacts with the Theatre of the Absurd is this book's main road to reinvigorating this past avant-garde for the contemporary moment. By "modern-day spectator", I do not mean a living, breathing person sitting in front of the visual piece and reacting to it, but a theoretical construct. Psychoanalysis is a particularly apt tool in hypothesizing spectator reaction because responses are often not informed by rational thought processes but are instinctual and outside of reason. It is a school of thought that focuses on desire, affect, and the unconscious and therefore equips us to anticipate spectator response in all its complexity and unexpectedness.

The idea of the theoretical spectator was first ventured by psychoanalytic film scholars in the 1970s and was since adopted in theatre studies. My book takes inspiration from film and theatre's psychoanalytically constructed spectator, but it also updates the construct used in these writings. Post-1970s psychoanalytic visual studies scholars understood the unconscious and psychoanalytic desire as conservative entities, which have to be eliminated in order for the spectator to become politicized by watching film and theatre. Spectators need to be ultra-conscious and rational, and quash their desire and unconscious, as this school of thought puts forward. Since my book fleshes out the subversions of contemporary social norms made possible by the Theatre of the Absurd, it is necessary to turn to a more politicized form of the unconscious, which has been propounded by Lacanian critics Jennifer Friedlander and Todd McGowan. Coupling a radical theory of the spectator's unconscious with Absurdist plays will enable us to pinpoint viewer responses to this past body of avant-garde theatre that challenge dominant ideologies relating to race, gender, and sexuality.

But before all this, it is necessary to take a few steps back and explain the beginnings of the theoretical spectator and its contemporary mutations. In 1975, feminist film scholar Laura Mulvey named a "male gaze" of cinema spectatorship in an essay that, not unlike the place occupied by Peter Bürger's 1974 book in the adjacent field of avant-garde studies, was foundational for the sub-discipline of psychoanalytic visual studies. Mulvey's essay, "Visual Pleasure and Narrative Cinema," proposed that the male film spectator, sitting in front of a Hollywood movie at the cinema, was led by his ego in what he did with the actress in front of him on the screen.

Mulvey extracted her idea of "the ego" from Lacan who, in turn, developed his theory based on colleague Henri Wallon's observations on the infant's first self-recognition in the mirror. Subjectivity, Lacan ventured, was premised on a founding lie (a "misrecognition") that we tell ourselves in the earliest months of our lives: we see ourselves in the mirror, whole-bodied and assuming a central place, and convince ourselves that we have control over the people and contents of our surroundings. This "mirror stage" or "Imaginary" register of the psyche repeats itself throughout life, without the aid of a mirror necessarily to create the illusion of self-autonomy (and deluded self-aggrandizement at its most extreme) later in life.

Mulvey insisted that the Lacanian mirror stage was operative in Hollywood cinema and it was inextricable from the machinations of patriarchy. The spectator's ego, she argued, "projects its fantasy onto the female figure" (Mulvey 19). Hollywood actresses, she persisted, shore up the patriarchal unconscious as, conventionally beautiful and alluring, they connote a "*to-be-looked-at-ness*" (19) that assures their reduction to an object, or "fetish" as psychoanalysis terms it, for the pleasures of the all-controlling, self-assured viewer.

Much has rightly been unpicked and problematized in Mulvey's account of the fetishized actress who is made subject to the will of the male spectator's ego. Critics have complained of the reduction of actresses to the status of patriarchal puppets who are devoid of agency. Mulvey's detractors have also bewailed the lack of conceptual space for forms of cinematic spectatorship that challenge patriarchy *via* the unconscious (and not in spite of it) (McGowan 2007; Friedlander 2008). However, accounts that have interlinked the Lacanian ego, the act of spectatorship, and objectification by dominant power structures have prevailed in psychoanalytic theatre and performance studies. They have done so because Mulvey's theoretical spectator hammered home the centrality of patriarchy in our visual economies. The spectator's unconscious internalization of patriarchal ideologies propounded by Mulvey may be unwelcome news but it still holds value in a world where male hegemony, gender-based wage inequality, and a worldwide sex industry dominated by girls and women persist despite the hard-won gains of feminism at the start of the twentieth century and in the 1970s.

The task before us is not to dismiss Mulvey's and her theatrical followers' accounts but to update them with theories of the unconscious that may also challenge the internalization of dominant ideologies from within the very same unconscious processes. To name just three examples of Mulvey's theatrical followers: Jill Dolan (1988) argued that the feminist spectator has no choice but to reject her unconscious and her ego, since she "is unwilling to leave her ideology outside the theatre and look at the work through the male gaze" (58); Barbara Freedman (1988) insisted that theatre relies upon a "scopic regime of [the male's spectator's] voyeurism and [the female actor's] exhibitionism" (381); and Peggy Phelan's *Unmarked* (1993), which compellingly expounds upon the resistant power of the invisible in performance, was emboldened by the Lacanian mirror stage in spectatorship (6).[8]

This dominant trend in psychoanalytic theatre studies, however, does not disclose the full story on Lacanian thought, as critics, mainly from non-theatrical sub-sections of cultural and visual studies, have been quick

---

[8]   Elsewhere, a backlash against Lacan in theatre studies has taken the form of a return to Freud. Paul Julian Smith (1998) attributes "the apparent exhaustion of Lacanian or *Screen* theory" (9) to his choice of Freudian methodology for a rereading of Spanish playwright Federico García Lorca's oeuvre. Meanwhile, Elin Diamond, in an analysis of Ibsen's *Hedda Gabler* (1890) as a proto-feminist text for historical spectators, argues that Freudian thought potentially construes identification as "caus[ing] the I/ego to be transformed by the other", whereas in the Lacanian model "the perceived other is always a version of me" (409). Ann Pellegrini, similarly, turns to a Freudian apprehension of spectatorial identification, arguing that Freud's "richly complicated understanding of the way unconscious identifications form and are continually transforming the character of the ego [...] unhinges self-identity to open up the space between" (69-70). Paul Julian, Smith. *The Theatre of Garcia Lorca: Text, Performance, Psychoanalysis*. Cambridge: Cambridge UP, 1998; Elin, Diamond. "The Violence of 'We': Politicizing Identification." Eds. J. Reinelt and J. Roach. *Critical Theory and Performance*. Ann Arbor: University of Michigan Press, 2007; Ann, Pellegrini. *Performance Anxieties: Staging Psychoanalysis, Staging Race*. New York: Routledge, 1997.

to note. Their counterargument constitutes a starting point for this book. Displacing the conceptual value allotted to the Lacanian ego, critics such as Jennifer Friedlander and Todd McGowan have instead focused on a system of the spectatorial unconscious that is radically separate from the mirror stage. Mulvey asserted in the 1970s that desire, particularly desire based on sexist objectification, and the ego were intertwined and mutually reinforcing.[9] This premise, Friedlander and McGowan point out, is based on a misreading that psychoanalyst Joan Copjec has labeled a "Foucauldinization of [Lacanian] desire" (19), where unconscious desire is deemed inseparable from power in its various guises. But, as Lacan retrospectively postured: "What did I try to get across with the mirror stage? That whatever in man is *loosened up, fragmented, anarchic*, establishes its relation to his perceptions on a plane with *a completely original tension*" (my emphases) (*Sem II* 166). "Original tensions" and "anarchic" undersides undermine the ego's reduction of its surroundings to a mirror image of itself. This is key to a politicization of Lacanian thought.

Lacan, in fact, battled against the "ego psychology" of his day. It was ego psychology, and not Lacan, which proposed the possibility of a "cure" to the unconscious in the form of a strengthened ego. By sharp contrast, a strengthened ego, for Lacan, meant the reinforced position of the individual in the world as it currently is – in other words, a strengthened ego nestles itself in the normative (capitalist, heterosexist, misogynist, racist) values that inform our society and oppress those (poor, LGBT, female, racialized) individuals who do not fall inside these norms. Lacan's self-professed "Freudian Revolution", a "return" to Freud in his most radical manifestation as he determined it, was set in motion in Marienbad in 1936 where he introduced the fourteenth congress of the International Psychoanalytic Association (the IPA) to the *pitfalls* of placating the ego, a paper that caused such a stir that it was cut short by British psychoanalyst and Freudian disciple Ernest Jones. The minutiae of Lacan's theory of the mirror stage runs as follows: the ego-driven

---

[9]   Mulvey's position was also shared by Jean-Louis Baudry and Christian Metz. Together these critics propounded a conservative theory of the unconscious in viewing film. Jean-Louis, Baudry. "The Apparatus: Metapsychological Approaches to the Impression of Reality in Cinema." Ed. P. Rosen. *Narrative, Apparatus, Ideology: A Film Theory Reader.* New York: Columbia University Press, 1986, 299-318; Christian, Metz. *The Imaginary Signifier: Psychoanalysis and the Cinema.* Bloomington: Indiana University Press, 1977.

"Imaginary" register of the psyche, which asserts a strong ego ensconced in and informed by normative values, may periodically operate at full throttle in life; this instills a misguided sense of unified self-centrality, but it haphazardly covers over a more profound split in the individual, which is signaled by the fact that the individual's ego relies on exterior objects in order to confirm its autonomy, strength, and supremacy. Every time that the individual is reminded of this reliance on the outside world, they are reminded of their split and precarious subjectivity. This reminder is capable of disrupting the normative values that a strengthened ego had sought to placate. The emergence of split subjectivity destabilizes the locus of dominant ideologies, named "the Other" in Lacanian parlance.

Returning to this conceptual coup engineered by Lacan as starting premise, Todd McGowan's *Film Theory After Lacan* (2007) and Jennifer Friedlander's *Feminine Look* (2008) insist that certain situations of spectatorship are capable of inducing moments when the individual, or "subject", realizes his or her split and divided nature. These in turn lead to moments when the unconscious is capable of subverting normative ideologies. Specifically, McGowan and Friedlander source potential from what Lacan called "the Real". This is the third "register" that makes up the psyche alongside the Imaginary (the preserve of the ego) and the "Symbolic". The latter is the psychical domain housing internalized ideologies, which the ego or "Imaginary" also works to support. In Lacan's structuralist model of the individual or "subject" of psychoanalysis, subjectivity is produced by language and discourse – it is linguistically composed. The Real dimension of our psyches stands outside of language: that is, it escapes both the Symbolic and Imaginary registers of our psyches and the external ideological "Other", since ideology depends on language for its production.

The Real is, as queer theorist Tim Dean observes, "a barrier to subjective or symbolic realization, but also the impossibility against which symbolization is constantly being elaborated" (50-51). As the extra-linguistic rents within the fabric of the ideological Other, the Real is "generative, not simply constraining" (Dean 50-51), functioning in such a way that it prompts individual subjects to question and interrogate the Other. McGowan and Friedlander consider situations in films from *Citizen Kane* (Orson Welles, 1941) to *Lost Highway* (David Lynch, 1997), and photographs from André Kertész's *Broken Plate* (1929) to Marcus Harvey's *Myra* (1995), where, through specific formal and/or thematic conditions of the text in question, the viewer's interrogatory Real may be incited.

It would be inaccurate to state that this Real version of Lacan, as it were, has not seen the light of day in theatre and performance studies. Eileen Fischer (1979), Mark Pizzato (1990), and Catherina Wulf (1997) have considered the two most canonized playwrights' oeuvre examined in these pages, Samuel Beckett and Jean Genet, in terms of their negotiation of the Lacanian Real. However, these critics' tendency toward pronouncements on "human desire" turn us to the rightful critique that a psychoanalytic toolkit can be ahistorical and monolithic if inattention is paid. These accounts therefore differ significantly from the methodology that I elaborate. The current book centers on the materially specific, implications of a past avant-garde for current discriminatory practices and dominant ideologies.

Elsewhere in theatre and performance studies, Anthony Kubiak's *Agitated States: Performance in the American Theatre of Cruelty* (2002) detects the presence of the Real throughout the history of American theatre from Puritan John Winthrop, to Eugene O'Neill, Edward Albee, Sam Shepard, and Tony Kushner. But, differently from McGowan and Friedlander, Kubiak detects "less material history than history's immaterial nightmares" in these plays, criticizing their lack of theatricality as the starting point for his argument that America betrays a "blindness to its theatres" (11) in its wider (ultra-violent) society. Kubiak's contention, though fascinating and original in its linkage of theatre chronology to some of the broader social implications of American history, is premised on the traumatic dimensions of the Real, which have been developed in detail by post-Lacanian philosopher Slavoj Žižek. This distinguishes itself from the subversive version of the Real propounded by Dean, Friedlander, and McGowan that I am taking up in this book. The Real is not necessarily or even mainly a traumatic force in the chapters that follow, since trauma is often something so overwhelming that it can disconnect spectators from critical or politicized thought processes. Rather, the Real elaborated in the chapters that follow enables the subversion of contemporary ideologies relating to gender, sexuality, and race.

Elsewhere in theatre studies, Lacanian-inflected analysis has tended toward the phenomenological – that is to say, as distinct from the spectator's affective trajectories that McGowan and Friedlander chart with regard to the specificities of the visual text in question. Herbert Blau, Alain Badiou, and Timothy Murray, for instance, have explored a version of Lacanian desire distanced from Imaginary mastery in their philosophical reflections on theatrical ontology and the structural division of the spectator from the stage.[10] Going beyond abstract accounts of the isomorphism linking Lacanian desire and theatrical ontology, Friedlander and McGowan read the contents of a visual text in terms of the psychical structures that they resemble. This is a method that the current book borrows in order to anticipate the contemporary spectator's unconscious processes as Absurdist avant-garde plays unfold. For McGowan, for instance, excessive paternal authority in Eisenstein's *Battleship Potemkin* (1925) situates the viewer in terms of Lacanian fantasy (39). As another example, Friedlander takes visual artist Jamie Wagg's ink-jet reprints of the CCTV footage of the kidnappers and killers of British child James Bulger. In the juxtaposition of the photograph's stark video surveillance aesthetic and its hyperbolic claiming of the status of "art" (the work is entitled "History Painting"), Friedlander discerns an antagonism that potentially enables spectators to "traverse" (69) an ideological fantasy as Lacanian discourse puts it.

Pinpointing the forms of the unconscious that the visual text conjures, these revisionist Lacanian critics then imagine the subversive dimensions of these viewing positions. I find the strategies developed by McGowan and Friedlander in the parallel visual fields of film and photography useful for my own project for reimagining Absurdist theatre

---

[10]   Alain Badiou proposes the idea of the "event" in theatre, extolling the virtues of medium's simplicity in an age of digital hegemony. Theatre represents "a kind of illumination [éclaircie]" "separat[ing] what is mixed and confused", and this a partial echo of a Lacanian ethics of not ceding on the path of one's desire (*ne pas céder sur son désir*) (72-73). Timothy Murray observes that a not inconsiderable body of poststructuralist thought on theatricality, from Derrida to Lyotard, was suffused with Lacan's "elaborate formula of desire revolving around his theory of the mirror stage" (16). Herbert Blau argues that resistant theatre hinges on an unsealed, Lacanian-inflected "original splitting", where "the audience which has delegated itself to the stage discovers in its fantasmatic figures that something has been surrendered to an unforeseen authority [...] which only produces more desire" (10). Alain, Badiou. *Handbook of Inaesthetics*. California: Stanford UP, 2005; Blau. *The Audience*. Baltimore: Johns Hopkins UP, 1990; Timothy, Murray. "Introduction." Ed. Timothy Murray. *Mimesis, Masochism, and Mime: The Politics of Theatricality in Contemporary French Thought*. Ann Arbor: University of Michigan Press, 1997. See also Patrick, Campbell and Adrian, Kear (eds.). *Psychoanalysis and Performance*. London: Routledge, 2001; Samuel, Weber. *Theatricality as Medium*. New York: Fordham UP, 2004; Georges, Balassa. "A Psychoanalytic Model for the Stage," *Performing Arts Journal* 3 (1978), 35-39; Sigmund, Freud. "Psychopathic characters on the stage," *The Tulane Drama Review* 4 (1960), 144-48; André, Green. *The Tragic Effect: The Oedipus Complex in Tragedy*. Cambridge: Cambridge UP, 1979.

and its subversive potential today. The plays that follow have been chosen in part because, in their thematic and formal composition, they resemble certain psychical structures. These psychical structures are "perverse", "psychotic", or pertain to a "supplementary enjoyment" (or "*jouissance* beyond the phallus*" to put it in technical Lacanian terms). For instance, *The Blacks* (1959), by Jean Genet, and *And They Put Handcuffs on the Flowers* (1969), by Fernando Arrabal, both evince a baroque profusion and speed in their visuals. These qualities resemble Lacan's theory of "supplementary enjoyment", which, too, relies on baroque excess to overwhelm the production of meaning with the proliferation of visual and acoustic signs, as shall be investigated in the fourth and fifth chapters of this book. The psychoanalytic concepts detected in these plays have, in turn, been selected for their potential to subvert the ideologies that structure our lives in the twenty-first century. For instance, the spectator's supplementary enjoyment produced by *The Blacks* and *And They Put Handcuffs on the Flowers* subvert the oppression facing black women (chapter four) today and the ideologies surrounding the modern-day Prison Industrial Complex (chapter five), which imprisons disproportionate numbers of racial, gender, and sexual minorities.

Lacanian psychoanalysis enables various re-readings of the Theatre of the Absurd as creating a space for racial, gender, and sexual minorities. However, this approach would not be possible in the chapters that follow by staying unquestioningly "true" to Lacan himself – a cis-gendered (as opposed to transgender), white, heterosexual, middle-class male whose writings cannot be dissociated from the privileges and blindspots that this position entails. I do not hold fast to some of Lacan's or his followers' ideas which connote, in my view, pathologization, misogyny, racism or other discursive prejudices. I inflect Lacan with contemporary queer theory and a form of feminism that investigates the intersection of race, gender, and class (called "intersectionality").

I discuss at certain points in this book how the Theatre of the Absurd "queers" dominant ideologies relating to gender, sexuality, race, religion, and class. It is therefore important to unpack this term and situate it historically and theoretically. "Queer theory" or "queer studies" is a discipline that began to flourish in American academia at the beginning of the 1990s, following second-wave feminism in the 1970s and the AIDS crisis of the 1980s. Activist groups such as Queer Nation rescued the term "queer" from its historical role as a slur against LGBT individuals, using it instead as a powerful rallying tool uniting LGBT individuals. Queer

Nation's slogan was, "We here, we're queer, get used to it!" From its activist origins, queerness therefore pertains to no sexual or gendered identity in particular, but instead blurs the divisions between them as a force for social change. This identitarian blurring was also taken up in American academia, notably in English and Comparative Literature departments. Judith Butler's *Gender Trouble: Feminism and the Subversion of Identity* and Eve Kosofsky Sedgwick's *Epistemology of the Closet*, both published in 1990, argued that the gender and sexual binary oppositions operated as "presiding master term[s] of the past century" (Sedgwick 11). Oppositions such as "man-woman" and "homo-heterosexual" reduce the complexity of individuals in order to reinforce pre-existing forms of "social organization" (Sedgwick 11). Butler argued in *Gender Trouble* that second-wave feminism, whose heyday was in the 1970s, had been wrong to hold tenaciously to the identity label "Woman" behind which women rallied in order to militate for social change. The label "Woman" did not account adequately for variations in sexual orientation between women, and was a concept based on heterosexual assumptions or "heteronormativity", Butler insisted. For this critic, the imperative is to re-conceive identity not as a stable construction but "as an *effect*, that is *produced* or *generated*", and that can simultaneously be subject to "strategies of subversive repetition" including via the "[p]ractices of parody" (Butler 146-147). Parody as a tool for queering gender and blurring the distinctions between "man" and "woman" is a theme we will see in chapter one on Ionesco's *The Bald Soprano*.

Because of its origins in grassroots LGBT activism and feminist studies, queerness is a concept most commonly associated with the destabilization of gender and sexual ideologies. However, as Donald Hall and Annamarie Jagose note in *The Routledge Queer Studies Reader*, queer is "potentially attentive to any socially consequential difference that contributes to regimes of sexual normalization" (xvi), including the overdetermination of individuals according to dominant ideologies of race, class, nation, citizenship, religion and more. José Muñoz's *Disidentifications: Queers of Color and the Performance of Politics* (1999) is just one example of a body of work that considers how queerness can be used as a concept to destabilize the notions of race and ethnicity.

Therefore, when I talk about the Theatre of the Absurd "queering" identity, I mean the destabilization of precepts, norms, and stereotypes relating to *all* identity labels, including racialized identities such as "black women" (explored in chapter four on Genet's *The Blacks*). In chapter one, I argue that *The Bald Soprano* queers gender and sexual orientation, or the rigid divide that society sets up between men and women, by means of cross-dressing women. When I talk about institutions such as marriage (chapter one) and prison (chapter five) being "queered", I allude to the unsettling of gendered, sexual, and racialized identities that these institutions rely on. In the United States, black men and transgender individuals are particularly susceptible to a stereotype of criminalization that sends them in disproportionate numbers to the institution of the prison. In chapter five, I explore how Arrabal's *And They Put Handcuffs on the Flowers* queers the stereotype of the prisoner as racially and sexually "deviant" or "degenerate". The play reveals racialized characters that are capable of enacting social change via non-heterosexual eroticism. They also demonstrate that sexual identity is subject to change – some prisoners are both heterosexual and practice homoeroticism.

The writings of US-based queer theorist Jasbir Puar inform the arguments of chapters two and three, which discuss, respectively, how Adamov's *Off Limits* destabilizes a Western nationalist ideology of "docile patriotism" and how Beckett's *Not I* unsettles a dominant ideology of "gender exceptionalism". Both terms have been coined by Puar, who is an associate professor in the Women and Gender Studies' department at Rutgers University and who has written on the interlocking nature of surveillance culture and militarization with dominant ideologies of race, gender, sexuality, and religion. Docile patriotism (chapter two), as Puar writes with new media scholar Amit Rai, denotes a social attitude that has set in since the twin tower attacks of September 11, 2001. It consists in public tolerance of European and American war-waging in foreign, often Islamic, territories. The ideology of gender exceptionalism (chapter three) defends Western feminism and believes that Muslim women are fundamentally submissive and incapable of asserting their own agency; it is only the Western world that believes itself capable of liberating Islamic women as Puar writes and critiques in *Terrorist Assemblages: Homonationalism in Queer Times* (2007). Adamov's *Off Limits* and Beckett's *Not I* unsettle these ideologies of gender exceptionalism and docile patriotism as named by queer theorists.

In brief, my methodology combines Lacanian psychoanalysis with queer theory to hypothesize unconscious reactions to the Theatre of the Absurd that make subversive interventions on the ideologies that shape our current world. I go into a fuller description of these subversive interventions in the chapter outlines in the following and final part of this introduction.

Chapter Outlines

The first chapter of this book argues that Eugène Ionesco's *The Bald Soprano*, one of the first examples of the Theatre of the Absurd published and staged in 1950, ignites a mode of viewing guided by the psychoanalytic concept of perversion. *The Bald Soprano*, true to the Absurdist ethos, is an uneventful play: two married couples, the Smiths and the Martins, converse on inconsequential and tenuously linked matters until their discourse descends into the senselessness of individual letters and random words, after which the dramatic action ends where it begins in an endless cycle of nonsense. Ionesco considered this play "a tragedy of language" (*Notes & Counter-Notes* 86). However, this chapter returns to the playwright's shock at finding that audiences, time and again, interpret *The Bald Soprano* as a comedy. This forms a basis for my argument that the play encourages the perverse unconscious in viewing. Audiences turn something unpleasant (the stuff of tragedy) into something pleasurable (a comedy), which closely resembles the psychoanalytic concept of perversion where sexual pleasure is elicited from unexpected, non-normative sources. Perverse viewing queers contemporary restrictive scripts on gender and heteronormativity represented by the play's two married couples, the Smiths and Martins. The multiplication of actors playing one role, parody, and female-to-male and male-to-female drag costuming are identified as key performance methods that enable this queering of gender and sexuality to occur.

The second chapter posits that Arthur Adamov's *Off Limits* stimulates a mode of viewing resembling the psychical state of psychosis. *Off Limits* centers on the topic of the Vietnam War (1955-1975). Corresponding to Absurdist senselessness, the play depicts a party-going group of New York socialites who re-enact the depictions of Vietnam via "happenings" – short, abstract sketches in vogue among the American avant-garde of the 1960s and 1970s. The play sits alongside other "Vietnam Protest Theatre" (Norma Alter's term) such as Armand Gatti's *V Comme Vietnam* (1967) that emerged in Europe in the late 1960s and throughout the 1970s to provide a critical lens on the American invasion of the Southeast Asian country. It is argued that psychotic viewing is encouraged by the play's production of audience hostility. Audiences are made to react angrily to the cast of characters who espouse radical anti-war stances in the happenings and commit racist acts in their "real" lives. Hostility reverses the complacency of a post-millennial Western public's "docile patriotism", a term coined by Puar and Rai as explained earlier, which denotes the lack of large-scale protest against Western military intervention in non-occidental territories such as Iraq, Syria, and Afghanistan.

Similar to chapter two, the third chapter of this book argues that Samuel Beckett's *Not I* encourages a psychotic form of spectatorship. This galvanizes spectators to reject "gender exceptionalism", a dominant ideology also defined by Puar to describe Western feminism's false belief that it holds the key to Muslim women's enlightenment in a post-9/11 age. As part of Beckett's late plays, *Not I* reflects the Theatre of the Absurd's assault on language and character depth in the extreme: a lone woman, simply named "Mouth", launches into a monologue at lightning speed while a silent woman in a North African djellaba, "Auditor", can only wave her arms silently alongside her. Audiences were shocked at the visual and acoustic intensity of the play when it first debuted in 1972. Actress Billie Whitelaw, who played Mouth, described audiences' "inner scream", which culminated in people fleeing to the toilets. Spectators tried to get away from the rambling orifice in the dark that threatened to swallow them whole with its domineering presence. An audience "inner scream", resembling a psychotic unconscious process of hostility, may be targeted at rejecting the play's depiction of the white Mouth's domination of her silenced, djellaba-clad Auditor. Mouth's domination of Auditor in *Not I* conjures the ideology of gender exceptionalism in which Western women are held to be more enlightened and capable of rescuing their Muslim sisters. However, the psychotic "inner scream" may be directed at rejecting such domination in order to overturn gender exceptionalism. Various performance conditions and staging techniques are identified as encouraging this reading. By analyzing three productions of *Not I* featuring Billie Whitelaw, Lisa Dwan, and Jessica Tandy in the role of Mouth, the chapter insists on the need to divide the spectator's attention equally between Mouth and Auditor in order to ensure that the power discrepancies informing gender exceptionalism are made visible and are challenged.

Chapter four turns to Jean Genet's *The Blacks* (1958), a play about a black community's emancipation from white hegemony. It is argued that the play conjures a viewing reaction guided by the unconscious formation of "supplementary enjoyment", and this permits spectators to challenge contemporary forms of gendered racism. Written during a time of worldwide decolonization and the struggle for Civil Rights in the United States, *The Blacks* (1958) depicts a black community's celebration of the funeral rites of a white woman, Marie, murdered by black man Village. Marie's funeral acts as a ceremonial conduit for black liberation. With speed and myriad plots that collapse in on themselves – notably the revelation that white Marie's murder never actually occurred – *The Blacks* is notoriously hard to follow for audiences. This difficulty of comprehension, it is argued, reflects the baroque complexity of what Lacan called "supplementary enjoyment", a mode of the unconscious that falls outside of discourse as a method to "unlearn" ideological scripts. In the case of Genet's *The Blacks*, gendered racism, the form of discrimination that black women face doubly for their gender and race, is unlearned or reversed. Deconstructing gendered racism is a key project for the post-millennial battle against anti-racism. Mainstream media attention on the Black Lives Matter movement in the US has focused on state-sanctioned police shootings of black men at the expense of treating the violence that African-American women face, as black feminists such as Tamara Winfrey Harris have suggested ("Ain't I A Woman: Making Black Lives Matter"). Throughout the fourth chapter, various production and performance techniques that encourage the unlearning of gendered racism are identified. These techniques include the use of musicality, rhythm, and rap.

In the final chapter on Fernando Arrabal's *And They Put Handcuffs on the Flowers*, supplementary enjoyment as a viewing position is explored again. By taking as its premise the idea that spectators of Arrabal's play experience supplementary enjoyment, the chapter argues that the ideologies idealizing the institution of the prison in our contemporary society are unlearned and undermined. Arrabal's play tells of the atrocities experienced by political prisoners of an unnamed dictatorship. The play was inspired by Arrabal's internment at Carabanchel penitentiary in 1967 under Spanish tyrant General Francisco Franco's regime. Despite these origins, *And They Put Handcuffs* makes no attempt to anchor itself in a specific timeframe and constitutes more of a cross-historical snapshot (from Ancient Greece onwards) of the cruelty that prison has exacted on inmates. Timelessness, a typical feature of the Theatre of the Absurd, enables the recuperation of this play for the present moment. *And They Put Handcuffs on the Flowers* destabilizes the common belief that prisons work as the harbinger of society's wellbeing, instead suggesting that penitentiaries perpetuate violence and injustice rather than solving it. This is relevant for post-millennial America, which has the highest rate of incarceration in the world (despite falling crime rates) and whose "Prison

Industrial Complex" (PIC) has become a profit-driven business aiming to maximize internment in the name of making money. The chapter proposes that the spectator of *And They Put Handcuffs* is positioned to unlearn the modern-day idealization of the Prison Industrial Complex via supplementary enjoyment. I focus on the play's baroque elements of intricate plotlines and high speed, which bear a resemblance to the psychoanalytic concept of supplementary enjoyment. Indeed, I argue that the play presents spectators with a queer aesthetic that accords dignity to prisoners as they enact non-normative forms of eroticism, which act as a motor for social change and a model of alternative justice found outside of the prison. The Theatre of the Absurd's destabilization of the modern-day Prison Industrial Complex is the final way in which this book's argument is confirmed: an avant-garde play from the past can assume subversive meaning for today's setting.

Comedy in Unexpected Places:
Ionesco's *The Bald Soprano* (1950)

This chapter argues that Eugène Ionesco's *The Bald Soprano* (1950) ignites a mode of viewing guided by the psychoanalytic concept of perversion. Perverse viewing disrupts ideological scripts on gender and heterosexuality in our contemporary world. Though we find ourselves a half-century away from the second wave of the feminist movement that swept the world in the 1970s and made hard-won gains for women's equality in areas such as the workplace, queer and feminist critics have written on the persistence of restrictive gender and sexual norms. In the West, women are still expected to be passive, beautiful and submissive as critics of "postfeminism" have indicated (e.g. McRobbie 2008; Tasker and Negra 2007), and men are urged to be strong, emotionally stoic, and dominant (e.g. Connell and Messerschmidt 2005). Moreover, reproductive heterosexual coupledom is still the norm as queer theorists who have studied "heteronormativity" confirm (e.g. Butler 1990; Halberstam 2011). Perversion, on the other hand, seeks sources of pleasure that diverge from these sexual and gender norms. Fetishes, BDSM and other practices of perversion disrupt heteronormativity and other restrictive scripts on gender and sexuality. Feminist critics have extended the practices of perversion beyond the bedroom to the arena of performance (Lorraine Gamman and Merja Makinen [1994]). Following this, I identify in this chapter theatrical strategies in *The Bald Soprano* that are perverse in nature. These strategies enable spectators to escape into the realm of non-normative fantasy beyond the social ideals of the feminine woman, masculine man, and heterosexual marriage. These strategies challenge gender norms and constitute the first way analyzed in this book in which the past movement of the Theatre of the Absurd has subversive value today.

The argument that *The Bald Soprano* can subvert gender and sexual norms seeks to separate the work of Ionesco from critics' tendency to universalize the significance of his oeuvre.[1] Ionesco's output has been associated with an anti-realist designation of "anti-theatre" (Hayman 50), focused, notably, on a form of language that fails to makes rational sense. Critics have tended to present Ionesco as representing gender-neutral individuals in metaphysical crisis because their language fails them. Critics have stressed the playwright's latter-day "humanist" plays (*The Killer* [1957], *Rhinoceros* [1959], *Exit the King* [1962], and *The Pedestrian of the Air* [1962]) in which the recurring character of Bérenger finds himself struggling against encroaching Fascism. Bérenger is alone in contesting a regime that seeks to reduce individual thought to doublespeak and mass crowd psychology. As Martin Esslin wrote in *The Theatre of the Absurd* "loneliness and isolation of the individual" characterize Ionesco's work because his characters have "difficulty in communicating with others" and find themselves "subjected to degrading outside pressures, to the mechanical conformity of society as well as to the equally degrading internal pressures of [their] own personality" (Esslin 197). Bérenger or Ionesco's other characters are not considered for what they say about gender or sexuality in this argument. Indeed, limited work has been done on Ionesco's commentary on gender and sexuality. Critics have preferred to read the play that shall be analyzed in this chapter, *The Bald Soprano*, as demonstrating a gender-blind crisis of language.[2] More broadly, critics have instead favored the oeuvre of queer playwright Jean Genet, whose

---

[1]   The works of Rosette Lamont, who discusses Ionesco's work in terms of gender-neutral "essential essences", is notable in this respect. Rosette, Lamont and M.J., Friedman. *The Two Faces of Ionesco*. Troy: Whitston Publications, 1978; Rosette, Lamont. *Ionesco's Imperatives: The Politics of Culture*. Ann Arbor: University of Michigan Press, 1993. Though too numerous to list in full here, there have been interesting works on the presence of the unconscious in Ionesco's work, but these have tended to resist an analysis of gender. See Gisèle, Féal. *Ionesco: un théâtre onirique*. Paris: Imago, 2001; Marie-Claude, Hubert. *Langage et corps fantasmé dans le théâtre des années cinquante: Ionesco, Beckett, Adamov*. Librairie José Corti, 1987.

[2]   For instance, Richard Schieber maps a Heideggarian paradigm onto Ionesco's play. *The Bald Soprano*, he argues, eclipses an authentic form of being (Heideggerian *Dasein*) behind the play's babble. Schieber, "'Bavardage' et 'silence' du langage dans *La Cantatrice chauve* d'Eugène Ionesco," *The South Carolina Modern Language Review*, 3 (2004). See also Alan, Mandel. "The Bald Soprano Sings: The Concept of the Absurd in the Works of Ionesco and Selected Musical Compositions," *The European Legacy*, 2 (1997), 170-74; Zoran, Milutinovi. "The Death of Representation and the Representation of Death: Ionesco, Beckett, and Stoppard," *Comparative Drama*, 40 (2006), 337-64; Cristina, Scarlat. "Le Spectacle comme forme de résistance: Eugène Ionesco, Jean-Luc Lagarce et *La Cantatrice chauve*," *Philologica Jassyensia*, 14 (2011), 353-61.

The Blacks we shall cover in the fourth chapter of this book, for a reading of gender in the Theatre of the Absurd.

Yet as Esslin himself wrote, "Ionesco's most frequently recurring basic pattern is the married couple" with "the woman usually play[ing] the part of an admiring, but nagging, supporter of the husband" (Esslin 197). Marriage, as queer theorists document, is one of the foundations of heteronormativity, which, in turn, is ideally constituted by gender-normative ideals of the masculine man and feminine woman (Butler 1990). The omnipresent theme of marriage makes Ionesco's theatre ripe for a critical exploration of gender and sexuality. *The Bald Soprano* is one such "marriage" play mentioned by Esslin, alongside *The Chairs* (1952) and *Amédée, or How to Get Rid of It* (1954). Heterosexual marriage is presented as in crisis, as couples cannot communicate meaningfully with one another or seek to escape their spouse. Marriage is a wasteland of miscommunication bereft of all sentimentality and emotion.

The Bald Soprano (1950), Ionesco's début play, features two married couples, the Smiths and the Martins. The play might best be glossed, true to the Theatre of the Absurd's common motif, as a play in which nothing in particular happens. Along with a Fire Chief and a maid, two married couples, the Smiths and the Martins, address each other with empty niceties, clichés, homonyms, repetition, and false syllogisms, fundamentally failing to communicate with one another. The characters' discourse eventually breaks down into a flurry of random words and individual letters before the play ends where it starts, with the roles of the married couples reversed, opening the curtain onto Mr. and Mrs. Martin who adopt the roles that Mr. and Mrs. Smith had enacted at the start of the play. The interchangeability and homogeneity of the heterosexual couple are suggested in this plotline. The Smiths and Martins suggest that hetero-normative marriage and its attendant gender ideals of the "perfect" woman and man are in crisis.

Despite the potential for gender and sexual subversions in the plotline of *The Bald Soprano*, the play has been interpreted as depicting the individual in linguistic crisis, which, as mentioned above, is a theme that dominates the secondary criticism on Ionesco. The characters of *The Bald Soprano* are not considered in terms of their gendered and sexual specificity. Perhaps inspiring critics' tendency to cast Ionesco's oeuvre as the representation of the individual in a linguistic crisis, Ionesco himself dubbed *The Bald Soprano* a "Tragedy of Language" in his autobiography *Notes and Counter-Notes* (1964) (86). Yet, empirically speaking, *The*

Bald Soprano has not garnered audience pity and fear, as Aristotle argued that tragedy conjures. It has generated laughter from audience members, casting the play firmly within the realm of comedy. It is this audience reaction of converting a "Tragedy of language" (Ionesco) into a comedy that I argue resembles the psychoanalytic concept of disavowal, a mechanism of perversion. With the play's critique of marriage and the gender norms subtending it, I further argue that such perversion distorts social expectations of gender and sexuality.

It is performance technique (drag costume, gesture, masks, and so on) that tends to stress the humor of *The Bald Soprano*. It is, therefore, three forms of performance strategy that structure the chapter's analysis: performances that parody femininity, those that assail masculinity, and those that attack both masculinity and femininity together. With comedy ignited in these performance strategies, the spectator is able to "disavow" (as psychoanalysis terms it) or refute gender norms. But first the chapter begins with a fuller explanation of the mechanism of perverse disavowal at work in *The Bald Soprano*, focusing on Ionesco's shock at finding that audiences interpret *The Bald Soprano* as a comedy rather than a tragedy. Spectators' efforts to turn something unpleasant (the stuff of tragedy) into something pleasurable (a comedy) closely resembles the psychoanalytic concept of perversion where sexual pleasure is elicited from unexpected sources.

A caveat is necessary before proceeding: while various perverse strategies (parody, drag costume, and multiple casting) are made to support my argument that the play unsettles restrictions on gender and sexuality, this does not mean to imply that such strategies are empirically produced. Some amateur productions likely deployed certain techniques in order to respond to practical demands, such as the necessity of simultaneous casting of numerous actors in one role so as to meet pedagogical requirements that all students enrolled in a theatre class perform in the production. However, as a collateral effect of pragmatic choices, strategies such as simultaneous casting may be used theoretically in the service of the chapter's argument that the spectator's perverse response will contest dominant views of gender and sexuality.

When the "Tragedy of Language" became Comedy

Infernally circuitous, uneventful, and lacking any real communication between its depthless characters, *The Bald Soprano* was Ionesco's self-styled "Tragedy of language" (*Notes & Counter-Notes* 86). When he wrote the play, Ionesco was inspired – or perhaps un-inspired is a better way to term it – by the Assimil method that helped him to learn English, which consisted in the repetition of banal phrases that he heard from the company's tapes. From this, the playwright described being "overcome by a proliferation of corpse-like words, [and] stunned by the automatism of conversation" (*Notes & Counter-Notes* 86). In *The Theatre of the Absurd* (1961), Martin Esslin contextualized *The Bald Soprano*'s empty language as a broader translation of the existential anxiety of the post-war period. The Enlightenment project linking the language of reason to ideas of social progress had failed society by the mid-twentieth century, having been pressed into totalitarian ends by Nazism and Communism. Ionesco targeted the failure of reason in *The Bald Soprano*, aiming to "drai[n] the sense from the hollowest clichés of everyday language" and to convey a disconcerting "strangeness that seems to pervade our whole existence" (*Notes & Counter-Notes* 27).

Firmly set in the playwright's mind as a "Tragedy of language", *The Bald Soprano* dismayed and surprised Ionesco when it debuted at the Théâtre des Noctambules in Paris. The play did not meet with audience disgruntlement, pity, or fear as an Aristotelian view of tragedy would venture. What it precipitated instead was laughter. This was no one-off incident either. *The Bald Soprano* has garnered chortles, giggles, and guffaws wherever it has been since its 1950 debut, and it has travelled the world over an unquantifiable number of times by now. While Samuel Beckett's *Waiting for Godot* may be the best-known and discussed example of the senseless Theatre of the Absurd, Ionesco's *The Bald Soprano* beats it to the title of the movement's most performed play. Since 1957, French producer Nicolas Bataille's version of the play has been performed uninterruptedly at the small Théâtre de la Huchette on Paris's Left Bank, a production that is currently coordinated by the theatre's administrator Gonzague Phélip and managing director Frank Desmedt.[3] The longevity of this performance run has earned the Huchette a place in the Guinness

---

[3] More information on the history of this remarkable production can be found in Gonzague, Phélip. *Le Fabuleux roman du théâtre de la Huchette*. Paris: Gallimard, 2007.

Book of Records for hosting the world's longest-running play in any one theatre. Not only this, but Ionesco's text has inspired a number of small-scale experimental productions all over the world, such as Brat Production's 24-hour version in Philadelphia (1998, 2007, 2010, 2012). The play has given rise to, as I have written on elsewhere, a continued "spirit of the avant-garde", because producers continue to enlist daring or experimental production methods long after the play's debut on the vanguard scene (Cox 2013).

The Bald Soprano was not the tragedy that the playwright had hoped. While Ionesco conceded that he must have been an "unconsciously comic author" (*Notes & Counter-Notes* 86), he never fully reneged on the topic of the tragedy of banal language, pegging *The Bald Soprano* as an "expression of the unusual" which "can spring only from the dullest and most ordinary daily routine and from our everyday prose, when pursued beyond their limits" (*NCN* 171-172). There is a risk of overvaluing the author's take on his play. Indeed, the dramatic characters of *The Bald Soprano* fit, to a degree, some classic theories of comedy without effort. Their robotic exchanges resemble Henri Bergson's (1944) dictum that comedy was to be found in "the mechanical encrusted on the living" and the laughter that their stiff conversation elicits exemplifies French critic and poet Boris Vian's claims that comedy functions as the "politeness of desperation" (*la politesse du désespoir*).[4]

Nevertheless, casting a glance over some of the contemporary productions of *The Bald Soprano*, recordings of which abound on YouTube, something rings undeniably true in Ionesco's insistence that what he had penned was a tragedy. *The Bald Soprano* is no riotous, laugh-a-minute affair. Certainly, there are conventionally funny bits that pivot on the comedic tropes of repetition and pun. A doorbell scene, for instance, depicts Mrs. Smith's repeated to-ing and fro-ing between the stage and the front door offstage while she utters the same phrase "There must be somebody there. I'll go and see" (Ionesco 22) (no one is, in fact,

---

[4]   Indeed, similarities with the latter position *The Bald Soprano* in a genre of dark or black comedy, since the quotation in fact originates not from Vian but, as Bernard Gendrel and Patrick Moran point out, from Belgian Surrealist Achille Chavée. Chavée deemed specifically "l'humour noir" capable of eliciting audience's "politeness of desperation". Bernard, Gendrel and Patrick, Moran. "Humour: panorama de la notion," *Fabula: la recherche en littérature*, May 24, 2007, http://www.fabula.org/atelier.php?Humour%3A_panorama_de_la_notion.

at the door).[5] Elsewhere, the maid Mary recites a self-penned poem "The Fire" in which she enumerates numerous objects that "caught fire" from a stone to "everything" (37) (including the fire itself). After the poem, Mrs. Martin puns that "That sent chills up my spine" while her husband continues the play-on-words with a "And yet there's a certain warmth in those lines..." (37).

Other than these sporadic examples, however, laughter – judging from my own experience of sitting in on various Parisian productions as well as from YouTube clips – is facilitated mostly via physical gesture. For instance, a group of students that I took to Caroline Raux's production at the Comédie St. Michel (analyzed later in the chapter) reacted with laughter to moments best described as physical slapstick but these same students betrayed bafflement and confusion at some of the more obscure lines of the piece. Obscure or baffling lines in fact occupy most of the playing time. Without the physical addenda of gesture these lines can and do easily fall flat, comically speaking. To cite only a few of these lines: "Dogs have fleas, dogs have fleas", "I'd rather lay an egg in a box than go and steal an ox", "Ah! Oh! Ah! Oh! Let me gnash my teeth", "Crocodile!" (40).

In other words, let us take seriously Ionesco's contention that *The Bald Soprano* is a "Tragedy of Language" to assert that the play treads a thin line between tragedy and comedy. This reflects Michael Bennett's argument, in *The Cambridge Introduction to Theatre and Literature of the Absurd*, that the blended genre of "tragicomedy" is at the heart of a definition of the Theatre of the absurd. His contention is that Absurd theatre contains an "everyday sense of the ridiculous" but the movement's "flattening out of the dramatic/narrative arc" (20) frustrates the possibility of interpreting them as unmitigated comedies. Absurd plays tend to lack a proper plotline, as is exemplified by *The Bald Soprano*'s robotic couples who repeat the same phrases that they began with instead of ending the play. "[N]o, or very little exposition" and "an ambiguous and/or hanging ending" (Bennett 20) provides a non-humorous counterweight to Absurd drama, even if an "everyday sense of the ridiculous" (Bennett 20), such as the meaningless rhetoric of *The Bald Soprano*, is laughable.

We might therefore think of certain plays of the Theatre of the Absurd as falling flat as comedies and becoming tragedies when they are

---

[5] References to the play in the text are to the following edition: Eugène, Ionesco. *The Bald Soprano & Other Plays*, trans. Donald M. Allen. New York: Grove Press, 1958.

performed in ways that fail to be comic, for example via missed timing or a lifeless reproduction of the text. So how might we go about assuring that Absurdism's tragic elements are turned into comedy? Indeed, why might this be desirable? The psychoanalytic theory of disavowal becomes appropriate here. This is because the theory of perversion is also a study of how the unconscious is capable of turning a tragic or anxiety-provoking situation into something pleasurable or comic. As feminist cultural studies critics Lorraine Gamman and Merja Makinen write in their book *Female Fetishism: A New Look* (1994), the pervert is "always the optimist" (220). More than this, the pervert uses pleasure, normally erotic pleasure, to go against heteronormativity, the set of norms that make heterosexuality into a social ideal. Women studies specialist Elizabeth Grosz, in her book *Space, Time, and Perversion: Essays on the Politics of Bodies* (1995), has described perversion as a "disavowal [defiance] of social reality so that change becomes conceivable and possible" (51). Fetishes, bondage, sadism, masochism are just a few of the examples of non-normative sexual practices explored by psychoanalysis as forms of perversion that diverge from heteronormativity, which insists on the primacy of heterosexual reproductive sex, and thus create the potential for change. Perversion also applies to various strategies in performance as Gamman and Makinen write in their book on feminist appropriations of perversion *Female Fetishism* (1994), which allows us to extend the theory of perversion from the realm of erotic practice to the arena of the theater and *The Bald Soprano*.

The theory of perversion fuses both the defiance of gender and sexual norms with the process by which anxiety is turned to pleasure, or, if we analogize *The Bald Soprano* as a case of perversion, the process where tragedy gets turned into comedy. Based on his case study "Little Hans", Freud posited that the male child conjures an object, the "fetish", as a means of diffusing "castration anxiety" (Freud Vol. 23). On seeing his mother, the child fears castration since he supposes that the mother's lack of penis is the result of forced removal, a fate that could befall him too. He "disavows" (*Verleugnung* as Freud terms in German) the mother's lack of penis, continued Freud, in order to avert anxiety, an act which allows him to derive pleasure. Lacan, in his turn, de-biologized the Freudian theory of disavowal. Signifiers or the individual signs of language function as the pleasurable "fetish" object to diffuse anxiety in Lacan's model. In his Sixth seminar on desire, Lacan wrote that perversion could be understood as a series of signs and images "cut off from the development of the drama" (*Sem VI* 310). The Lacanian model insists that errant and non-normative forms of language – off-the-wall jokes, idioms, even individual morphemes, which appear outside of a formal structure or plot – avert the anxiety of "symbolic" castration. Symbolic castration denotes the feeling of severe restriction under dominant ideologies such as those of sexuality and gender.

A Lacanian theory of perversion is particularly applicable to *The Bald Soprano* because errant signs and images "cut off from the development of the drama" (Lacan 310) are to be found in abundance – to the extent, indeed, that they stop the drama from reaching a satisfying conclusion as Mr. and Mrs. Martin merely take up the same nonsensical language that Mr. and Mrs. Smith had begun with. *The Bald Soprano* thus contains the ingredients to feed perversion according to the Lacanian model. But the errant signs and images aren't necessarily taken as producing pleasure in either *The Bald Soprano* or in the theory of perversion. Disavowal, like *The Bald Soprano* falling flat comically and rebounding into tragedy, treads a fine line between anxiety and pleasure. Disavowal is a mechanism that holds two contradicting pieces of information simultaneously – in the Freudian context, "I know that I am castrated" but "I will create sources of pleasure to defy this reality", and in the Lacanian one, "I know I am symbolically castrated or oppressed" but "I will create sources of pleasure to defy this oppression". One false move on the part of the source of pleasure, or on the part of Absurd comedy as I am analogizing, and the individual is reverted to anxiety, and the "tragic" reality of their symbolic castration by dominant ideologies.

My theory is that in the creation of pleasure, or in the experience of Ionesco's play as a comedy to return to my analogy, *The Bald Soprano* will enable spectators to experience perverse disavowal, and this will defy oppression. But what are the circumstances that will accord spectators a "disavowal of social reality so that change becomes conceivable and possible" (51) as Grosz describes? The following will explore productions of *The Bald Soprano* that have enlisted comic technique in order to enable spectators to defy symbolic castration or oppression. Specifically, these comedic techniques have worked in the service of destabilizing gender and sexual oppression. Comedic technique in *The Bald Soprano* parodies ideals of women as ultra-feminine, and masculinity and its attributes (strength, rationality, etc.) as being the exclusive preserve of man. Comedy helps spectators to derive pleasure in a realm beyond these gender norms and restrictions.

Parodies of Femininity

In Western visual culture, women are expected to arrest viewers with their beauty and looks. As cinema critic Laura Mulvey described in her "Visual Pleasure and Narrative Cinema" (1975), beautiful Hollywood actresses connote a "*to-be-looked-at-ness*" (19) and incarnate idealized womanhood. Greta Garbo, Audrey Hepburn, Marilyn Monroe, and modern-day avatars such as Scarlett Johansen and Natalie Portman all exude a "classic" (white) feminine beauty that would fit with Mulvey's view that feminine "*to-be-looked-at-ness*" is tailored box-office success based on male desire. They encourage voyeuristic desire on the part of the spectator who looks on with a "male gaze". The male gaze reduces these women to an object for the pleasures of the all-controlling, self-assured (male) viewer.

By contrast, *The Bald Soprano*'s female characters are not normatively beautiful or coquettish; indeed, they often conjure spectators' laughter through de-eroticized physicality and gesture. This was seen, for instance, in the Alambic Comédie production of *The Bald Soprano* in Paris between 2009 and 2014 (I saw a performance in 2011), which was directed by Alain Lahaye. A Union Jack provided the backdrop to the Alambic *mise-en-scène* to remind viewers of the hyperbolically "English" nature of the Smiths and Martins.[6] The short black dresses of Mrs. Smith and Mrs. Martin recalled the mini-dresses of swinging 1960s London, a time of sexual freedom in a country that had been shaped hitherto by Victorian moral condemnations of desire.[7] The two wives could have encouraged a "*to-be-looked-at-ness*" (Mulvey 19) that views women through a lens of male desire in this setting and in their dresses. However, the presence of the maid Mary inhibited this. Mary wore a dress that was so all-encompassing that it resembled a drape, which de-eroticized the character and encouraged spectators to view the women in a way that was not sexualized. The contrast between a fully clothed Mary with the short dresses of Mrs. Smith and Mrs. Martin was comic in its extremity. The contrast also enabled spectators to view the dresses of the wives, and their catering to male desire, with a more critical eye, parodying the norm that dictates that women should be beautiful and sexualized.

---

[6] Mrs. Smith opens the play with observations about the "English salad" and the "English water" (9) that she and her husband have consumed.

[7] For more on this production, see the interview with the director Alain Lahaye, http://www.dailymotion.com/video/xmwaxg.

Alambic's Mary continued a parody of femininity when she recited an obscure poem "The Fire" in which everything from a "stone", to a "castle", "forest", "men", "women", "birds", and tautologous "ashes", "smoke", "fire" "caught fire" (37):

MARY: I'm going to recite a poem, then, is that agreed? It is a poem entitled "The Fire" in honor of the Fire Chief:

The Fire

The polypoids were burning in the wood
A stone caught fire
[...]
The ashes caught fire
The smoke caught fire
The fire caught fire
Everything caught fire
Caught fire, caught fire. (37)

Mary's announcement that she would recite a poem in honor of the Fire Chief's arrival is followed by a moment of bathos as she describes nonsense and impossibility (fire, ashes, and stone catching fire). This poem itself may not be obviously funny for spectators. Poetic senselessness conjures what Ionesco described as the "Tragedy of Language" (*NCN* 86) where language no longer retains sense. Alambic Comédie stressed the humorous elements of the moment, however, via Mary's heightened gestures. She accelerated her pace of recitation to the extent that she demonstrated the gradual loss of bodily control as her limbs shot up in staccato movements.

This is one example among many when unfunny, or at least limitedly funny, moments are converted into comedy via performance, and comedy is directed at a disavowal of the norms surrounding the way women are expected to look and act. A bathetic, nonsensical poem "The Fire" becomes highly amusing by virtue of Mary's uncontrolled bodily gesture. In psychoanalytic terms, we could label this conversion of unhumorous elements to comedy "perverse" since it resembles the psychological defense mechanism of "disavowal" that is present in cases of perversion. Disavowal is targeted at a defiance of the norms of femininity: Mary's recital of "The Fire" in the Alambic production challenges the idea of the "feminine" women. Her indelicate, and "unfeminine", gestures when she recited the poem in Alambic's production fit into a pattern of perverse escape fantasies from the heteronormative ideal of the delicate, bashful, and unassuming woman. The delicate gestures that women are supposed to enact in order to connote a *"to-be-looked-at-ness"* (Mulvey 19) were overturned with Mary's maladroit limbs shooting in all directions. In laughing at Mary's multi-limbed, goofy, recital of the poem "The Fire", audiences are encouraged to disavow "social reality" (Grosz 51) that binds women to femininity. Laughter thus subverts gender dictates surrounding femaleness and femininity.

In their study of the way women use perversion for feminist ends, *Female Fetishism: A New Look*, Gamman and Makinen name "kitsch, camp, pastiche and parody" as "post-modern aesthetic strategies" that enable "lesbian, bisexual as well as heterosexual women [...] [to] get pleasure" (182) and to escape from patriarchal reality into a realm of non-normative fantasy. More specifically anchored in the realm of parody that Gamman and Makinen describe as enabling women to derive pleasure through perversion, Mrs. Smith of the student production of *The Bald Soprano* in Lucy Cavendish College, Cambridge (date unknown), elicited audience amusement via a parody of femininity.[8] It was not un-feminine gestures that she played with like Alambic's maladroit Mary but an *exaggeration* of femininity or hyper-femininity. Cavendish's Mrs. Smith incessantly watered a vase of flowers attached to the wrist of one hand with a watering can tied to the other while commencing her uninspiring opening speech to her husband on the very "English" nature of their lives: "We've drunk the soup, and eaten the fish and chips, and the English salad. The children have drunk English water" (9). These lines typify the "boring art" that filled the post-war avant-garde period in both Europe and the United States as avant-garde studies critic Mike Sell describes in relation to American playwright Jack Gelber's *The Connection* (1959), which featured a cast of characters waiting for the arrival of their drug dealer or "connection" (*Avant-Garde Performance and the Limits of Criticism* 84). Waiting is a notable feature of the Theatre of the Absurd, as the cue for boredom, the audience's and the characters', is also present in Beckett's *Waiting for Godot* in which the cast wait for the title character who never appears. It is also reflected in the lines just cited in *The Bald Soprano*, particularly since Mrs. Smith launches into the very "English" nature of their lives after "*A long moment of silence*" and against a backdrop

---

[8]   A recording of this production is available in seven parts on YouTube, beginning with http://www.youtube.com/watch?v=1upwbgBOkrw.

in which "*The English clock strikes 17 English strokes*" (9) to mark the uneventful passing of time.

Such boredom hardly connotes laughter. Indeed, it might rebound spectators on the play's "tragic" elements of Absurd "tragicomedy" if we recall Michael Bennett's definition since they frustrate plot development and "flatte[n] out [...] the dramatic/narrative arc" (Bennett 20). However, the Cavendish college production of *The Bald Soprano* managed to make the moment funny by embedding Mrs. Smith's monotonous lines in the same character's repetitive watering-can gesture. This gesture was so frequent that it appeared as an automatism or a nervous tic. Audiences were presented with a moment of physical comedy, which was dependent on ridiculing Mrs. Smith's flaws. She reflects what Alenka Zupančič describes as comedy's emphasis on the split between "material, physical conditions" of the body and the "pure discarnate intellect" (*The Odd One In* 46) that defines human existence as distinct from other species. Archetypal comedic scenes such as a man tripping on a banana skin remind us that the "materiality of the body is what stops [the intellect] from going beyond a certain limit" and thus "counterbalances idealistic escapes" of human intelligence and social convention (Zupančič 47). Indeed, since Mrs. Smith's commentary on the "English" nature of her life with her husband is not highly intellectual – she subsequently launches into truisms such as "[p]otatoes are very good fried in fat" (9) – it could be argued that the watering-can tic of Cavendish's Mrs. Smith drew out and emphasized the text's *a priori* limit on "pure, discarnate intellect" (Zupančič 47). The moment was another instance in which boredom or a lack of pleasure was turned into comedy as audiences laughed, suggesting again spectators' disavowal of the unhumorous in order to focus on comedic pleasure. Pleasure was targeted more specifically at a disavowal or refusal of the norms governing femininity, as the act of being bound to and constantly touching the watering can for reassurance appeared a vulgar exaggeration of the ideology that women are attached to aesthetics, in this case symbolized by flowers.

I have argued so far that audiences of *The Bald Soprano* were encouraged to disavow the norms governing the way women should look and act in Alambic production's de-feminization of the maid Mary and Cavendish's hyper-feminization of Mrs. Smith who appeared obsessively, nervously, concerned with flowers as she caressed her watering can. In other productions, women are made sexual objects following classic cultural expectations. However, simultaneously counter to dominant expectations, women's eroticization is exaggerated to the extent that, again, it becomes laughable and susceptible to perverse disavowal. Laughter or disavowal divests normative femininity of authority. The amateur troupe of Coral Reef High School in Miami (2010-2011) tripled the number of actors playing each of *The Bald Soprano*'s characters, including the two housewives, Mrs. Smith and Mrs. Martin.[9] The play's wives betrayed a demonstratively "sassy" attitude involving finger wagging and hip shimmies in the Coral Reef production, conjuring a form of feminine coquettishness that fits with cultural expectations about women. However, the sheer number of Mrs. Smiths and Mrs. Martins on the stage also hinted at the homogeneity of this social role that women are expected to perform. Ionesco scholar Cristina Scarlat (2011) has written on the homogeneity of the petit bourgeoisie (*la petite bourgeoisie européenne*) (354) that *The Bald Soprano* spotlights in its depthless, robotic married couples of the Smiths and the Martins. Coral Reef's proliferation of hip-shimmying wives brought to audience's attention the gendered nature of the homogeneous upper middle-class discussed by Scarlat.

The multiplication of different actresses to play the same character suggests that women are homogenous, and act according to a predefined script or ideological role. Coral Reef fused this critique of homogenized femininity with comedy, encouraging audiences to disavow the ideological models accruing to women. At one point, the three Mrs. Smiths of the Coral Reef production uttered the play's lines in the doorbell scene, "Men are all alike! You sit there all day long, a cigarette in your mouth, or you powder your nose and rouge your lips, fifty times a day, or else you drink like a fish" (13). Accusations of men being "alike" hinted at the same homogeneity of the "perfect woman" who is expected to be delicate and sexy in our culture. The homogenization of women according to a standard of beauty was additionally stressed by the numerous Mrs. Smiths saying their lines to a backdrop of feminine shimmies and hip-popping. The audience expressed evident pleasure at this criticism of gender roles as loud laughter and clapping erupted in the auditorium, again indicating perverse defiance of gender codes through the pleasures of comedy.

---

[9]   A full version of this production can be viewed on YouTube at https://www.youtube.com/watch?v=V_QPaavaz4U.

The Mrs. Smiths also went one step further in railing against the normalization of gender roles since their accusations against the play's men were nonsensical; after all, men are *not* expected to "powder [their] nose and rouge [their] lips" (13). As queer theorists such as trans theorist and activist Julia Serano have written, men find themselves disproportionately punished for an appropriation of feminine codes as the Mrs. Smiths describe. Serano observes that women are freer to don trousers and tomboyish behavior, because their appropriation of the masculine valorizes the dominant gender category of masculinity. On the other hand, a valorization of femininity, whether by men or other women, tends not to be desired as femininity is the non-dominant category. As Serano writes, this double standard and denigration of femininity extends to the LGBT community: "[i]n today's queer communities, masculinity is praised while femininity remains suspect" (54). Butch and tomboyish identities dominate in queer communities of the Western world, whereas "feminine" accouterments such as lipstick, make-up, and dresses are deemed frivolous by both mainstream and queer communities.

The audience laughter encouraged by Mrs. Smiths' hip-shimmying discussions of men rouging their lips urged spectators to escape to an alternative reality where dignity and pleasure are accorded to femininity, and notably the appropriation of femininity by men. This counters what is disparaged both by the dominant society and in queer circles alike: the trappings of femininity. Spectators could seek out new forms of pleasure in men queering the norms of masculinity via an appropriation of the "feminine" act of rouging one's lips and powdering one's nose. Indeed, this specific form of queer pleasure would seem to be anchored in a "camp" appropriation of femininity, which Gamman and Makinen describe as one of postmodern aesthetic regimes allowing "lesbian, bisexual as well as heterosexual women" in particular "[to] get pleasure" (182) as cited earlier, thus enabling women-centered pleasures to abound in spectatorship.

In addition to the queer pleasures attached to Coral Reef's hip-shimmying redefinition of men as "roug[ing]" their lips, the same production, in its improbable number of people playing one character, aimed at a "Gaga feminism" that queer theorist J. Jack Halberstam has written on as "find[ing] inspiration in the silly and the marginal, the childish and outlandish" for "big and meaningful forms of critique" (*Gaga Feminism* 22). Lady Gaga is known for the flamboyancy of her musical performances while communicating messages that aid the queer community. For instance, in her music video "Born this Way" Gaga is clad in a Halloween-esque skeletal costume as she champions universal social acceptance no matter one's sexuality ("whether gay, straight or bi [...] Baby I was born this way"). Such "gaga feminism" was emphasized in the Coral Reef production of *The Bald Soprano* by the fact that the production opened their version of Ionesco's play to the strains of Lady Gaga's music.

The title of Coral Reef production's Lady Gaga song choice, "Bad Romance", in particular directed spectators to *The Bald Soprano*'s criticism, latent in Ionesco's text, of the model of heteronormative marriage, because the Smiths and Martins are unable to communicate with each other in a meaningful way. Lines from "Bad Romance", such as "You and me could write a bad romance" and "I want your psycho, your vertigo schtick" pointed audiences to the pleasures that Gaga's persona derives from overturning sexualized violence in her song. Gaga's active "want[ing]" of her love's "psycho" constitutes a parodic reference to Alfred Hitchcock's thriller *Psycho* (1960). It brings to mind the iconic close-up of a horrified Janet Leigh, who plays *Psycho*'s hapless secretary Marion Crane, in the shower scene immediately before she is slashed to pieces by a disguised figure later revealed to be the disturbed Norman Bates (played by Anthony Perkins). Gaga re-appropriates this reference via playfulness and, extra-textually, her allegiance to the LGBT cause, hence the "Gaga feminism" that Halberstam describes. Coral Reef enjoined audiences to derive similar inter-textual pleasure when viewing the multitudinous married couples of *The Bald Soprano* to a backdrop of Gaga's "Bad Romance".

In other productions of *The Bald Soprano*, a sexualization of the play's maid Mary has been disavowed and subverted via laughter. A number of other productions have clothed this character in almost-pornographic ensembles. For instance, Mary wore a French maid's outfit in Antonio Morillas Rodríguez's production in Seville, Spain, in 2013 and in Les Polycandre's *mise-en-scène* (2013-2014), directed by Caroline Raux and performed at the Comédie St. Michel in Paris (the latter production I saw with students in 2014).[10] In Gianni Leonetti's 2011 production in

---

[10] A recording of Antonio Morillas Rodríguez's production is available on YouTube at https://www.youtube.com/watch?v=x2VL913tFjQ.

Genoa, Italy, Mary evidently aimed at seductiveness with her long, glossy hair and her red, silk gloves that extended up her arms.[11]

This performance strategy of a near-nude or sexualized Mary gives spectators the opportunity to avert the male gaze and laugh at – and ridicule – the objectification of the female body to which it tends. Turning in greater detail to *Les Polycandre*'s Mary, an almost-naked Mary sat incongruously with the more modest outfits of the rest of the cast. The husbands wore suits, the wives flouncy 1950s dresses, and the Fire Chief a plain black polo shirt. Disavowal of the male gaze was elicited from audiences as they were encouraged to laugh not *at* the near-naked Mary, but *with* her. The presence of "Ionesco", a character who sat at the corner of the stage, was crucial to this. With a self-satisfied air indicated by his head held high up, "Ionesco" interrupted proceedings at numerous points with magician-like hand gestures, which implied his authority as creator of the cast of characters. Mary's objectification was made glaringly obvious as the almost-nude maid enacted puppet-like gestures, implying that she was under the exclusive control of her "master", the playwright Ionesco. The male gaze was made visible to audiences by the presence of Ionesco's objectification and control of the maid Mary. It was made risible because of Ionesco's evident and unfounded sense of self-importance. Audience laughter was directed at overturning the male gaze and Mary's objectification.

Re-appropriations of Masculinity

While the productions just discussed make normative expectations attending femininity risible, this section explores a *mise-en-scène* of *The Bald Soprano* that leverages laughter to disavow cultural expectations about men and masculinity. In the following I detect moments when gender norms surrounding men become the subject of critical laughter and pleasure for spectators. They may be read as moments when, as queer theorist Jack Halberstam describes, masculinity as a social construct, as opposed to something natural or essential, becomes "legible" (*Female Masculinity* 2-3). "Hegemonic masculinity", a term coined by Australian sociologist Raewyn Connell to describe the dominant ideologies surrounding men, rely on the idea that men are "naturally" strong,

---

[11] A part of this production is available on YouTube at https://www.youtube.com/watch?v=NfFfT5KmMn8.

robust, and stoic. I suggest that it is subverted in my analysis of Rita Cofiño's Spanish-language production of *The Bald Soprano* in this part of the chapter.[12]

Cofiño's production of *The Bald Soprano* at the University of Cantabría in 2013 queered hegemonic masculinity via female-to-male drag enactments of the play's Fire Chief. In the original play-text, the character's masculinity is emphasized by his uniform, and his unexpressive demeanor. He enters in the middle of the dramatic action *"wearing an enormous shining helmet"* (24). The improbable dimensions of the Fire Chief's helmet draw attention to his professional activity, the job of a fireman, which remains a highly gendered job largely done by men. The size of the helmet (*"enormous"*) also indicates a certain level of masculine pride the Fire Chief takes in his job. In the text, the Fire Chief plays the taciturn mediator in an argument between the married couple Mr. and Mrs. Smith, uttering one-line phrases such as, "Well, what it is all about?" (24) and "Go right ahead" (25) when the tension mounts between the married couples who argue over whether, when someone rings at the door, there must always be someone there. The Fire Chief's taciturn nature curries favor with the cultural expectation about hegemonic masculinity, which demands that men remain stoic, minimally expressive of their emotions, and rational.

Cofiño's female Fire Chief parodied the masculinity of *The Bald Soprano*'s Fire Chief, as she made no attempt to "pass" for a man but she was also not entirely feminine. She had a robust frame – deemed unfeminine in Western culture – yet she was clad in garish red tights and an all-encompassing skirt that marked her explicitly as a woman. Her helmet, red too, appeared ridiculous, as it was too big for her and covered her eyes. This hinted at a mockery of the text's reference to the Fire Chief's masculine pride in his *"enormous shining helmet"* (24). Cofiño's Fire Chief's garish and awkwardly masculine attire resisted her alignment with normative scripts of women as hyper-feminine, delicate, and coquettish. She also retained the "masculine" personality traits of Ionesco's character. Cofiño's Fire Chief retained the calmness, dignity, and sobriety of Ionesco's original character as she paced solemnly across the stage.

---

[12]   A recording of this production is available on YouTube at https://www.youtube.com/watch?v=0oMD5PI5VDQ.

Incongruous or non-hegemonic forms of masculinity were emphasized by Cofiño's characterization of the Fire Chief as a gendered melee with her red tights, oversized helmet, and stoic overtones. She generated audience laughter in her incongruity, sparking disavowal of the norms surrounding masculinity. Her anecdotes also garnered laughter and they subverted the expectation that men's discourse should be rational and logical. The expectation that men should be the paragons of reason is one of great historical weight in Western culture, dating back to the Enlightenment and German philosopher Immanuel Kant's instruction (1784) that men should enlist a "public use of reason" (Kant 1). The Fire Chief's fables, far from resembling a historically-anchored masculine rationality, are utterly illogical. For instance, the Fire Chief recounts "'The Dog and the Cow,' an experimental fable": "Once upon a time another cow asked another dog: 'Why have you not swallowed your trunk?' 'Pardon me,' replied the dog, 'it is because I thought that I was an elephant'" (30). The lack of moral meaning, which defines the role of the fable in our society, provides the final polish on the senselessness of "The Dog and the Cow". When Mrs. Martin asks for the moral, the Fire Chief replies: "That's for you to find out" (30).

While the text of *The Bald Soprano* provides a parody of rationality (reflecting the play's dimensions as a "Tragedy of Language"), Cofiño's depiction of the Fire Chief's illogical "experimental fables" parlayed irrationality into a laughable disavowal of masculinity. She recounted her nonsensical anecdotes with her head held up high and her hands behind her back, emphasizing the position of male authority that this character is supposed to have over the rest of the cast. Her unfazed and authoritative demeanor appeared unjustified and overblown given the absurdity and nonsensical quality of her lines. The fact that a woman enacted the Fire Chief's authoritative masculinity further queers the norm of male reason, drawing attention to the performed nature of the norms governing how men are expected to act in our society.

Cofiño's Fire Chief could best be described as "masculine" or "butch" woman – the latter term often being used to refer to a sub-category of lesbian identity. The Fire Chief's "butch" persona was made palpable when placed in tandem with the maid Mary, who was highly feminine in appearance and could thus be designated as a "femme", another sub-category of lesbian identity. The butch-femme coupledom of the Fire Chief and Mary in the Cofiño production was made particularly prominent in the reunion scene between the pair, and it gave the play an added female homoerotic or queer sub-text. In the original text, this reunion scene is heterosexual in its guise; Mary enters the dramatic action after the Fire Chief finishes recounting a series of nonsensical fables ("the cold", "the snake and fox", "the cow and crushed glass", etc.). The pair instantly recognize that they are long-lost lovers and reunite with a kiss ("*Mary throws herself on the neck of the Fire Chief*" (35)). In the original text, this moment elicits reproving comments from Mary's employers, which betray their classist prejudice: "MRS. SMITH: [...] I don't like to see...here among us. /MR. SMITH: She's not been properly brought up" (35). In the Cofiño production, the butch Fire Chief's retort "Oh, you have too many prejudices" played not only on class differences between the working Mary and the married couples, but it also targeted the hetero-normative preconceptions harbored by the Smiths. The Smiths cast judgment on the reunion between two long-lost lovers of the same gender. The Martins and the Smiths were dressed in identical outfits, which further targeted the bourgeois, heteronormative mold to which they belong by connoting their incapacity for individual thought.

The reunion scene in Cofiño's production evoked the kind of perverse viewing that I have been championing, which may leverage laughter and disavowal to poke fun at the pretensions of heteronormativity, in particular those that cast aspersions on the possibility of erotic love between two women. The audience was given to laugh at the outraged, exaggerated gestures of the married couples expressing their moral panic when they witnessed the lesbian kiss between the "femme" Mary and the "butch" Fire Chief. The production managed to avoid the recuperation of lesbian love by the male gaze as one might see in mainstream pornography where a man must intervene in the end to conclude the erotic play between two women, a plotline that belittles or disparages the possibility of female homoeroticism separate from men and male pleasure. What was belittled, rather, were the horrified couples, who were cast as unable to accept the chaste kiss between the Fire Chief and Mary.

Parodies of Gender Norms and Post-Gender Alternatives

As sociologists Raewyn Connell, who coined the term "hegemonic masculinity", and James W. Messerschmidt remind us, "[g]ender is always relational, and patterns of masculinity are socially defined in contradistinction from some model (whether real or imaginary) of femininity" (848). "Emphasized femininity", as Connell and Messerschmidt term it, buttresses "hegemonic masculinity" and vice versa. Given the mutually reinforcing nature of feminine and masculine gender norms, it behooves us to look at productions of *The Bald Soprano* that move beyond separate parodies of masculinity and femininity, as we have seen so far in analysis. Instead, let us look at productions that queer and destabilize both sets of gender norms simultaneously. Two productions, the Lucy Cavendish College production at Cambridge University (date unknown) and Jean Berutti's 2004 *mise-en-scène* proved themselves capable of doing this.[13]

Perhaps more out of necessity than choice, the Lucy Cavendish College production at Cambridge University (England) had all six characters of *The Bald Soprano* played by women. The production was at an all-women's college in Cambridge. The cast nonetheless used this all-female cast as the starting premise for an ironic deconstruction of masculinity throughout playing time. For one, the Fire Chief was dressed in male drag. "He" additionally adopted a blustery stance and a "Queen's English" accent. The performer parodied masculinity in a different way to Cofiño's Fire Chief who, as we saw earlier, imbued the character with somber sobriety.

Elsewhere, during a reunion scene between the other married pair of *The Bald Soprano*, Mr. and Mrs. Martin, the couple ended their discourse (in which they adopted robotic, disinterested voices) by standing to seal the end of their estrangement with a kiss. This act revealed a drastic height disparity between the two. Mrs. Martin towered over her husband Mr. Martin. This disparity contravenes hetero-normative standards of the "tall and dashing Prince Charming" of typical reunion scenes. These standards also continue to pervade late twentieth-century and post-millennial narratives as modern-day career women wait for and seek out physically robust and strapping men. One need only think, for instance, of Carrie's "Mr. Big" in *Sex and the City* (1998-2004) and Bridget's neo-Austenian hero, the brooding and mysterious "Mark Darcy" in Helen Fielding's *Bridget Jones's Diary* (1996). In contrast to the physically strong hero of these accounts, in the Lucy Cavendish production a small Donald Martin kissed a towering Elizabeth Martin. The moment reversed gender

---

[13] A version of Berutti's production is available on DVD: *La Cantatrice chauve*, dir. by Stéphane Lébard. Compagnie lyonnaise de cinéma, 2005.

norms, which peg physically weaker women against strong men. This reversal was imbued with irony as Donald exclaimed, "You are my little darling!". Lucy Cavendish's drag-king Mr. Martin impugned the codes that pertain to masculinity in contemporary hetero-patriarchy – notably, those of physical strength and stature. The moment was evidently designed to foster laughter from the audience, permitting audience's perverse disavowal of heteronormative coupledom, in which the man is expected to be physically stronger than the woman, via comedy and pleasure.

Spectators were also encouraged to eschew, by means of laughter and disavowal, white male authority by virtue of the Lucy Cavendish production. As the Martins froze in the end embrace, a highly comical Mary, who was of Southeast Asian ethnicity, intervened. She affected a broken accent and played up a stereotype of excessive servility that white Western society tends to allot Asian women. As writer and Asia cultural and business specialist Sheridan Prasso writes, in her book *The Asian Mystique* (2005), women of Southeast Asian descent are typically reduced to a "China Doll" stereotype, which associates them with the idea of the passive and delicate "Lotus Flower", "Geisha Girl" or "Madame Butterfly" (59). Mary of the Cavendish production performed a race- and gender-conscious form of humor through the exaggeration of this stereotype. A highly broken and accented form of English emphasized her foreignness and distinction from a white Western paradigm.

It was mentioned earlier that Mary recited a nonsensical poem entitled "The Fire", in which ashes, stones, and fire impossibly and tautologously catch fire. Mary's recitation of the poem in the Cavendish production played up the servility of the "Lotus" or "Geisha" girl stereotype, and brought into question the Western prejudices underpinning it. Mary's gestures became uncontrollable and her employers, not wanting to lose face at the sight of their maid's indiscretions, brusquely dragged her from the scene. This emphasized – to a brutal degree – Western society's view of the totalized passivity and disposability of Asian "China Dolls". The moment when she was dragged off-scene by her racist employers was one that elicited spectators' allegiance with Mary. Laughter that was provoked in this act was turned toward a defiance and disavowal of Mary's employers, who were mocked for their concern for social appearances and desperate embarrassment in having a maid who cannot keep control of her limbs.

Mary encouraged spectators to defy the China Doll stereotype not only by exaggerating it, but also by taking distance from it. For instance, in the reunion scene between the long and lean Mrs. Martin and her vertically challenged, estranged husband, Mary revealed that she possessed higher knowledge that the couple in fact do not know each other at all. The whole premise of the couple's reunion was based on false logic since their children have different colored eyes. In the text of *The Bald Soprano* Mary declares that she is aware of the differences between Mr. and Mrs. Martin's respective children, a prior knowledge that undermines the couples' reunion. She steps aside to freeze the dramatic action and defines herself as the "Sherlock Holmes" of the play:

> He believes in vain that she is Elizabeth. She believes in vain that he is Donald – they are sadly deceived. But who is the true Donald? Who is the true Elizabeth? [...] My real name is Sherlock Holmes. [*She exits*] (19)

Cavendish's choice to cast an Asian Mary to utter these words position the maid as challenging a "China Doll" stereotype that would peg her as passive and devoid of intellect.

Stereotypes at the intersection of gender and race were called into question by means of comedy in Cavendish's Southeast Asian Mary. This production also mocked the norms surrounding men and masculinity with an exchange between Mrs. Smith, and Mr. Smith and Mr. Martin. Mrs. Smith recounted the anecdote of a fiancé who gave his beloved a bouquet of flowers. The anecdote in the original text mocks the act of heterosexual courtship in which a man is expected to offer the female object of his affection a bouquet of flowers; Ionesco's anecdotal suitor snatches the offered flowers back from his fiancée before engaging in the impossible and absurd feat of going "off in all directions" (32). The Lucy Cavendish production queered the heterosexual nature of the ritual of offering flowers, as lines that were meant to be uttered by the play's male characters are instead voiced by the women characters of the play. In the text, Mr. Smith observes after his wife's anecdote: "My wife is intelligence personified. She's even more intelligent than I. In any case, she is much more feminine, everyone else says so" (31-32). In the Cavendish production, it is *Mrs.* Smith who uttered the line, wresting them from her husband, in an adapted format: "*They* say my wife is intelligence personified. She's even more intelligent than I. In any case, she is much more feminine" (my emphasis). As she recounted these lines, she sat slouching in her chair, opening her legs wide. Mrs. Smith thus appropriated Mr. Smith's lines from the text for her own purposes, parodying a man's words in this act ("*They say* my wife"). Her slouching posture enabled her to appropriate a masculine gesture as her own. Masculinity was thus disavowed for spectators, as they were encouraged to laugh at the clearly male gestures and lines enacted by Mrs. Smith.

Indeed, Mrs. Smith's performance in this moment overturned Mr. Smith's further attempts to objectify her. At the same time that she poked fun at the pretensions of her masculine interlocutors by appropriating Mr. Smith's lines and gestures (just described), Mr. Smith endeavored to dismiss Mrs. Smith with the line (present in the original text), "My wife has always been romantic" (31). The word "romantic" may be rooted in the misogynistic reduction of women to sentimentality and the realm of emotion. This reduction also dates back to the Enlightenment and Kantian thought (described earlier), as the dialectical opposite of male reason. Mrs. Smith's parody of masculinity as her husband uttered words about his wife's "romantic" nature had the effect of rendering the line an evidently male judgment of women. The gendered nature of Mr. Smith's comments on his wife was also made clear by the fact that he was performed by an actress in male drag – a performance technique that emphasized the social construction of masculinity behind the judgment. Spectators were encouraged to disavow Mr. Smith's judgment by laughing at him.

In sum, Cavendish College blended femininity and masculinity to mock social norms pertaining to both genders. They showed that female masculinity was possible in the drag-king enactments of the Fire Chief, Mr. Martin, and Mr. Smith. The production's ironically-servile-yet-canny Southeast Asian Mary, Mrs. Martin who towers over her husband, and slouching Mrs. Smith who mocks her husband also encouraged spectators' defiant laughter at stereotypes that hold women to be weak and irrational, and deem men to be rational and authoritative. Indeed, the cast seemed intent on moving beyond the circumscription of human gender altogether by adding animal noises into proceedings as the play drew toward its end chaos. The production's decision to end playing time in animal bleating stressed the absurdity of the original text while garnering audience laughter and emphasizing the comedy of the piece. Animal noises represented the opportunity for spectators to disavow gender codes and move towards an alternative, de-gendered visual economy.

Similar to the Lucy Cavendish production, Jean-Claude Berutti's version of *The Bald Soprano* in 2004 conjured a world in which the norms of sexuality and gender were abolished altogether. A DVD was released featuring an interview with Berutti and a recording of a performance of the production at Saint-Genest-Lerpt in the Loire region. As Berutti stated, his aim was to deconstruct the class divides surrounding the avant-garde. He set out to destabilize the elitism of avant-garde theatre, which tends to be staged in and around world capitals and major cities. Berutti took *The Bald Soprano* out of Paris and the big cities where it is usually performed and toured the French provinces with it. He established "pop-up theatres" (*théâtres ambulants*) in which to stage the play wherever he went. A portable theatre, consisting of a boxing ring with a trap door-hole right of center-stage where the characters entered and departed the dramatic action, facilitated Berutti's tour. The recruitment of non-professional young actors at each stop cemented this production's anti-elitist gesture of making avant-garde theatre available to a wide public. In making Ionesco's play accessible to people in the non-Parisian provinces, Berutti demonstrated the potential of the avant-garde to defy boundaries of class and region.

Berutti's aim to challenge class boundaries in taking *The Bald Soprano* out of its metropolitan stomping ground was matched by the production's destabilization of gender and sexual norms. Indeed, as with the other productions we have seen, this production allows spectators to derive comedic pleasure from queering gender and sexual stereotypes. For instance, the choice of set proved propitious in a destabilization of the norms surrounding heterosexual marriage. In the film recording of the production, Berutti established a makeshift boxing ring in a community hall in Saint-Genest-Lerpt. This choice of set placed emphasis on the fact that *The Bald Soprano* is at base about two, heterosexual, married couples, the Smiths and Martins, who fail to comprehend each other and are locked in marital battle. In the text the couples make persistent jibes at one another (for instance: "MR SMITH: Don't interrupt, my dear, you're disgusting" (21)). This may be interpreted as a queering of heterosexual marriage idealized in our culture. Berutti's addition of the boxing ring allowed the comparison of the couples to boxers in a fight. The analogization of wives and husbands as boxers in a ring exaggerated the play's marital conflicts and, in the ludicrousness of the analogy, made the institution of marriage appear risible. The set choice enabled audiences to derive pleasure, through laughter and humor, from the text's destabilization of the matrimonial institution.

Dehumanization of the cast of characters also generated humor and audience pleasure. Berutti's production dehumanized the married couples of *The Bald Soprano*, positioning them beyond the restrictions of gender conventions in a similar way to the Lucy Cavendish production's addition of animal noises emitted by the couples at the end of playing time. In Berutti's *mise-en-scène*, the Smiths and the Martins were clad in white and wore impersonal masks. These masks de-gendered the couples; only certain markers that appeared superimposed onto the characters showed their gender. The superimposition of these markers helped to construe gender as arbitrary and artificial. Mrs. Smith's and Mrs. Martin's gendered trappings were visually more prominent than the men's as they donned longer wigs and skirts. Femininity was thus associated with aesthetics and needless froufrou. The overlaying of wigs and skirts on strikingly white bodies brought to spectators' attention the patriarchal view of women as superficial and vacuous. With their clinically white body suits, all of the characters' appearances resembled those of a clown. This further allowed spectators to take comedic pleasure from the de-gendered figures before them, as it referenced the comic tradition of harlequins and fools in Western culture. The move also poked fun at racial norms. The masks donned by the cast signaled the racial homogeneity of the bourgeois couples. Meanwhile, the cast's hyperbolically white nature ridiculed white domination, moving beyond a world of privilege based on skin color and racial distinction.

The Berutti production also eroticized the "reunion" scene between Mr. and Mrs. Martin discussed earlier in the chapter, generating laughter in order to destabilize the sexual expectations surrounding men and women in heterosexual coupledom. In the text of *The Bald Soprano* the reunion scene between the Martins is undermined by Mary's higher knowledge that the couple does not know each other at all, and their "reunion" is in fact a first meeting. This stresses *The Bald Soprano*'s parody of the institution of marriage, as the couple is unable to recognize each other at first. The couple discovers that they have numerous points in common despite drawing a blank at the level of physical recognition:

> *Mr. and Mrs. Martin sit facing each other, without speaking. They smile timidly at each other. [...]*

MR. MARTIN: Excuse me, madam, but it seems to me, unless I'm mistaken, that I've met you somewhere before.

MRS. MARTIN: I, too, sir. It seems to me that I've met you somewhere before too. (15)

Slowly the Martins discover that they live in the same town, on the same street, in the same house, that they sleep in the same bed, and that they have a child in common.

Berutti's production took the parody of the scene to another, sexualized, level. Both Mr. and Mrs. Martin of Jean-Claude Berutti's 2004 production infused the process of marital de-estrangement with exaggerated gesture. Starting at opposite ends of Berutti's makeshift boxing ring, Mr. and Mrs. Martin begin their exchange in breathless voices that might better find their home in soft-core pornography. Mrs. Martin leant coquettishly back on the ring's wires, connoting sexual receptivity to her partner, while Mr. Martin sat forward with his legs open wide, implying the character's more active stance. These positions coupled with the breathless voices suffused the scene with erotic charge. The voices became increasingly excited as if to imply mounting sexual intensity. Mrs. Martin writhed and shook her chest as she crawled towards her "husband". The act of crawling stressed her submissive position, suggesting the capitulation to men's desire that women are expected to enact in heteronormative, male-centric sex. This power imbalance tipped toward Mr. Martin was stressed as the latter dominated his wife, shuffling towards her in a robotic but nonetheless quick and regular rhythm that insinuated his sexual climax. Both characters took the gendered nature of their gestures, which may be interpreted as an act of marital coitus, to hyperbolic proportions and enabled audiences to laugh at gender and sexual expectations. Mr. and Mrs. Martin "perverted" heteronormative expectations which deem women passive – exaggerated and distorted by Mrs. Martin's submissive crawling, writhing, and receptive leaning back on the boxing ring – and men active – hyperbolized by Mr. Martin's rhythmic shuffling towards his wife.

The objectification of women was, likewise, humorously destabilized in Berutti's *mise-en-scène* by means of the maid Mary. While in Caroline Roux's performance, as we saw earlier, women's objectification was parodied via the near-nudity of Mary, Berutti's production enlisted male-to-female drag performance. A lithe, pectoral man made no attempt to "pass" for a woman in his enactment of the maid.

Queer theorist Judith Butler opines in *Gender Trouble* that drag performance can bring to public attention the fact that gender is nothing natural but is secured via a series of performances and gestures. The "abiding gendered self", she writes, is thrown into disarray via a display of "the arbitrary relation between [performed] acts [of gender], in the possibility of a failure to repeat [such acts consistently], a de-formity, or a parodic repetition" (Butler 141). With wiry hair, an improbably pale face, over-plucked eyebrows, and a body tightly clothed all in black to highlight her masculine frame, Mary of the Berutti production appeared to be the drag "de-formity" that Butler describes of the norms surrounding women. With only one hand in a washing-up glove, Mary also demonstrated a "parodic repetition" (Butler 141) of the norm confining women to domesticity and the kitchen. Mary's improbable appearance also generated much laughter. This laughter permitted a disavowal of normative female beauty standards that pressure women in Western patriarchy to have poker-straight hair, tanned skin, delicately shaped but full eyebrows, and a slim figure with full breasts and hips.

Voice and discourse also enabled a "parodic repetition" (Butler 141) and comedic disavowal of normative femininity. Berutti's Mary had an evidently masculine voice with a deep and round timbre. She made no attempt to make it "feminine" by, for instance, speaking in a higher octave. Often when Mary spoke, she provoked audience laughter. She "de-form[ed]" (Butler 141) the norms surrounding the way women are expected to speak in a delicate, high register, and this encouraged spectators' laughter. Comedy was also emphasized by the actor's holding of a microphone, evoking the role of an emcee or stand-up comedian. Clutching her microphone, Berutti's Mary uttered the following story about the impossibility of the Martins' knowing each other with dramatic suspense and comedic pauses:

> Elizabeth and Donald are now too happy to be able to hear me. I can therefore let you in on a secret. Elizabeth is not Elizabeth, Donald is not Donald. And here is the proof: the child that Donald spoke of is not Elizabeth's daughter, they are not the same person. [...] Donald's child has a white right eye and a red left eye, Elizabeth's child has a red right eye and a white left eye! (Ionesco 19)

The story is not automatically funny but absurd, since having red and white eyes is improbable. Berutti's Mary encouraged laughter in her position as a stand-up comedian with a microphone. She also took pauses in various places to allow the audience to laugh at the absurdity of the couple's reunion. The comedy of the moment was cemented in her stance: with her hips tilted slightly forward, Berutti's Mary conjured a feminine stance when she told this anecdote but her evidently masculine appearance made this performance camp and effeminate.

This is another occasion when a limitedly funny moment in the text, the impossibility of the Martins' knowing each because their children do not have red and white eyes in the same places, is made highly comical in performance. The performance strategy used, moreover, is a camp one, centered on the drag queen enactment of Mary. As saw earlier, in their study of the forms of perversion that aid the cause of feminism *Female Fetishism*, Gamman and Makinen identify that camp performances, such as we can see with Berutti's drag queen maid Mary, form part of a host of "post-modern aesthetic strategies" along with "kitsch, [...] pastiche and parody" which allow contemporary "gay, lesbian, bisexual as well as heterosexual women (rather than men) [to] get pleasure" (182). One need only look at extravagant costumes and music videos of pop stars such as Kylie Minogue or Lady Gaga to see the popularity of camp in modern-day women's creative output and the simultaneous appeal of these artists to the LGBT community. It could be argued, then, that Berutti's production not only enabled a disavowal of the norms surrounding women in the comedic rendition of the maid Mary; a camp aesthetic regime provided the opportunity for forms of pleasure available to women and queer individuals especially.

In this chapter, I have argued that *The Bald Soprano* ignites perverse viewing in spectators, by urging them to convert unfunny or limitedly funny elements of the play into something highly humorous. The conversion of Ionesco's "Tragedy of language" (*Notes & Counter-Notes* 86) into a comedy mirrors the psychoanalytic process of disavowal, which aims to avert anxiety by deriving pleasure from unexpected, tragic, or anxiety-inducing places. Spectators' pleasurable perspective on the dramatic action disrupts or "perverts" ideological scripts on gender and heterosexuality. My argument of the possibility for disavowal has relied on performance technique, which stresses what is comedic in the plot. Exaggeration, parody, hip-shimmying, multiple casting, drag performance, and de-humanizing masks enable spectators' destabilization of the norms surrounding femininity (the subject of the first part of the chapter), masculinity (which we saw in the second part), and both feminine and masculine norms relating to gender and sexual presentation (the third part).

What are the possibilities for similar recuperations of other similar Absurdist offerings? The mechanism of perversion, where disavowal turns a traumatic scenario into a pleasurable one despite the odds, may be in operation in other Absurdist plays. This is because a wealth of other plays belongs to the blended genre of "tragicomedy" as discussed at the start of the chapter. As Ionesco scholar Roy Swanson notes, "tragicomic" strains proliferate in the Theatre of the Absurd canon. Absurdist plays often pivot on "unchanged desire" and "reiterated frustration" until finally we are "present[ed] [with] an absurdity which, when seen as such, becomes humorous indeed" (130), continues Swanson. The liminal space between comedy and tragedy brought up by the Theatre of the Absurd resembles psychoanalytic disavowal where trauma is turned into pleasure.

Indeed, resistant pleasures that are specifically perverse can be found in a number of the other "marriage" plays of the Theatre of the Absurd that waver between tragedy and comedy. The British playwright Harold Pinter, who has been associated with Absurdism, wrote *The Birthday Party* in 1957. The play starts in much the same way as Ionesco's *The Bald Soprano* as the exchange between married boardinghouse owners Peter and Meg is banal in the extreme. The American playwright Edward Albee also conjures the tragicomic marriage paradigm of Absurdist plays in *Who's Afraid of Virginia Woolf?* (1962). Set on a campus in a New England university, married couple George and Martha have become disenchanted enemies. These are two other examples of the Absurdist movement in which marriage is derided via Absurdist humor, and they present themselves as future candidates for application of the paradigm that I have developed in this chapter.

Remembrance Through Rejection: Active Nihilism, Vietnam, and Adamov's *Off Limits* (1969)

This chapter examines Russian-born Absurdist Arthur Adamov's *Off Limits* (1969). It argues that this play, about the Vietnam War (1955-1975), stimulates a mode of viewing that resembles the psychical state of psychosis. *Off Limits* provides a critical lens on the long, drawn-out conflict in Vietnam that lasted a total of two decades between the Soviet-supported North and the anti-communist South of the country, which was heavily reinforced by the United States. The conflict is believed to have caused anywhere up to 3.9 million fatal casualties, and constitutes one of the first controversial US military interventions abroad (Lewy 450-453). Vietnam has since been followed by a plethora of other American military interventions in foreign territory: the first gulf war (1990-1991), and the wars in Iraq (2003-2011), Afghanistan (2001-), and now in the civil war in Syria (2011-). Adamov's play may be connected to these subsequent conflicts via its critical stance on US military intervention overseas. Spectators of *Off Limits* may harness psychotic spectatorship to interrupt the Western public's "docile patriotism", which is a term that queer theorists Jasbir Puar and Amit Rai have coined to describe the post-9/11 climate (Puar and Rai 2002). Psychosis conjures anger, which counters the Western public's "docile" support of American military intervention. *Off Limits'* destabilization of Western docility is the second way in which a past Absurdist play may be recuperated for subversive ends in post-millennial times.

Arthur Adamov, born in Kidslovodsk in 1908 to Russian-Armenian parents who fled the Russian Revolution, was known among the playwrights of the Theatre of the Absurd for the overt political messages communicated in his theatre. With early Communist allegiances that gradually dwindled as the violence of Stalin's empire became evident, Adamov remained nonetheless a "man of immense [...] passion and commitment" (Esslin 127) throughout his life according to Martin Esslin in *The Theatre of the Absurd*. Adamov viewed theatre as a political forum to stimulate spectators' critical thought processes and to educate audiences. He wrote on such political subjects as apartheid in South Africa in *La Politique des Restes* (1967), the Paris commune of 1871 in

Printemps '71 (1961), and the Vietnam War in *Off Limits* (1969), the play under analysis in this chapter.

Off Limits should have been a roaring success among avant-garde audiences and critics, as it was written in 1969, a time when backlash against the Vietnam War was reaching its apogee before American withdrawal in 1975. What should have further cemented the play's popularity was that it was a sign of the times: the play emerged when Vietnam Protest Theatre, which as theatre scholar Nora Alter writes of in her eponymous book, was flourishing in the United States and Europe. George Tabori's *Pinkville* (1971), Peter Weiss's *Vietnam Discourse* (1970), Armand Gatti's *V Comme Vietnam* (1967) and André Benedetto's *Napalm* (1968) (Alter 1996) were just some of the plays similarly questioning America's unconscionable war abroad at around the same time as Adamov's *Off Limits*.

However, perhaps what is most surprising about *Off Limits* is that it was a flop. Reviewers of the play's only stage productions in Paris and Milan roundly condemned the play as unclear, unstructured, and evasive. It was "badly constructed, [...] incoherent, [and] spineless" (*Combat*) for Mathieu Galey, without "head nor tail" (*sans queue ni tête*) (*Le Figaro*) for Jean-Jacques Gautier, and gave rise to a "violent reactionary campaign" (*L'Humanité*) according to René Gaudy.

The plot of *Off Limits* is centered on a drive for annihilation and nothingness. This enervated critics who thought that vocal and clear protest against the Vietnam War was of vital importance. Written just one year before Adamov committed suicide in 1970 after being plagued by alcoholism and a barbiturates addiction, the play gave a snapshot of a group of wayward and dissolute American avant-gardists who reacted against the Vietnam War in a series of "happenings". Happenings were short performance pieces that were abstract and not fully scripted, and which became popular in the postwar period in the United States. In *Off Limits*, there is no one clear storyline to the piece but rather several subplots that do not lead anywhere but to destruction and annihilation. Alongside the heterogeneous and abstract happenings, spectators are presented with various wayward characters, who were inspired by Adamov's trip to the United States and his impressions of a broken country in the shadow of Vietnam:[14] teenager Jim suffers from a drug addiction and he is killed at the Mexican border escaping conscription; his girlfriend Sally is killed

---

[14]   Adamov described his trip to the US in his autobiographical *Ici et maintenant*. Arthur, Adamov. *Ici et maintenant*. Paris: Gallimard, 1964.

too and, together with the violated prostitute Molly, represents the long-suffering women of American society; television workers Humphrey O'Douglas and Doris Roan greedily wish to capitalize on dramatizing Vietnam, while the partygoers Luce, Dorothy and others undermine their own, vocal, objections to the war by committing racist acts towards their fellow Americans. The play ends not with the clearly resolved conclusion of any of these characters' fates but with a number of decimated Statues of Liberty strewn across the stage, symbolizing the broken nature of American society in the shadow of the Vietnam War.

For the seeming hopelessness and lack of direction demonstrated in *Off Limits* critics and audiences condemned the piece. The play in fact never made it into the canon of Vietnam Protest Theatre named by Alter. Indeed, the play's plotlessness recalls the Theatre of the Absurd, which was, as theatre scholar Arnold Hinchliffe described, a theatre of "nothing" (99).

However, it is precisely in this pursuit of nothingness that *Off Limits* may be politicized. Adamov's style of Absurdism, according to Esslin, showed a world devoid of meaning but, as he insists, this is with a "presupposition that the world *has* a meaning, although it of necessity is outside of human consciousness" (Esslin 97). Re-interpreting Esslin's words in my analysis of *Off Limits*, I argue that spectators are encouraged to engage in a critical quest for the truth of what happened in Vietnam "outside of human consciousness" (Esslin 97), in the realm of their unconscious. This unconscious reaction is guided by the mechanism of psychosis and a drive toward uncovering the truth obscured by social codes.

Journalist René Gaudy for the French leftist newspaper *l'Humanité* observed that *Off Limits* gave rise to a "violent reactionary campaign" (*une violente campagne réactionnaire*) in the play's stint at the Piccolo Theatre in Milan in 1969. Yet this "violent" reaction of rejection is taken positively in this chapter, and deemed essential for a recuperation of the play in post-9/11 times. The public reaction to *Off Limits* is read as a symptom of audience anger at the way *Off Limits* chose to stage Vietnam as a wound that primarily affected an American avant-garde and bourgeois elite, displacing the Vietnamese victims. Following feminists of color who have separated anger from the notion of irrationality and who have recuperated it as a legitimate feeling (Ahmed 2004), it is possible to read audience ire as providing a proverbial wake-up call from a state of post-millennial "docile patriotism". The latter, according to queer theorists Jasbir Puar and Amit Rai, marks the post-9/11 climate. However, it is equally as applicable to Vietnam. In a world where the American battle against Islamic fundamentalism reigns and invasion of territories such as Afghanistan, Iraq, and Syria has become normalized, Puar and Rai explain that the media infantilizes the public. It convinces them that they are in danger of an imminent threat from terrorist "monster[s]" (Puar and Rai 131-132) if America does not intervene abroad, and uses fear tactics to quell protest. Vietnam, the subject of Adamov's play, was the world's first "television war". It was the first instance in which the media manipulated the American public to quell protest and stir up support for the US's questionable actions abroad.

The hostile or "violent reactionary" campaign described by Gaudy against *Off Limits* potentially wakes spectators out of the stupor engineered by the media both in the post-millennial period and during the Vietnam War. This is because *Off Limits'* happenings are in fact highly critical of the mediatization of the Vietnam War. But the buck does not simply stop at a critique of the dominant media surrounding the war. The happenings, which demonstrate the media's shortcomings in accurately representing the war, act in concert with the play's dramatic action, which recounts the everyday lives of the American characters. Spectators are urged to a state of anger about the hypocrisy of the characters of *Off Limits* as they claim to be against the injustices of the war in their happenings while, in their own lives, they commit racist acts. This anger, it is argued, resembles the affect in operation in psychosis. Psychosis also stirs individuals into rejecting dominant social codes in what Lacan described as a process of "foreclosure". It is the foreclosure, or discarding, of American Liberalism that is encouraged at the end of *Off Limits* as we shall see in the second part of the chapter. Rather than simply meaningless, *Off Limits* enables the spectator's rejection of American Liberalism and opens them onto the questioning domain of the Real, which seeks to recover elided and unknown histories about the Vietnam War. This reflects Esslin's insistence that Adamov's Absurdism implied hope and meaning "outside of human consciousness" (Esslin 97) or, in this context, outside of what is heretofore known about Vietnam. The foreclosure of American Liberalism is also crucial for a politicized play about conflict in current times. As post-9/11 scholars such as Jaap Kooijman (2013) have noted, American Liberalism remains a pernicious ideology that places a stranglehold on public protest against the contemporary invasion of Islamic territories from both liberal and conservative sides (Kooijman 92).

In identifying the critical intervention that *Off Limits* can provide for spectators of a post-9/11 era, this chapter does not wish to collapse different historical moments into one. Vietnam and the post-9/11 era each have their own historical, cultural, and social specificities, a fact that must not be forgotten by readers throughout this chapter. However, my view is that *Off Limits* may be placed in the post-9/11 setting by virtue of "the uncanny momentary correspondences of history" (Harding 205), which avant-garde scholar James Harding describes in his book *Ghosts of the Avant-Garde* (seen in the introduction). Uncanny historical correspondences help us to link past vanguards to present moments as Harding recounts in the context of his analysis of American vanguard troupe Living Theatre and its production of *The Brig*. As also covered in the introduction, *The Brig* depicted the pitiable conditions for inmates of a Marine prison in the 1960s, but as Harding argues, it disturbed post-9/11 audiences learning about the events at Abu Ghraib. This chapter seeks out similar uncanny historical correspondences that link the Vietnam War and the way it is represented in *Off Limits* to our post-9/11 world.

The chapter contains two main parts. The first part analyzes the anger of audiences, which I argue is psychotic in nature. The characters take a stand against the Vietnam War in the abstract happenings, but they commit racist acts against African Americans on their own doorstep. It is the hypocrisy of the characters' anti-war stance in the happenings and their real-life prejudice that stirs spectators' anger. This mirrors the way delusion, in psychoanalytic theories of psychosis, encourages a reaction of hostility from the juxtaposition of unreal delusions with symbolic reality. The second part of the chapter focuses on the central mechanism of the psychoanalytic theory of psychosis: foreclosure. It argues that audiences "foreclose", or reject, American Liberalism in the play's ending. Such foreclosure is relevant to the era post-9/11, because American Liberalism allows the West to continue supporting American military intervention abroad. Together, both parts posit that *Off Limits* enables the spectator's rejection of current America-centered versions of the Vietnam War, opening them onto the questioning domain of the Real that seeks to recover elided and unknown histories about the conflict.

I ground both parts mostly in theoretical reflection. This is because *Off Limits* has a very limited performance history to draw on. The play has only been produced twice – once by Gabriel Garran in Paris and the second time by Klaus Michel Grüber in Milan. Both staged their versions of Adamov's play immediately following the text's publication in 1969. In other words, the modernization of *Off Limits* for post-9/11 audiences has not so far been explored in performance. The conclusion of the chapter nonetheless turns to hypothesize production and performance methods that future *mises-en-scène* may harness to draw out the links between past and present and encourage the psychotic form of spectatorship theorized here. Flashing images and the theatrical concept of "liveness", which places emphasis on action in the present tense, are discussed in this concluding part.

Audience Anger and Psychosis

This part of the chapter will analyze how *Off Limits* stirs a form of anger in spectatorship that is akin to psychosis. My analysis is two-pronged, because *Off Limits* contains two main dramatic components: the "happenings", which are abstract avant-garde performances, and the dramatic action that depicts the "real" lives of the characters outside of the happenings. Local violence depicted outside of the happenings highlights the hypocrisy of the characters' protests in the happenings. This stokes an unconscious anger in spectators, because the happenings and dramatic action mirror the co-existence of delusion and reality in psychosis, which gives rise to what Freud and Lacan both described as a hostile critique of reality.

"Happenings" in Adamov's *Off Limits* remember the events of the Vietnam War through a prism of inaccuracy and, in some cases, flagrant falsity. As the character Lisbeth states, "in all our happenings, we are trying to translate into gestures and cries a…dilapidated…form of thought" (75-76).[15] However, the "dilapidated" thought and untrue versions of Vietnam told in the happenings are not gratuitous: they are related to the ways that the American media recounted the war, suggesting that the lies issued from the mediatization of Vietnam rather than the cast. A considerable proportion of the play's characters work in American television (Humphrey O'Douglas, Reynold Day, Doris Roan, George Watkins) while the characters James Andrews and a newspaper seller work in print media. The characters enacting the happenings make a commentary on the mediatization of the war. Additionally, Gabriel Garran's and Klaus Michael Grüber's productions of *Off Limits* in

---

[15]   References to the play in the text are to the following edition: Arthur, Adamov. *Off Limits*. Paris: Gallimard, 1969. All translations of the text are my own. Original: "nous essayons, dans tous nos happenings, de traduire en gestes et en cris cette pensée…vétuste."

1969 visually framed *Off Limits'* happenings as views of what was being reported to Americans in the media. They did this by staging the cast's happenings against a backdrop of the Channel 5 American television studio that some of the characters work in. Part of Garran's production, which took place in the Parisian suburb of Aubervilliers, depicted a studio while individual television screens were interspersed throughout the auditorium. Grüber's production in Milan, more non-naturalist than Garran's, similarly consisted of a stage littered with television screens against a clinically white backdrop (Gaudy, *L'Humanité*). The scenography of the Grüber production, moreover, emphasized the false nature of the stories circulated by the media that were re-told in the happenings. Television screens were positioned alongside a number of toilets, sinks, and bidets, implying that media narratives about the war were tantamount to excrement.

Klaus Michael Grüber's production of Off Limits in Milan's Piccolo Teatro in 1969

Copyright © Photo Luigi Ciminaghi/Piccolo Teatro di Milano – Teatro d'Europa

Against a backdrop that emphasized media constructedness and falsity, the cast enacted historically inaccurate or exaggerated events relating to the Vietnam War. In one happening, teenager Jim, who throughout the play avers his militant stand against American intervention abroad, cries out: "Na...na...na...na...na...pal...palm. (*Shouting:*) Napalm! Death to the children! Death to those younger than 13! All are hit! Victory is ours!" (76).[16] Jim luxuriates in the acoustics of a word that caused mass death and injury in order to criticize, via exaggeration, the American mediatization of the use of napalm by the US army. Jim's cries of the US victory enabled by the chemical weapon napalm ("Victory is ours!") reflects media and communication studies scholar Joanne Garde-Hansen's summary of the official image and news releases that were submitted to the American media by the US military and government at the time of the Vietnam War. These dominant US news stories "produced the Vietnamese civilians as subhuman insurgents and [American] soldiers as heroes" (Garde-Hansen 111). Stressing the media's focus on US military prowess, Jim downplays and displaces the Vietnamese victims in his focus on the sonorous pleasures that the word napalm produces ("Na...na...na...na...na...pal...palm"), reflecting the "sanitised images, editing, brevity and framing" (Garde-Hansen 111) on the part of the government-backed, pro-war American media.

Despite the media's glorification of napalm referenced in *Off Limits*, in reality, the devastation wrought by the American military's use of the chemical is never more readily illustrated than with the story of "Napalm Girl", Kim Phúc. Phúc was captured in a photograph running, severely scalded, from her village in 1972 after American deployment of the chemical. The photograph sent shockwaves around the world and turned people against American involvement in Vietnam as Canadian economist and writer Denise Chong (2001) argues. Yet before 1972 the American media downplayed the violence caused by napalm and even later films on Vietnam sanitized the US legacy of chemical weaponry in Vietnam. For instance, *The Deer Hunter* (Michael Cimino, 1979) glamorized "with wicked virtuosity" (Franklin 39) the use of napalm, as US cultural historian Bruce Franklin explains, twisting the facts by claiming it was North Vietnamese forces that deployed the chemical on a South Vietnamese village rather than the Americans. Jim's inaccurate depiction of the American deployment of napalm, in this view, only exaggerates the callous glorification of the use of napalm that was already circulated in the real-life media and film. His rejoicing in the word "napalm" turns spectators to a critique of the role of the media in the war.

---

[16] "Na...na...na...na...na...pal...palm. (*A tue-tête*) Napalm! Mort aux enfants! Mort aux moins de treize ans! Tous atteints! Victoire acquise!"

The Cold War, in which US intervention in the Communist north of Vietnam may be contextualized, is also distorted in a later happening in order to underline the false stories of the American media. The agent of this later happening is the American media mogul, Humphrey O'Douglas, who is, as the stage directions read, "debonair, almost always drunk, industrial, [and] the director of Channel 5" (13). A television channel director, Humphrey champions the American values of liberty and freedom in his praise of the "fundamental liberties of man and the citizen" (139).[17] In this stance, Humphrey becomes the embodiment of the media narrative that US intervention in Vietnam was necessary to liberate the Vietnamese from the threat of Communist tyranny in the north of the country. As he states, US military intervention in Vietnam is necessary in order to create "a world where one can say what one thinks, without fear, a world unknown in Peking, Havana, Moscow, a free world" (139).[18] As a dislikeable "debonair" and "drunk", however, spectators are already primed to view his words with skepticism.

Spectators' critical eye on American media narratives about US liberation of oppressed peoples is cemented immediately after with Humphrey's re-enactment of the Hungarian Uprising against the character Lazlo, a Hungarian immigrant. During the Hungarian Uprising, over 2,500 Hungarian civilians lost their lives in an unsuccessful revolt against the Soviet Empire. Yet, in this happening, it is the embodiment of American "liberty", Humphrey, who commits violence against a Hungarian and not the Soviets. Humphrey declares vituperatively to Lazlo, "Confess that you stole my wallet" while violently frisking the Hungarian character for evidence of his suspicions. Finally, when Humphrey finds his wallet, he shouts: "So that's how property is stolen, in the Hungarian style?... Well, if the Russian tanks had run you over, that would have made one more victim but one less thief" (140).[19] While it was the Soviets who committed the events of the Hungarian Uprising of 1956 that Humphrey references with his mention of the "Russian tanks" running over the

---

17   "Débonnaire, presque toujours saoul, industriel, [et] directeur de la Cinquième Chaîne de T.V." "Les libertés élémentaires de l'homme et du citoyen."

18   "Un monde où on peut dire ce qu'on pense, sans peur, un monde inconnu à Pékin, à la Havane, à Moscou, un monde libre."

19   "Avoue que tu as piqué mon portefeuille, avoue victime! (*Humphrey fouille Lazlo Dery, trouve son portefeille dans sa poche; Lazlo Dery tremble de tous ses membres.*) Tiens, je découvre une vieille connaissance. (*Pause.*) Alors c'est comme ça qu'on file, à la hongroise?...Eh bien, si les tanks russes t'avaient passé dessus, ça aurait fait une victime de plus mais un voleur de moins."

Hungarians, it is a representative of the US media who is exposed as a hypocrite and even the agent of violence against the Hungarians in this happening. Humphrey's violence holds his previous championing of the "fundamental liberties of man and the citizen" (139) up to scrutiny. Humphrey undermines his own discourse about the fundamental right to liberty of those living under Communism in his violent and oppressive actions against Lazlo. The media narrative about American liberty as a justification for military intervention in Vietnam is exposed as hollow and empty. Indeed, in Humphrey's contradictory actions, it is America impositions of "liberty" on the rest of the world that is shown to be the true agent of violence.

Vietnam is re-told in a distorted way in *Off Limits'* happenings in order to cast a critical eye on the American media. Jim signals media glorifications of the use of napalm, and Humphrey reveals the violent reality behind the media's claims of America liberating the world from the threat of Communism. As such the play's happenings reflect what avant-garde studies critic Mike Sell describes as the "bad memory" (*Avant-garde Performance and the Limits of Criticism* 163) that characterized the happenings when they flourished in post-World War II America. The happenings were "event art" or short performances that were not scripted or staged, reflecting a move towards non-theatrical forms of performance that had been gathering momentum throughout the early decades of the twentieth century in Europe and America, as exhibited by movements such as Dadaism. Since they were short, often plotless and abstract, sketches or performances, the happenings disallowed "traditional kinds of history or criticism" (Sell 163). This "bad memory" is illustrated, for instance, by feminist performance artist Carolee Schneemann's happening, entitled *Meat Joy*, which she enacted at the Festival of Free Expression in Paris in 1964. *Meat Joy* centered on a group of semi-naked women who writhed on a floor covered in raw meat and fish juices. The performance was rife with suggestions of women's confinement to the domestic sphere throughout history. However, its abstraction opened spectators to a view of history that was not accurate but rather premised on affect and "the contradictory feelings evoked [...] disgust and titillation" (Sell 135) at the sight of women bathing in meat juices.

"Bad memory" is invoked in the details of *Off Limits'* happenings, such as Jim's rejoicing in the word "napalm" and Humphrey's enactment of the Soviet atrocity of the Hungarian Uprising as a representative of the American media. Spectators grasp a non-traditional view of history

(Sell), which criticizes the role of the American media in reporting the war. The strategy of the happenings to cast history and memory in a non-traditional light is a particularly relevant one for debunking the various myths surrounding the Vietnam War as they were constructed by the US media. As US cultural historian Bruce Franklin (2007) describes, Vietnam was "something that divided, wounded, and victimized America" (34) in the American cultural imaginary. It was the first conflict in modern history that was played out on screens across American homes from start to finish, and thus became known as the world's "first television war". Typically, the media legitimized American intervention in Vietnam under the banner of an all-American heroism. It was deemed up to the Americans to "rescue" South Vietnam from the communist North. Even where the media was more critical of US military intervention, America – rather than the Vietnamese victims – was omnipresent. A liberal-radical strand of the media protested American involvement in Indochina in defense of "romantic version of Maoist revolution" (394) as US historian Charles DeBenedetti noted. In both narratives and in all cases, the US media downplayed the number of Vietnamese civilian casualties, instead privileging Americans – the soldiers who lost their lives, the heroism of their armies, or a public back home divided between pro- and anti-war camps. Casting a critical eye on the US media, the "bad memory" of *Off Limits'* happenings may thus debunk the American "empire of memory" (206), as ethnographer Christina Schwenkel terms it, that dominated constructions of "Vietnam" for the American public.

The non-traditional view of remembering Vietnam, by way of the happenings, is similarly premised on affect and emotion as Sell describes with reference to Schneemann's *Meat Joy*. As we recall from critic René Gaudy's description, the play provoked a "violent reactionary campaign" (*L'Humanité*) when *Off Limits* was staged in Milan in 1969 by director Klaus Michael Grüber. History and memory of Vietnam are accessed by means of spectator anger in *Off Limits*. However, it is not simply or even mainly the American media, held up to scrutiny in the happenings, that spectators are encouraged to be angry at; rather, it is the *cast* of the characters, described by Philippe Madral as "masochistic and bohemian intellectuals fascinated by their own derailing" (*L'Humanité*), that stoke audience ire.[20] The happenings are re-inscribed in the dramatic action

---

[20] My translation. Original: "[i]ntellectuels masochistes et bohèmes, fascinés par leur propre déroute".

and a depiction of the "real" lives of the characters. In this re-inscription, spectators are exposed to the cast's hypocrisy, as they criticize the American media's glorification of the Vietnam War in the happenings while in their own lives they commit racist acts.

As an illustration of this, anti-war teenager Jim, who critiqued the American media's representation of the use of napalm in the happening described above, manifests little concern for a badly beaten black man returning from the Vietnam War. Indeed, Jim accuses the returning soldier of being the "lackey of American imperialism" (*le laquais de l'impérialisme américain*) (131). This comment refers to the disproportionate presence of African Americans sent to fight in Vietnam. The disproportionate enrollment of African Americans, in fact, stems from structural discrimination in the US, which exempted many whites from conscription. As American historian James Westheider writes, white middle-class individuals were more eligible for deferment of their conscription than economically disadvantaged minorities as the American government exempted many skilled workers and students from the roll call (Westheider 22). Jim refuses to confront the structural nature of American racism, which promoted and encouraged the disproportionate drafting of African American individuals to Vietnam, in his bitter accusations against the nameless African-American war veteran. His harsh judgment of black Americans as "lackeys" of the American government's imperialist intervention in Vietnam shows little sympathy with the reality of African Americans, who were left more vulnerable to conscription than whites because of economic and racial disadvantage. Jim's lack of sympathy, indeed racism, is held in tension with his protests against US involvement in Vietnam in the "Napalm" happening described earlier. Jim is free to criticize the American media's glorification of the deployment of napalm, because he has eluded conscription, fleeing to the Mexican border with girlfriend Sally. Later references to Jim's allowance (*pognon*) (52) from his father cements the role of white economic privilege in the character's anti-war stance.

In his happening, Jim critiques the violence meted out to the Vietnamese people on the part of the American media and its glorification of the chemical weapon. However, in his "real" life dismissal of the veteran black man, Jim shows himself to be just as much the agent of violence against racialized bodies as the media was to the Vietnamese. *Off Limits* draws out the contradictions between the characters' actions in the happenings and in their real lives to demonstrate that the characters are thus not simply passive recipients of the news but are active agents who are complicit in the American media's biases. Domestic racism becomes indissociable from US military violence on foreign terrain. It is from this that spectators' anger is stirred.

Off Limits uses the happenings to underline the violence committed by Americans in their real lives. This mirrors the mechanism of psychosis, which as both Freud and Lacan noted, similarly generated hostility, aggression and anger in individuals. We may analogize the happenings, which form "bad memories" of Vietnam such as Jim's indulgence in the word napalm and the American enactment of the Hungarian Uprising, as what Lacan called the "irréalisation" (*irréalisation*) of delusion (*De la psychose paranoïaque* 238). Delusion is the symptom of psychosis, which is premised on a false or "irreal" language as Lacan stated. Yet delusion works in tandem with symbolic reality, as is illustrated by Lacan's observations on his patient, "Aimée". Lacan wrote on Aimée's ability to retain a relatively normal life even as she experienced delusion: "alongside [her] professional life where her ability to adapt is relatively well preserved, the patient leads as she says another 'irreal' or 'entirely imaginary' life" (*De la psychose paranoïaque* 238).[21] This psychotic double life, as Freud pointed out, enables individuals to see the injustices and contradictions of symbolic reality. As Freud said of his psychotic patient Dr Schreber, "the human subject [who experiences delusion] has recaptured a relation, and often a very intense one, to the people and things in the world, even though the relation is a *hostile one now*, where formerly it was hopefully affectionate" (my emphasis) (Vol. 12, 70-71). Delusion enables the psychotic's "hostile" stance on symbolic reality where before it was "affectionate".

Returning to *Off Limits*, it is only with the help of the "irreal" happenings purporting to denounce American media representation of Vietnam that spectators are able to react in a hostile manner to the characters in their everyday lives. Spectators are repeatedly confronted with the hypocrisy between what the characters say and what they do. Spectators are made to react angrily against these "masochistic and bohemian intellectuals fascinated by their own derailing" (Madral *L'Humanité*) in their "real" lives. It is in this way that we may analogize *Off*

---

21 My translation. Original: "A côté de cette vie professionnelle où l'adaptation est relativement conservée, la malade mène une autre vie 'irréelle' nous dit-elle ou 'entièrement imaginaire'."

Limits as creating a psychotic form of spectatorship, which explains the audience anger and "violent reactionary campaign" (Gaudy *L'Humanité*) that the play provoked when it was staged.

Another example of the play's critique of the characters' "real" lives lies in the juxtaposition of the opening happening with the characters' racist preconceptions. The play begins with a happening that involves the opening and closing of books. Characters are instructed to empty their minds of thoughts. This set of instructions symbolizes the self-blinding to knowledge, education, and information on the part of the American public. As the play hints that the happenings are distortions of media narratives about the war, these commands also scrutinize the media's part in encouraging public ignorance and self-blinding to the atrocities of Vietnam. But a journalist, named James, points out the cast of characters' domestic racism when he asks Lisbeth, the main agent of the opening happening, if she has ever been to Harlem. She responds in the negative, adding with evident discomfort that she could not stand the looks of hatred that faced her growing up as a white woman in the Deep South. Lisbeth's exact words are, "But just one look of hatred is enough to make me ill…" (26).[22] A black nursemaid, who remains silent, then enters the scene with a pushchair carrying the daughter of one of the happening's participants, Dorothy. As James asks why Dorothy would employ a black woman to take care of her daughter if she fears (*craindre*) black people, Dorothy retorts: "Because blacks love children. And also, when they are not together, they aren't dangerous" (26).[23] Dorothy, like Lisbeth, reduces black people to a racist vision of dangerous criminality, which she clarifies is extinguished when black people are separated in order to rear the offspring of whites. Lisbeth's covert racism – her fear of crossing black people in Harlem – is equated with Dorothy's overt bigotry, which is evident in her claims that black people when separated are not dangerous. Through this equivalence, the hypocrisy of the happening that occurred moments before is revealed in its full light: Lisbeth, all too willing to criticize the American media's creation of a passively ignorant and self-blinding public in relation to the Vietnam War, is unable to confront the race-based iniquities on her own doorstep and, indeed, her own racism. Distant violence on foreign shores is connected to white supremacist micro-aggressions on the stage.

---

[22]   "Mais un seul regard de haine suffit à me rendre malade…"

[23]   "Parce que les Noirs adorent les enfants. Et puis, quand ils ne sont pas ensemble, ils ne sont pas dangereux".

Local violence depicted *outside* of the happenings highlights the hypocrisy of the characters' protests *in* the happenings. Emulating the way delusion creates a hostile view on symbolic reality, *Off Limits* encourages spectators to look angrily on the characters' real-life actions by means of the unreal happenings. Hypocrisy sparks spectators' rage and a criticism of the characters' actions. This rage could undermine post-millennial ideologies, were Adamov's *Off Limits* to be staged today. This is because the psychotic hostility that audiences are made to feel as a result of the characters' hypocrisy acts as a remedy to public "docile patriotism" (Puar and Rai 132), which queer theorists Jasbir Puar and Amit Rai describe as reigning in a post-9/11 world.

Rai and Puar, writing on post-9/11 constructions of the terrorist in the media, name "docile patriotism" as the principle trait allowing the global West to keep waging war on Islamic fundamentalism in far away lands. They describe the production of docility via media scare tactics: the terrorist is made an abject "monster" of deviant sexuality. He is a "Monster Terrorist Fag" as these critics explain in their eponymous article,

> On CNN, FOX News, BBC, or ABC we hear terrorist experts, psychiatrists, state officials, and journalists use the figure of the terrorist-monster as a screen to project both the racist fantasies of the West and the disciplining agenda of patriotism. Infantilizing the population, they scream with what seems to be at times one voice: 'The terrorist is a monster. The monster is the enemy. The enemy must be hunted down to protect you and all those women and children that you do not know, but we know.' (Puar and Rai 131-132)

Though it does not center on the figure of the "monster terrorist" as Rai and Puar describe, *Off Limits* signals a similar domestication of the American public through the media's lies, which are recounted in the happenings by the world's "first television war", Vietnam. The self-blinding to the brutal reality of Vietnam as a result of mediatization of the war, symbolized in the aforementioned happening by the opening and closing of books, exposes a similar "infantilizing [of] the population" described by Rai and Puar in a post-9/11 world of FOX News, CNN, ABC and the BBC. Though Vietnam and the post-9/11 climate of the global West's war against Islamic fundamentalism are historically separate moments, the media's omnipresent role in relaying conflict to an American public serves to unite them. A number of works in Media and Communication studies have been written on the links between mediatization of the Vietnam War – the world's first television war – and the global War on Terror following 9/11, and the media's role in public desensitization with regard to both conflicts.[24] The anger stirred by *Off Limits'* critique of the American media and the characters' hypocritical bigotries may thus counter Western patriotic docility both then and now.

But more significantly than the play's potential links to media representations of post-millennial conflicts, *Off Limits* implies that domestic prejudice cannot be disassociated from international atrocity in Vietnam. As long as the cast continue to hold preconceived ideas about the racialized people around them, they will not counter the lies told by the media, try as they might in the happenings through a strategy of exaggeration and distortion of American media narratives. In other words, to return to Rai and Puar's comments above, *Off Limits* demonstrates that "the racist fantasies of the West" (131-132) projected in the media are the accumulation of racist preconceptions and practices held and enacted by each member of white American society. The characters are shown to be complicit in American media biases and active agents in the version of the war that was peddled by the media in this maneuver.

Being active agents may not show white America in its best light, but it does accord the public a certain degree of agency to combat the media's mythologizing. In showing the cast as active agents in the media's lies about war, *Off Limits* demonstrates that the public's "docile patriotism" and "infantilization" at the hands of the media (Puar and Rai 131-132) are not passive states, nor are they inevitable. Each individual member of the public can change media falsity by looking to themselves and their own prejudices. The spectator of *Off Limits* is encouraged into a position of hostility toward the characters' individual prejudices, and they are thus accorded the agency needed to combat the docile patriotism spun by the media.

Anger is a feeling that is often disregarded in a Western society constructed in the shadow of the Enlightenment and its stress on reason and rationality. Yet, as queer feminist of color Sara Ahmed reminds us, anger such as we see in spectators of *Off Limits* is not a fruitless emotion. In her phenomenological study of emotion as a source of insight for feminism, *The Cultural Politics of Emotion* (2004), Ahmed insists that

---

[24]   For instance: Robin, Anderson. *A Century of Media, A Century of War*. New York: Peter Lang, 2006; Jennifer, Good *et al. Mythologizing the Vietnam War: Visual Culture and Mediated Memory*. Newcastle: Cambridge Scholars, 2014, 38.

"[b]eing [angry] against something is also being for something, something that has yet to be articulated or is not yet" (175). Spectators' psychotic hostility towards the dramatic reality of *Off Limits* may be taken, then, as not only a stance against the characters, but also the start of "something that has yet to be articulated" (Ahmed 175), an alternative quest for non-hegemonic memories of the Vietnam War. We turn to this quest for alternative memories now.

Foreclosure and Alternative Memories

We have seen that *Off Limits* calls upon a reaction of psychotic hostility in the spectator in order to question white Americans' role in media constructions of Vietnam. Audience anger counteracts public docile patriotism to American war-waging abroad. In this part of the chapter, I want to situate anger in further details of the psychoanalytic theory of psychosis in order to understand how spectators may build on anger to recover forgotten memories of Vietnam.

Off Limits' encouragement of audiences' fury may be associated with what Lacan described as "foreclosure", and what Freud before him termed "Verwerfung", a symptom that accompanies the onset of delusion. Foreclosure is an active form of nihilism that opens spectators onto the interrogatory domain of the Real. According to Lacan, after delusion enables a critique of symbolic reality, the psychotic individual is guided by an imperative to reject or "foreclose" social codes into the domain of the Real, the psychical realm where nothing signifies and meaning is cast into oblivion. The psychotic sees the world as fundamentally flawed and seeks to divest it of meaning by way of the "foreclosure" or jettisoning of symbolic codes into the Real. Lacan described the psychotic's conviction in the wrongfulness of the world as both "radical" and "unshakeable" (*inébranlable*) (*Sem III* 133). Entering the Real, as discussed in the introduction, is not simply about "symbolic impossibility" but is also "generative" (Dean 50-51) of alternative codes that do not adhere to dominant ideologies. Applied to the spectatorship of *Off Limits*, foreclosure carries with it the idea of a radical rejection of prevailing codes on Vietnam, which is at the same time generative of new forms of memory surrounding the conflict.

Foreclosure would seem to be the driving force behind the ending of *Off Limits* especially. The characters' partying comes to its climax. The exclusively visual closing scene betrays an apocalyptic tone. As the final stage direction reads: "*A shattered Statue of Liberty. Then a second Statue of Liberty shattered. And a third one, shattered as well. Scores of shattered Statues of Liberty. Deafening music. Sounds of the end of a world*" (180).[25] The apocalyptic summoning of the "end of a world" symbolized by the decimated statues of Liberty is not dissimilar from what Freud described as the delusional "world catastrophe" (Vol. 12, 69) envisioned by his psychotic patient Dr Schreber. Schreber imagined that he needed to transform into a woman in order to spare the world of its sins. Spectators of *Off Limits* are likewise exposed to a vision of the end of the world or "world catastrophe" (Freud 69), or at least the end of the world defined by America and its ideals as the stage becomes replete with broken symbols of the country.

The ending symbolizes a rejection of America-centered ways of remembering Vietnam. This is because the State of Liberty references America's declared motive for intervention in Indochina. The end scene lays waste to the American values of liberty and freedom, which are referenced in the Declaration of Independence (1776) under the description of Americans' rights to the "life, liberty and the pursuit of happiness". American Liberalism was also exploited in order to justify US intervention in Vietnam. The US, under the banner of constitutional rights to self-determination and civil liberty, claimed that it was "rescuing" Vietnam from a communist threat.

The decimated statues of the play's climax suggest a foreclosure of the nationalist narrative purporting to "save" Vietnam and the American Liberalism that underwrites it. Spectators are encouraged to foreclose this narrative into the Real. Perhaps this is what makes *Off Limits* most pertinent for a deconstruction not only of Vietnam but also wars on post-9/11 terror. Media scholar Jaap Kooijman, in his book *Fabricating the Absolutely Fake: America in Contemporary Pop Culture* (2013), observes that American Liberalism is depicted as a self-evident and universal ideal in post-9/11 popular culture in the US. This untouched ideal ultimately undermines skepticism or outright opposition to America war-waging abroad. Kooijman gives the example of U2 front man Bono's appearance on *Oprah*, a show that aired several episodes questioning the morality and purpose of the War on Terror:

---

[25] "*La statue de la Liberté fracassée. Puis une seconde statue de la Liberté fracassée. Puis une troisième, fracassée, elle aussi. Des dizaines de statues de la Liberté fracassées. Musique assourdissante. Bruits de la fin d'un monde.*"

Although both Americans and non-Americans may oppose the actual politics of the nation-state USA, that does not necessarily lead to a questioning of the idealism embodied by an imagined America. Particularly after the terrorist attacks of September 11, 2001, this distinction became explicitly visible. In spite of the controversial policies of the Bush administration (the Patriot Act, the War on Terror, Guantánamo Bay), "America" still remains to many the Beacon of Freedom and Democracy, which, as Bono told Oprah, is "an ideal that's supposed to be contagious." (Kooijman 171)

An unerring faith in American "Freedom and Democracy" extends from conservative circles supporting post-9/11 invasions of Islamic territories to, as Kooijman suggests, anti-war veterans such as Bono. *Off Limits* moves to destroy the ultimate symbol of American "Freedom and Democracy" (Kooijman 171), the State of Liberty, and this deals a blow to the "idealism embodied by an imagined America" (171). Casting American Liberalism into the Real by foreclosure, spectators are guided to seek memories of Vietnam and other conflicts that remain eclipsed by American idealism.

A reading of psychotic foreclosure serves as one way of re-politicizing *Off Limits* because it encourages spectators' "radical" and "unshakeable" (*Sem III* 133) conviction in the wrongfulness of America's way of remembering conflict. Not only this, the access to the Real that foreclosure enables is a source of potential creation. As Tim Dean reminds us, the Real is not only "a barrier to subjective or symbolic realization [...] [but also] the impossibility against which symbolization is constantly being elaborated" (50-51). There are elements within the text of *Off Limits* that, if stressed, press the play's "symbolic impossibility" (Dean) into the formulation of new codes and meanings.

A turn to the characters of prostitute Molly and Jim's girlfriend Sally in *Off Limits* elucidates this. Both characters insist at various points on the quest for truth outside of what spectators see in the play. Molly refuses the hegemony of American representation, which *Off Limits* is premised on: "America, Molly hates you. She won't forget" (142).[26] Her refusal to "forget" Vietnam stands apart from the mediatized memories that the play consigns to the proverbial dustbin. Similarly, Sally interjects between two party scenes in a direct injunction to spectators: "Open your eyes and search and find/An independent matter/Managed effortlessly BY

---

[26] "Amérique, Molly te hait. Elle n'oubliera pas."

YOU/Which works all by itself FOR YOU" (83).[27] Her words are located outside of the party scenes and the happenings that occur within them. Spectators are pushed to foreclose all forms of representation of Vietnam – whether they come in the form of the happenings or the characters' dramatic reality – given in the play. They are opened onto a form of representational black hole or aporia, which resembles the Lacanian Real, that nonetheless refuses to "forget" (Molly) and encourages spectator to "search" and "find" (Sally) matters or memories that fall outside of American representation.

In sum, two operations are at stake in *Off Limits*: the play demands the foreclosure of all American representation of the Vietnam War and it further elicits the replacement of a representational black hole with ongoing inquiry into heretofore-unrepresented histories. This combination moves *Off Limits* from the realm of "passive" to "active" nihilism. Active nihilism, according to post-Lacanian philosopher Alenka Zupančič, constitutes "a fight against semblance, as an attitude of exposing the 'illusions', 'lies' and imaginary formations *in the name of the Real*" (emphasis original) (*The Shortest Shadow* 63). In other words, *Off Limits* spends its time deriding and undermining all American forms of representing the Vietnam War in order to "fight against semblance" (Zupančič) in the search for truth. It is in this way that the play's nihilism, its opening spectators to a representational nothingness or black hole, may be considered an active, ongoing, and ever-questioning quest for truth. The critical anger and sense of vehement rejection sparked by the play, when re-modeled on this paradigm of active nihilism, imbues it with new subversive clout. With the symbol of American representation (the Statue of Liberty) left in tatters in the closing tableau and Sally's and Molly's words on the imperative to remember outside of dominant and selective memory, *Off Limits* obliges spectators to think about Vietnam and other mediatized wars such as the War on Terror outside of the "'illusions', 'lies' and imaginary formations" (Zupančič) that have dictated public reception.

This chapter has separated the backlash elicited by Adamov's *Off Limits* from critics' accusations in 1969 that it was bad quality theatre. When reconsidered as symptomatic of a rejection of racist prejudice

---

27   "Ouvrez les yeux et cherchez et trouvez / Une affaire indépendante / Gérée sans peine PAR VOUS / Qui marche toute seule POUR VOUS."

formed on both American domestic terrain and foreign shores, outraged audience response earns *Off Limits* a rightful place under the rubric of "Vietnam Protest Theatre" from which it was unceremoniously expunged (or indeed never allowed access to). My argument has imputed value specifically to the notion of anger. I have suggested that anger bears the potential to counteract the docile patriotism of the post-9/11 climate. The play encourages us to reject, with anger, the racist micro-aggressions that feed distorted media narratives about the conflict in a move that emulates psychosis. Like the psychotic's conviction in the wrongfulness of the world, the play also opens the spectator onto the domain of the Real to recover elided memories of conflict outside of what is presented to them.

Something that remains for future scholarship to explore is the precise production and performance methods that would animate the audience's active nihilism and the connections of past warfare to a post-millennial counterpart that I have hypothesized in these pages. Very little is known of *Off Limits* at a level of staging because of its disappearance from view, to a chorus of critical scorn, after the Parisian and Milanese productions mentioned earlier. The lack of details about this play's production history is the reason I have concentrated on recuperating lost subversive energies from the text.

However, *Off Limits* could benefit from borrowing some of the techniques from the canon of Vietnam Protest Theatre named by Nora Alter to highlight its critique of the way Vietnam is remembered in America. Vietnam Protest Theatre often deployed mixed-media strategies. The documentary plays *Pinkville* (George Tabori) and *Vietnam Discourse* (Peter Weiss) incorporated lesser known news reports and images into the dramatic action for the purposes of educating audiences and exposing them to news stories that the American media had chosen to keep from the public (Alter 10). Similar visual clues could be dispersed throughout *Off Limits*. Images of the aggressions that were committed in faraway Vietnam could be flashed before spectators' eyes while the cast enacts localized racist violence on characters such as the nameless African-American veteran of Vietnam and the equally anonymous black nursemaid who is a victim of Lisbeth's and Dorothy's racism. This would emphasize the interconnectedness of domestic discrimination and the American military intervention abroad. Moreover, when Jim cries out "Na...na...na...na...palm", the photograph of "Napalm girl" (Kim Phúc) could appear momentarily before spectators' eyes. Such a "flashing" technique holds the merit of enabling viewers to take stock of the aggressions committed on far-off terrain and its links to Jim's words. The image could also be flashed before spectators' eyes when he dismisses the African-American veteran as a "lackey of American imperialism" (131) in order to remind spectators of his earlier anti-war stance against napalm and the hypocritical lack of concern that he shows for racialized individuals on his own doorstep. Images from more recent American military intervention abroad would, moreover, enable the association of Vietnam with the post-9/11 climate of docile patriotism.

Finally, it is prudent to heed Nora Alter's words when it comes to the subject of Vietnam Protest Theatre:

> [T]heatre [...] hold[s] – perhaps to a degree that television does not – the sense not only that "you were there" but that "you are here." And that is to say the intolerable sense both that you can do nothing about the (television) war and *that you must do something about it.* (My emphasis) (Alter xx)

As Alter stresses throughout her book, Vietnam Protest Theatre leveraged its uniquely live nature to trouble the desensitizing effects of other forms of media on public understandings of Vietnam. Theatre is an art form that inhabits the present and depends on "liveness", unlike the recorded images of cinema or photography and the past moment that such recordings index. If we wish to look again at *Off Limits* as a candidate for stage production, the power of theatrical liveness would best not be ignored. As Alter's words indicate, liveness emphasizes the sense of our existence in the present moment ("you are here"), and it connotes urgency ("you must do something about it"). Perhaps, in the context of Adamov's play, live urgency would be engendered by the stressed timbre of Molly's and Sally's voices as they articulate the need to keep on inquiring and the refusal to forget. Or perhaps it would involve an accelerating pace of the destruction of the statues of liberty in the end scene as opposed to the fixed tableau that Adamov originally suggested. Whatever the answer, a sense that the present ("you are here") is imbricated with the past ("you were there") also seems crucial to recuperating this Absurdist play for today's post-9/11 climate where wars still rage in far-off countries and the media still plays a major hand in inoculating the Western public against mass-scale protest.

Psychotic recuperations of a multi-racial feminism in Beckett's *Not I* (1972)

This third chapter examines Irish playwright Samuel Beckett's *Not I*, published in 1972. Similar to the last chapter, it is argued that the play encourages a psychotic form of spectatorship. Psychotic viewing foments audience rejection of dominant values, such as the American dream and how it shapes our understanding of conflict as discussed previously. In this chapter psychotic rejection targets "gender exceptionalism", another dominant ideology defined by queer theorist Jasbir Puar to describe the post-9/11 age. Feminism, as Puar writes, has been coopted in the West's self-declared War on Terror. Western feminism has been deemed in an appropriate position to "save" Muslim women from Islamic patriarchy. Women's liberation in the Western world is understood to be already accomplished in contrast to the Islamic world's approach to questions of women's rights, which is often framed as "backwards" by dominant Western media. As Puar details, this has resulted in the West's sense of its own exceptionalism when it comes to feminism, or its own "gender exceptionalism" (Puar 5). Gender exceptionalism relies on racist and neo-imperialist takes of the Islamic world as primitive. *Not I*'s subversion of gender exceptionalism is the third way that I explore in this book in which the Theatre of the Absurd subverts the ideologies of our contemporary times.

Not I features the mouth of a woman suspended in darkness. Spectators cannot see the rest of the character's body. "Mouth" re-tells her life story at lightning speed and in disjointed sentences. The speed conveys urgency, and this leads audiences to understand her extreme distress. Mouth is accompanied by a silent Auditor who is cloaked in a North African djellaba and who shrugs periodically in a gesture that signals the inability to help "Mouth" in her plight. The play typifies the aesthetic of negativity of Beckett's theatre. Numerous Beckettian characters lay bare to spectators their entrapment in a mental wasteland of repetition and bleakness, while never finding themselves able to escape from it. Before *Not I*'s Mouth, Vladimir, Estragon, Lucky and Pozzo of *Waiting for Godot* (1949) find themselves in a no man's land as they wait interminably for the title character "Godot", who never appears. Mouth of *Not I* typifies Beckettian negativity but she is also symptomatic of the gendered shift that Beckett took in his latter-day plays. The character of Winnie in *Happy Days* (1961) relentlessly chatters away to her husband while trapped in a mound of dirt, while *Footfalls* (1975) and *Rockaby* (1980) also feature women who labor on endlessly in a discourse that serves no satisfying conclusion (Jeffers 138). Similarly, while Mouth conveys an extreme distress in her lightning-speed monologue, she carries on interminably and concludes where she started, babbling quietly behind the curtain. She reflects Martin Esslin's characterization of the Theatre of the Absurd as analogous to the myth of Sisyphus, who was condemned infinitely to pushing a rock up a hill only to watch it fall back down again.

While most critics focus on the significance of the character of Mouth in an analysis of *Not I*, this chapter turns to the character of Auditor – the mute character who stands beside the protagonist – and the effect that she has on Mouth's monologue. Auditor's importance has been somewhat of a moot point for critics and it is rare indeed to see the character given primary importance in critics' analysis, but this chapter insists on her importance.[1] Auditor's presence potentially targets the contemporary ideology of gender exceptionalism, coined by Jasbir Puar as just described. The social script of gender exceptionalism asserts that the women of the non-Islamic West bear more agency – are putatively freer and more liberated – than Muslim women in the non-West. This idea is evoked in the visuals of *Not I* since the white Mouth launches into a monologue at lightning speed while Auditor, who is implied to be a North African woman as I shall explain, can only wave her arms silently alongside her. Gender exceptionalism is evoked but crucially also rejected through psychotic viewing in spectatorship. This reading is informed by Puar's theory of Western gender exceptionalism, but also with the help of other postcolonial feminists who have commented on the racial and ethnic privileges that favor white women in the Western social hierarchy, notably Chandra Mohanty (1984) and Sara Ahmed (2006). Fusing postcolonial feminism with Lacanian theory, we shall return to the concept of foreclosure, the mechanism of psychosis explored in the last chapter, and discuss the "enigmatic void", another psychotic symptom, in order to argue that the spectator casts the visual imbalance

---

[1]   For instance, Mary Bryden argues that Auditor is an unnecessary (male) presence that eclipses Mouth. Mary, Bryden. *Women in Beckett's Prose and Drama: Her Own Other.* Basingstoke: Palgrave Macmillan, 1993.

between Mouth and Auditor and the ideology of gender exceptionalism that underwrites this imbalance into the meaningless psychical domain of the Real as Lacan conceptualized. Spectators are placed in a position, by virtue of psychotic viewing, where gender exceptionalism does not signify and is de-naturalized.

The first part of the chapter explains why psychosis is evoked in viewing. Audiences are encouraged to reject the representational reality of *Not I* via the creation of their "inner scream", a term that Beckett's chosen actress for the role of Mouth, Billie Whitelaw, coined.[2] The protagonist tells her tragic life story with such speed and intensity that the play becomes an endurance test for audiences. Spectators' inner scream is predicated on the need to flee from Mouth and the story that she re-tells. This need to escape potentially propels the audience's eschewal of the dynamic between Mouth and Auditor, between the domineering white protagonist and her subordinate playing partner who is marked out as a racial and religious Other in her djellaba. Psychotic viewing precipitates a condemnation of the power differentials that favor Mouth over Auditor. Overturning power differentials between Western and Muslim women is key to subverting contemporary gender exceptionalism. The chapter then moves onto performance conditions and staging techniques that would encourage a psychotic rejection of contemporary gender exceptionalism, concentrating on productions featuring Billie Whitelaw, Lisa Dwan, and Jessica Tandy in the role of Mouth. The need to divide the spectator's attention equally between Mouth and Auditor is essential, since visual balance corrects the power discrepancies informing gender exceptionalism, where Western women are favored as more empowered than the women of the Islamic world.

Psychosis and Gender Exceptionalism in *Not I*

Not I, one of Beckett's latter-day plays, may be considered less for the story it tells than the striking effect that it has on spectators. The play takes the Theatre of the Absurd's dissolution of traditionally, psychologically complex, and unified characters to an extreme end point, as the lone mouth of a woman is all that is visible of the protagonist. Mouth recounts her life story at breakneck speed for ten to fifteen intense

---

2   Whitelaw coined this term in the interview recorded in association with the BBC production of *Not I*. *Beckett At the BBC: Not I*, dir. by Tristram Powell. BBC, 1975.

minutes. Her lines are uttered so quickly that they blend into each other and are hard to follow. As spectators, we can only patch together snippets and impute assumptions about what happened to the protagonist or why she has ended in a frenzied state: she was abandoned by her parents in childhood, at some point may have committed a crime that landed her on trial, and lives her remaining days alone. But it is less what Mouth says than *how* she says it: the image of a lone mouth suspended in the darkness recounting her story at lightning speed has left spectators astonished and stupefied. As the late British actress Billie Whitelaw (1932-2014), who played Mouth in Beckett's own production of the play in 1973, recalled in the BBC version of *Not I* in 1975: "people tried to escape into the loo to get away from this relentless mouth that wouldn't let go" (*Beckett at the BBC*). Whitelaw qualified that what *Not I* unleashed in spectators was an "inner scream" (*Beckett at the BBC*).

This "inner scream" of the spectator, which was so violent among some that they felt compelled to flee the auditorium as Whitelaw recounts, provides the basis for my assertion that *Not I* encourages a viewing regime guided by the psychical state of psychosis as psychoanalysis defines it. *Not I* appears to disallow a dialectic based on listening and exchange between the actors and audience, appealing instead as Beckett insisted, to "the necessary emotions of the audience rather than appealing to the intellect" (qtd. in Fischer 102). Via the replication of Mouth's inner scream in spectators, the play seeks to impose Mouth's worldview on audiences. As Whitelaw recounted in her memoirs, spectators were positioned "to be sucked into this rioting, rambling hole" (Whitelaw 118) along with Mouth.

It is Mouth's "rioting, rambling hole" (Whitelaw), reproduced in spectators, that emulates the condition of psychosis. With the bullet-paced speed of her monologue, Mouth bears progressively witness to a state where language passes her by and its function of producing meaning fails. As Beckett scholar Brian Gatten remarks, Mouth relates a "coherent", albeit "disjointed, staccato" (Gatten 94) monologue that moves from a description of her reality at the start of the play to a state in which language overwhelms every aspect of her lived experience. She voices her monologue entirely in the third person, indicating a lack of control over the recounting of her own life story, and she becomes overwhelmed by a "steady stream...mad stuff...half the vowels wrong" with her "whole body like gone…just the mouth" (222).[3] This reduction of the protagonist to "just the mouth…like maddened" (222) whose discourse has no purpose or makes no sense resembles what Lacan called the "enigmatic void" (*le vide énigmatique*), which is particular to the advanced stages of psychosis. As indicated previously, the function of language to produce meaning is rejected by a process of "foreclosure" (for Freud *Verwerfung* and for Lacan *forclusion*). Foreclosure involves the rejection of ideology by evacuating it of meaning, casting it into the psychical realm that Lacan called the "Real". At a certain point, foreclosure becomes so totalizing that all language is reduced to pure materiality – nothing can signify and sustain meaning. Language undergoes an evacuation of meaning; all social codes lose their ability to signify as the subject experiences what Lacan called the "signification of signification" (Écrits 451) – in other words, individuals under the sway of psychosis are pushed to see that language is constructed and produces meaning artificially.

Mouth experiences the enigmatic void or language as pure materiality in her inability to voice anything but a "steady stream…mad stuff…half the vowels wrong" (222) and in the reduction of her body to a mouthpiece for her nonsensical language. But it is important to remember that the spectator, pushed to sympathize with and replicate Mouth's "inner scream" as Billie Whitelaw said, is sucked into the protagonist's "rioting, rambling hole" (Whitelaw 118) of the enigmatic void too. They too are urged to glimpse the enigmatic void's "signification of signification" (Lacan 451), the constructedness of language. Espying the way that discourse is constructed, spectators are pushed potentially to realize that ideologies make up language and the production of meaning.

Not only revealing the ideologically constructed nature of language, the enigmatic void also involves the radical rejection of ideology into the realm of the Real. As Lacan noted in his *Écrits*, psychotic rejection of discourse and ideology into the Real mounts with a "degree of certainty [that] takes on a weight proportional to the enigmatic void" (Lacan 451). With the inner scream of the protagonist foisted upon spectators, those who watch *Not I* are also positioned to reject ideology and discourse in the same "enigmatic void" as Mouth.

---

[3] References to the play in the text will be to this edition: Samuel, Beckett. "Not I," in *The Collected Shorter Plays*. New York: Grove Press, 1984, 213-224.

The value of this form of reception lies in what spectators will potentially be pushed to cast into the abyss of the meaninglessness, into the Real, as a result. With the dynamic between Mouth and Auditor, *Not I* creates a dynamic that speaks to the ideology of Western gender exceptionalism, which maneuvers Western feminism into an appropriate position to "save" Muslim women from Islamic patriarchy. The enigmatic void thus potentially reduces gender exceptionalism to meaninglessness. In such a schema, spectators are positioned to reject gender exceptionalism, to cast it into the Real so that it does not signify and it is de-naturalized.

It is necessary at this point to analyze in detail how *Not I* conjures the ideology of Western gender exceptionalism, before turning back to the spectator's enigmatic void divesting this ideology of meaning. Beckett was inspired by a mix of cultural references in creating *Not I*, both Western and non-Western, a fact that enables us to connect the play to gender exceptionalism. The playwright's personal letters revealed that Mouth reminded him of one of the "old crones, stumbling down the lanes, in the ditches, beside the hedgerows" (qtd. in Brater 24) who surrounded him as he was growing up. Beckett scholar Jennifer Jeffers deploys this memory to read *Not I* as the staging of Anglo-Irish national trauma. As Beckett came of age in the 1920s in the Dublin suburb of Foxrock, he witnessed the impoverishment of Anglo-Irish communities following the withdrawal of the British and the formation of the Free Catholic State in 1922. Mouth, interpreted against this historical backdrop, becomes a cipher for a body of people divested of social standing (Jeffers 145). The inspiration for Auditor, meanwhile, who accompanies Mouth and is not visible to audiences except for her djellaba, came from a moment when Beckett was sitting alone in a café in an unspecified country in North Africa during the late 1960s or early 1970s. He saw, as Beckett scholar Enoch Brater recounts, the "solitary figure" of an "Arab woman" "completely covered in a djellaba, leaning against a wall [...] in a position of intense listening" (Brater 24) as she waited for her children to return from school.

Given the mix of occidental and non-occidental references that inspired the characters of Mouth and Auditor, the theme of racial difference between women is built into the fabric of *Not I*. Not only this, the theme of power differentials separating a white woman from a woman of Islamic confession who is most likely to be of color is presented to spectators. Mouth reaches the climax of her discourse in four punctuating moments when she screams: "what?...who?...no!...

she!..." (216, 218, 221, 222). Against the voluble protests of Mouth, Auditor can do nothing else but respond with "a simple sideways raising of arms from sides and their falling back" (215). This gesture highlights the fact that while Mouth suffers, she can do so through the privileges of voice and language. Meanwhile, Auditor is disallowed such privileges. By extension, Auditor may be deemed subject to a more extreme form of oppression than her white playing partner, Mouth.

Given that Beckett's letters reveal that Auditor was at base a Muslim woman of North African origin and Mouth was a white Irish woman in her advancing years, it could be argued that the protagonist holds more social clout than her Muslim playing partner. This is particularly the case if we re-situate Absurdist characters in post-9/11 times, as this book aims to do. Our current climate is shaped by the legacy of 9/11 and a widespread Islamophobia in the Western world, which indiscriminately touches all Muslim communities. Islamophobia spikes every time the extreme acts of the fundamentalist few are committed. Given the *Zeitgeist*, we could surmise that Mouth's whiteness serves to privilege her over Auditor or at most, we might take Mouth's age and class (the fact that she is meant to be an "old crone" (Brater 24)) as factors that peg her as equally disempowered as her mute interlocutor.

A reading of racial and religious difference between the women of *Not I* has been missed by a majority of critics, who have understood the protagonist as requisitioning power from Auditor. That is, Auditor has been placed in a position of *a priori* dominance over the protagonist. This assumption rests on a reading of Auditor that occludes her racialized and gendered origins. Beckett scholar Mary Bryden, for instance, who reads Auditor as male, opines that the almost imperceptible character encapsulates an "extraction [...] of the judgemental male" (Bryden 119). Others have analogized Auditor as a male psychoanalyst (more on that later) debarred from power by the analysand Mouth who refuses to be silenced.[4]

If we return to the original inspiration for the characters and re-position them in modern times, it is possible to argue that *Not I* demands that spectators reckon with the juxtaposition of a white woman against a

---

[4] See Shane, Weller. "'Some Experience of the Schizoid Voice': Samuel Beckett and the Language of Derangement," *Forum for Modern Language Studies*, 45, No. 1 (2008), 32-50; Dina, Sherzer. "Portrait of a Woman: The Experience of Marginality in *Not I*." Ed. Linda Ben-Zvi. *Women in Beckett: Performance and Critical Perspective.* Urbana: University of Illinois Press, 1990, 201-207.

Muslim woman of color. Both characters evoke diminished selfhood but Mouth implies that she bears more agency than Auditor. The juxtaposition of the very vocal Mouth with the silenced Auditor chimes with the contemporary ideology of Western gender exceptionalism. Gender exceptionalism, a term coined by queer theorist Jasbir Puar in *Terrorist Assemblages* (2007), describes the effect of intensified Islamophobia on Western mainstream feminism. As Puar argues, Western feminism betrays a belief in its exceptional capacity "as a missionary discourse to rescue Muslim women from their oppressive male counterparts" (5). Eve Ensler's initiative "V-Day" provides a concrete example of how gender exceptionalism operates. In 2001, V-Day paid tribute to the women of Afghanistan at the same time as public support for a "War on Terror" was gathering momentum in the wake of the tragic events of September 11. Puar affirms that Ensler's V-Day and the War on Terror were not disconnected, because both bewailed the plight of Muslim women in Afghanistan. V-Day was, in other words, informed by the same neo-imperialistic claims of the United States needing to "save" the women of the Muslim world, and therefore constituted, Puar concludes, a "tokenistic liberal apology that often leaves uninterrogated a West/Islam binary" (7). Meanwhile, grassroots feminist associations existing in Afghanistan for decades, such as the Revolutionary Association of the Women of Afghanistan (RAWA), went systematically ignored by V-Day and its pundits. Puar makes the point that such examples of white feminism's belief in its superiority over feminisms of color, such as can be found in V-Day's act of ignoring RAWA and other Afghan feminist associations, is not only premature and unearned; it makes feminism as a whole ripe for conservative cooptation. Gender exceptionalism aids the warmongering of the West against the Islamic east, a point demonstrated perfectly by the coincidence of V-Day's focus on the women of Afghanistan with the "War on Terror" in the same country and year (2001).

Not I disrupts gender exceptionalism by implying the power that Mouth exercises over Auditor. Rather than being in a position to "save" women of the Muslim world, *Not I* curries favor with the idea that white Western woman are complicit in their oppression. Mouth tells her story of suffering through very audible and intense lamentation, while Auditor can only communicate oppression and pain through a helpless shrugging gesture, as she is deprived of voice. Auditor becomes the casualty of the predominant whitewashing of space in the Western world that postcolonial queer feminist Sara Ahmed describes in her phenomenological investigation of the normative dimensions of space in *Queer Phenomenology: Orientations, Objects, Others* (2006). As Ahmed explains, "To be black or not white in 'the white world' is to turn back toward oneself, to become an object [...] *being diminished as an effect of the bodily extension of others*" (my emphasis) (Ahmed 139). Reflecting this, Auditor, as a "not white" (Ahmed 139) Muslim woman, demonstrates an increasingly muted gesture. Her shrugging progressively "lessens" (Beckett 215), as the stage directions read, each of the three times that Mouth takes a pause in her discourse "till scarcely perceptible at third" (215). Meanwhile, Mouth displays in each of these pauses what is described as a "vehement refusal to relinquish the third person" (215). This stage direction indicates suffering but also a degree of agency – the act of decided or "vehement" refusal or saying "no" to the first person subject pronoun suggests that Mouth has *chosen* the way that she will tell her story to spectators. In each pause, Mouth utters the line, "what?... who?...no!...she!..." (216, 218, 221, 222) and does not, in fact, articulate any of her story in the first person. Against this backdrop, the muted Auditor, "in helpless compassion" (215), literally enacts the bodily diminishment "as an effect of the bodily extension" (Ahmed 139) of a white, Westernized Mouth making the voluble choice to express herself in the third person.

I argue then that Mouth illustrates white Western women's greater degree of agency and wielding of power over Muslim women, in line with the ideology of Western gender exceptionalism described by Puar. The point here is not to suggest that Western feminism is the sole cause of the oppression visited upon Muslim women or that Mouth enjoys the luxury of being free of oppression herself; rather it is to lay emphasis on the fruitfulness of the message that *Not I* calls forth that implies that Mouth is *both* oppressed and the oppressor. This undermines the self-satisfied contingent of white mainstream feminism in the West, which, as Puar explains, prefers to focus on the plight of an Islamic female Other, who is radically reduced, than the oppression that its own women still face. White feminist self-satisfaction relies on a vision of Western women as "modern, as having control over their bodies and sexualities, and the freedom to make their own decision" (Mohanty 337) as postcolonial feminist Chandra Mohanty described in her groundbreaking article on the ethnocentrism of Western feminism "Under Western Eyes: Feminist Scholarship and Colonial Discourse" in 1984. Mouth undermines this vision. *Not I*'s protagonist is hardly the picture of the emancipated

Western woman recounted by Mohanty. Mouth, too, inhabits the margins of society, as a self-described "old hag already" (Beckett 220). However, Mouth describes her in-between state of being "in control" and "under control" (218), and this leads us to understand that she is both oppressed and wields power particularly over the increasingly silenced Auditor. In brief, Mouth falls outside of the category of Western women who are uniformly emancipated and in a position to "save" their Muslim sisters, instead suggesting that she is both oppressed and the oppressor.

Let us return to the spectator's enigmatic void. I stated earlier that gender exceptionalism, which *Not I* evokes, could be divested of meaning by virtue of the spectator's experience of the enigmatic void. The latter involves the reduction of ideological codes to meaninglessness. But there is a tension inhabiting *Not I* that limits spectators' opportunity to strip gender exceptionalism of its authority. This tension emerges particularly in performance. Viewers are frequently led to focus disproportionately on one or other character of *Not I*, Mouth or Auditor, but not both simultaneously. This, as I shall explain in the following three parts of this chapter, which analyze three different productions of the play, limits spectators' capacity to eject gender exceptionalism into the Real and divest it of meaning. As I shall argue, directing the spectators' attention to a balanced and global view of Mouth and Auditor will bring forth the power differentials that peg Mouth as bearing more agency than Auditor. Balanced viewing of *Not I*'s two characters ensures that the spectator's compulsion towards an "inner scream" (Whitelaw *Beckett at the BBC*) will precipitate the enigmatic void that de-naturalizes the ideology of gender exceptionalism, which the image of the power differentials between Mouth and Auditor reveals.

Billie Whitelaw at the Royal Court (1973)

The imperative, I am arguing, for productions that wish to stir audiences' rejection of the contemporary ideology of gender exceptionalism, is to create a visual balance between Mouth and Auditor. Balance will enable spectators' visual comparison of Auditor and Mouth. Auditor's oppression will then be made visible. A clear representation of these power differentials between the two women would form a precursor to the experience of the enigmatic void that would enable spectators to reject the power imbalance and the gender exceptionalism that subtends it. In this sense, I adhere to Beckett scholar Enoch Brater's view that the spectator's eye must shunt between the two shadowy figures, Mouth and Auditor, so that "the rich itineraries of the audience's eye [...] mak[e] the full text of *Not I* emerge in performance" (Brater 34).

Nevertheless, imbalance and a tendency toward audiences' disproportionate emphasis on one or the other character – *either* Mouth *or* Auditor – are precisely where the technical challenge of this piece lies. Reviewing various performances of *Not I* for the *London Review of Books* Adam Mars-Jones remarks,

> Auditor and Mouth occupy different parts of the stage, one full-sized and motionless (except at crucial moments of disruption in the monologue, when the audience's attention will naturally be fixed on Mouth), the other a few inches across and moving constantly. Both are supposed to be illuminated faintly, with no change of lighting during the piece. How to make a single theatrical performance of two such opposed elements? When Beckett asked the impossible of a performer he was generally able to get his way. When the impossibility was technical he had to admit defeat. (Mars-Jones 22)

Mars-Jones contextualizes his last observation in Beckett's own, albeit reluctant, choice to dispense with Auditor in the 1975 production of the play in Paris, owing to the "technical" (Mars-Jones 22) difficulty of keeping spectators' gaze on both characters. Directors are continually confronted with a tradeoff, Mars-Jones asserts, between retaining the visual intensity of the piece – since much of *Not I*'s force comes from spectators' fixation on the floating mouth – and retaining both characters.

Details of the most canonized production of *Not I*, performed by Billie Whitelaw at the Royal Court in London in 1973 and directed by Beckett himself, point to a visual stress on the character of Mouth at the expense of Auditor. This is not necessarily exclusive to the signature production, as critics have remarked on the mystique that Mouth tends to cultivate. She has reportedly had a mesmerizing effect on audiences as an orifice apparently cast adrift from the moorings of her body. However, the evidence mounts against the Royal Court production for its galvanization of a particularly acute case of audience fascination and identification with the protagonist alone to the detriment of her stage partner, Auditor. As Whitelaw wrote in her autobiography, "All that *Not I* consists of is a mouth" (Whitelaw 123), forgetting Auditor altogether in this summary. Auditor, the "shadowy figure in a djellabah" (Whitelaw 123) only came as an afterthought in her memoir. As she posited, dropping the subject of Auditor soon afterward, "Sam [Beckett] [...] was fascinated by the figures of Moroccans in their djellabahs, standing still" (Whitelaw 123). Whitelaw was known as Beckett's actress of choice; she dominated the stage over Brian Miller, who played Auditor, in the Royal Court production in 1973.

As a consequence of Whitelaw's dominance over Miller, and relating more specifically to what went on in performance, Whitelaw described her frustration at "a lot of people [who] thought that [she] was pacing up and down, that the mouth was moving" (Whitelaw and Ben-Zvi 9). She described this optical deceit as similar to the effect of "looking at a star" for too long: "after a while it seems to be moving about" (Whitelaw and Ben-Zvi 9). Whitelaw's irritation stemmed from the fact that she was painfully immobilized on a rostrum, her head clamped into place by a vice. The effect of movement that audiences described effaced Whitelaw's efforts to convey disembodiment in remaining agonizingly static.

Whitelaw's suggestion that she appeared as a "star" (Whitelaw and Ben-Zvi 9) in the night-sky also bespeaks the protagonist's tendency toward the imposition of "dumbness and [...] attentiveness" (Bryden 133-134) on spectators, a description that Mary Bryden gives in her assessment of the piece in her book *Women in Samuel Beckett's Drama* (1993). Mouth's stupefying effect on audience members comes at the cost of a performance that would focus on the specificity of Auditor and her plight. When Mouth holds audiences spellbound, audiences may ignore or downplay the importance of the character of Auditor. Indeed, where Mouth holds audiences in thrall to her, her discourse risks overwhelming and absorbing Auditor's condition. To return to our reading of the play as evoking the power differentials between women of different religions, ethnicities, and races, Mouth's all-encompassing hold on audiences runs the risk of universalizing the condition of women's oppression. This cancels out the differences between Mouth and Auditor, which are implied in the text's emphasis on the volubility of Mouth and the silent, limited movement of Auditor. Productions that leave audiences to focus on Mouth may risk precipitating the merging of the two women's conditions and what Mohanty calls, in "Under Western Eyes," a "homogeneous notion of the oppression of women as a group" (Mohanty 337). Homogenization is counterproductive to a form of feminist criticism that addresses racial, class-based, and other differences between women.

Worse still, Mouth's ubiquity may strip both the protagonist and her listener of the specificity of her gender entirely. I make this contention based on Whitelaw's insistence that Mouth de-genders space. Whitelaw's version of Mouth shed "all of the manifestations of sex" (Whitelaw and Ben-Zvi 4). Whitelaw repeated to herself every night before she went on stage, "let the skin fall off; let the flesh fall off [...] you physically keep out of the way" (Whitelaw and Ben-Zvi 4). Mouth's evacuation of her gender from the story that she recounts risks missing the value of this piece as a representation of women's oppression. The evacuation of gender from *Not I* could well have been buttressed by the enactment of Auditor by a white man, Brian Miller, in the Royal Court production. This is because character conflation seemed a priority in the signature production. As Miller wore a black djellaba, Whitelaw was cloaked in a "great black Dracula-like cape" (Whitelaw 124) to cover the rostrum she was strapped onto. The similar costuming of Whitelaw and Miller likely created a mirroring effect, which would foster the audience's impression of the equivalence between the oppression faced by a white woman and a white man. The white male incarnation of Auditor also stamps out the specificities of Auditor's fight against oppression as a non-Western woman, relegating the origins of this character to invisibility and forestalling the possibility of reading this play as sensitive to the racial differences among women.

Whitelaw recounted "spiritually leaving the body" (Whitelaw 124) each night that she enacted the role of *Not I*. She spoke of the considerable physical strain on her body playing the part of Mouth. Disproportionate emphasis on Mouth not only, then, reinforces the erasure of Auditor and her plight; it entails a real-life dispensation of being and self on the part of the actress who plays Beckett's protagonist. This turns us to the ethical implications of a performance strategy that seeks to hold audiences spellbound with near-exclusive focus on Mouth. Whitelaw hyperventilated on more than one occasion. She attributed this to the forced immobilization of her body in the vice, which stoked a nervous energy that mounted in her head and had no means of escape. The actress broke a new record for the speed at which she recited Mouth's monologue, shaving three minutes off the running time of the play compared with its world debut with Jessica Tandy at the Lincoln Center the year before (described shortly). However, the effect of the rush of words coming from Whitelaw's mouth compounded with her immobilization and caused her head to shake violently. Whitelaw confessed to experiencing such disorientation that she had to ask to have a faint light (visible only to her) installed in the back of the auditorium in order to reassure her of her existence.

Theatre and performance scholar Gerry McCarthy observes, on the subject of performing *Not I*, that the piece reverses the habitual process by which an actor prepares to enter into character. Though actors typically describe the "reintegration of the self" and "the enjoyment of a virtual image of personality which arises from the actual application of the actor's energy resources" (McCarthy 464-465), *Not I* demands the actual and the virtual divestiture of selfhood. The play "arrives immediately back at the contemplation of the actor or actress expending energy, and in so doing, experiencing her actual and virtual conditions as an amalgam, an integrated state from which there is no escape, except to will the integration and press on" (McCarthy 465). While McCarthy contends that it is simply an onus of the actress playing Mouth to "accept the physical discomfort of performance" (McCarthy 460), this pain cannot only be averted, as covered in the following part of the chapter, it is unnecessary because it works in the service of privileging the trauma of the white heroine of this piece at the expense of the figure at her side.

Jessica Tandy at the Lincoln Center (1972)

If the Royal Court production points to a disproportionate emphasis on Mouth and her mesmerizing effect on the audience at the expense of Auditor, commentary surrounding the world debut of the play the year before, which starred British actress Jessica Tandy in the lead role, hints at an opposite imbalance tipped toward Auditor. This is equally counterproductive, as we shall explore here.

Jessica Tandy, in the role of Mouth, played alongside American actor Henderson Forsythe in the role of Auditor at the Lincoln Center in New York City in 1972. Both actors were well known by this time. In contrast to the super-human dimension of the stellar-like Mouth played by Whitelaw at the Royal Court, attention was drawn to a preternaturally large Auditor at the Lincoln Center. Enoch Brater gives a detailed account of the production in his book *Beyond Minimalism: Beckett's Late Style in his Theatre* (1987). As Brater remarks, Forsythe's Auditor was,

> elevated on a box, [and] steadied himself against a specially constructed railing to maintain a consistently even balance; the djellaba was draped over the railing to reach the floor of the stage itself. Cold stage lighting exaggerated his threatening verticalization. (Brater 31)

Auditor loomed large in the production at the Lincoln Center, imposing a "threatening verticalization" on spectators, in contrast to Mouth's ubiquity at the Royal Court.

Perhaps a visual configuration where Auditor towers over Mouth helps combat audiences' tendency to draw an equivalence between Mouth and Auditor, and the forms of oppression that they battle, which we saw before in a discussion of the Royal Court production. However, "threatening verticalization" is hardly a term denoting the neutrality of Auditor, and it does not obviate other fraught implications of the performance method. A power discrepancy tipped toward Auditor disallows an interpretation of the play that situates both Mouth and Auditor's diminished senses of self in an overall patriarchal structure while remaining attentive to racial specificity. "[T]hreatening verticalization" (Brater 31) indeed seems to tip the power differentials toward the character of Auditor, averting altogether the play's implication that Mouth is nonetheless at a social and structural advantage over the character of Auditor because of her racial privilege. As long as Auditor remains what Brater deemed a male "wordless giant who [stands] in mute contrast to the minimal image of the *panting orifice*" (my emphasis) (Brater 31), the chance for reading Mouth as having more agency than Auditor is lost. Brater's description of Mouth as a "panting orifice" assumes almost erotic dimensions, corresponding to feminist scholar Ann Wilson's account of *Not I*'s protagonist as aping the visual economies of pornography with the image of a mouth that "generat[es] so much saliva that it sprays […] and clings to her lower lip" (Wilson 191). Mouth, in this view, risks objectification by the male gaze, cancelling out the feminist reading at the intersections of racial and religious difference between the play's two women that I am putting forward in this chapter.

If Mouth is not reduced to a sexual object, the image of a "panting orifice" (Brater 31) in the shadow of an imposing male Auditor could alternatively imply that Mouth is the victim of sexual violence. Some lines from the text may feed this reading. Mouth alludes to a traumatic sexual experience that she believes is a form of divine "punishment…for some sin or other" (217). A binary opposition could be instated, in other words, between masculine aggression, embodied by the white male Auditor's "threatening verticalization" (Brater 31), and feminine passivity, incarnated by Tandy's "panting" (Brater 31) and subordinate Mouth, in the Lincoln Center production. In arguing this, I do not wish to deny the value of this performance method for another reading of the play. *Not I* could signal the oppression that women suffer at the hands of men in a performance scheme that accords Auditor disproportionate power over Mouth. However, this means that *Not I*'s potential for depicting womanhood in a more nuanced, multi-racial, light is disabled. As Puar reminds us, "[w]omen can be subjects of violence but also agents of it, whether it is produced on their behalf or perpetuated directly by them" (Puar 90). An all-female cast would enable a more complex reading of women as victims and perpetrators of marginalization in a hierarchy predicated on not only gendered, but also religious, racial, and class-based divides, with Mouth being the agent who reinforces Auditor's marginalization. But a male Auditor who imposes a menacing vertical stature limits a reading of the power differentials between women of different races and ethnicities. A male characterization of Auditor does not evoke the differences between women in the same way that a female Auditor would.

What is more, it is not necessarily a white male body that audiences understood in the Lincoln Center production. The sight of a djellaba indeed would signal to audiences the interpretation of this character, if he is visibly male to spectators, as a *Muslim* man. The image of a "threatening" male giant in an all-encompassing djellaba, a marker of racial and religious distinction since the clothing item hails from North Africa, is hardly a neutral one in a post-9/11 world where stereotypes of fundamentalist suicide bombers, who are nearly always coded in mainstream media as male, abound. Henderson Forsythe's white male enactment of the role of Auditor, re-situated in the post-millennial context, would be symptomatic of a Western appropriation of the Muslim man in this respect. Where Auditor towers over Mouth as in the Lincoln Center production, a sense of ominousness and foreboding is conjured. In the modern-day context, this plays into an Islamophobic prejudice against the masked and cloaked male body of the non-Western world. As Puar makes the point with reference to the wave of violence committed against Sikh men in the aftermath of 9/11 in the US, contemporary Islamophobic prejudice pays little heed to the specificity of religious practice or costume. Western fear is incited by anything from the North African djellaba to Sikh, Muslim, or Hindu turbans. A range of masculinities in non-Western religious dress is thus made susceptible to "perverse" "rescripting" (Puar 168) in the post-9/11 world as Puar continues. The sight of Mouth's unmitigated (white) victimhood at the hands of a male Auditor in North African dress could well fan the flames of an anti-Islamic trope of Western vulnerability to non-Western terror.

The problematic aspects of Auditor's role at the Lincoln Center aside, this production accorded Tandy a greater degree of selfhood in the role of Mouth than Whitelaw was granted. Located inside a box big enough for two, Tandy had a reading light and five prompt cards held up by a man who facilitated her performance of Mouth's dense, blistering monologue as Mars-Jones recounts (22). Tandy deigned to bring into effect, much to Beckett's purported chagrin, the "reintegration of the self" (464-465) that McCarthy argues is absented from *Not I*, as I described earlier. This bears potential inasmuch as it does not forsake the actress's integrity to perform the role of Mouth as we saw was the case in the Royal Court production and Whitelaw's self-confessed exhaustion after playing the protagonist.

However, Tandy drastically slowed down her pace to tell Mouth's story. This would seem to be the main reason for Beckett's disapproval of the Lincoln Center production, as he purportedly accused Tandy of "destroying" his play with her slow speed. This kind of method limits the chance that the spectator has to adopt Mouth's "inner scream" (*Beckett at the BBC*) as Whitelaw described. I argued earlier that Mouth's inner scream enabled the psychotic unconscious economy to be created in the spectatorship of *Not I*, since spectators, fleeing to the toilets to escape the din, feel the imposition of language and the need to reject the ideology behind language as viscerally as Mouth. But spectators of the Lincoln Center production have limited access to this unconscious form. Tandy recounted the narrative over the course of twenty-two minutes of playing time, in contrast to Whitelaw's fifteen minutes. This rendered the monologue comprehensible in its entirety and produced what theatre critic Cristina Cano Vara calls a "naturalized speech [that] hinder[s] the impression that [Mouth's] language is unnatural, almost mechanic" (27). Cano Vara notes this re-naturalization of Mouth's discourse in the parallel context of the Spanish production of the play at the autumn theatre festival in Madrid in 1991 (directed by Alvaro del Amo), which also set the running time of *Not I* at twenty-two minutes. Mouth, played by Spanish television star Marisa Paredes, encouraged "conventional modes of perception" (Cano Vara 29) involving empathetic identification with a "woman voicing her sufferings at last" (29). While the articulation and clear understanding of women's victimization is an important move prior to deconstruction of sexist oppression, Paredes's and Tandy's earlier eliciting of audience empathy hinges on a re-naturalization of Mouth's discourse. Re-naturalized discourse could end up reinforcing the meaning behind the discourse: in other words, it is Mouth's suffering that could be naturalized as inevitable. This is particularly so if audience empathy for *Not I*'s protagonist is not accompanied by a move to *de*-naturalize the female victimization implicit in Cano Vara's description of Mouth as a "woman voicing her sufferings at last" (29).

The spectator's psychotic response, by contrast, *would* cast female vulnerability into the oblivion of the Real and strip female disempowerment of all sense. This seems one channel that is unavailable to spectators of productions that emphasized audience empathy rather than the adoption of Mouth's "inner scream" (*Beckett at the BBC*). It is important, then, to draw the distinction between spectator's identification with the protagonist by means of empathy, and the wholesale assumption of Mouth's plight as the spectator's own through a more totalizing form of identification. Theatre and performance scholar Lindsay Cummings, in her book *Empathy as Dialogue in Theatre and Performance* (2016), reminds us that empathy "involves *more than one person*" (emphasis in the original) (59) and the "parity of exchange" (59) between actor and spectator. This is opposed to the "feelings of invasion and domination" (Cummings 59) that spectators experience in totalized recognition of themselves in the dramatic action onstage. Though it may seem ethically counter-intuitive, I am arguing that it is precisely the feeling of the spectator's "invasion and domination" (Cummings 59) by Mouth that is fruitful in *Not I*, provided that it is enriched by a subsequent rejection of the oppression facing women as the spectator's "inner scream" (*Beckett at the BBC*) of protest would seem to suggest. Mouth pushes language and, more importantly, the ideologies that make up language to their limits of meaning in her experience of the enigmatic void. Eliciting the same drive towards the evacuation of meaning from dominant ideologies in the spectator, the enigmatic void demonstrates one way in which visceral, non-empathetic identification might be used for subversive viewing, building on Beckett's own vision of his play as working on audience affect and emotion rather than reason (cited earlier).

Lisa Dwan on Tour (2005, 2009, 2014)

Irish actress Lisa Dwan's version of Mouth could be characterized as a continuation of the legacy that Whitelaw set in motion decades earlier when her performance mesmerized audiences at the Royal Court Theatre. Dwan commenced her stint in this role in 2005, with a reprised production at the Royal Court, directed by Walter Asmus. Dwan has also performed at the Duchess Theatre and the Southbank Centre in London, and in 2014, the production, which played to audiences together with Beckett's two other short monologues *Rockaby* and *Footfalls*, went on a worldwide tour. It might be argued that Dwan has been passed the baton from Whitelaw since Whitelaw even assisted Dwan in the rehearsal process.

However, one marked difference distinguishes the two actresses' incarnation of Mouth in *Not I*: Dwan does not perform alongside an Auditor in Asmus's production. For reviewer Mars-Jones, whose comments on Beckett's play being composed of "two such opposed elements" we saw earlier, the choice to remove Auditor from proceedings averted the hazardous technical terrain of having to negotiate the division of audience attention between the two characters. He opines that "[w]ith the Auditor out of the picture matters of staging are simplified – Dwan's Mouth couldn't be described as 'faintly lit'" (Mars-Jones 22). Beckett laid out in the stage directions that faint lighting should illuminate both Mouth and Auditor in the original text of *Not I*. Mars-Jones signals that the image of a lone Dwan in the Asmus production gained in visual intensity without the presence of Auditor, who for this critic brings an unwelcome "suggestion of kitsch" to proceedings in the gesture of "*helpless compassion*" (Mars-Jones 22) that she periodically makes. Auditor's dispensation was also deemed necessary to the successful functioning of the television version of the play where only the use of an artificial split screen would have enabled the simultaneous depiction of Auditor and the disembodied mouth, which needed to be in extreme close-up to be visible.

As in this BBC version of *Not I*, Dwan's mouth was clearly visible rather than "faintly lit" (215) as stipulated in the original text, an effect achieved with the aid of a spotlight. Dwan was blindfolded as Tandy and Whitelaw were before her, but she was strapped to a wooden wall, a cutout that made only her mouth and chin visible to audiences, unlike Tandy's box or Whitelaw's rostrum. The visual impact of Mouth's discourse is heightened in a setup uniquely consecrated to the protagonist. Focus on Dwan's mouth alone also has the benefit of remedying a situation where, as Beckett scholars James Knowlson and John Pilling note, an "obtrusive" Auditor stands alongside a "too precisely anatomical" (Knowlson and Pilling 198) image of Mouth, both of which threaten to diminish the play's effect.

Visual intensity was able to produce the "inner scream" and, according to my argument, the enigmatic void that comes with it. As with Whitelaw's performance at the Royal Court Theatre, one audience member prematurely exited the Asmus production because of a panic attack induced by Mouth's monologue. The play's capacity to incite this reaction indicates that this play is just as capable of producing the spectator's "inner scream" (*Beckett at the BBC*) today as it was four decades ago. As described earlier, such an inner scream illustrates the spectators' tendency toward the rejection of the dramatic action, literally fleeing it. Spectators' push towards a rejection of what they see could be harnessed to jettison the ideologies guiding the oppression of women, as I have argued, in the psychotic enigmatic void.

Before I get to the issue of Auditor's absence in this production, it is useful to consider the potential of the spectator's enigmatic void, which I argued underwrites the "inner scream" and the psychotic viewing unconscious, in this context. Notably, it is important to consider Dwan's own comments on her enactment of the role of Mouth, which emphasize the positive and emancipatory effects of playing the character. Dwan's speed of recital seems to be a key ingredient that enables the "inner scream" of actor and audience, setting in motion the enigmatic void that leads to a rejection of ideology. Dwan clocked in at a remarkable nine minutes of playing time, in contrast to Whitelaw's fifteen and Tandy's twenty-two minutes. Her speed on stage may be attributed to a meticulous but slow and steady rehearsal process. During the rehearsal period, Dwan would position her head between the banisters in her apartment as a "makeshift harness" (Dwan, "Beckett's *Not I*") to practice Mouth's speech. She was allowed the freedom to prepare in her own time. This was in contrast to Billie Whitelaw, who spent much of the period that she played Mouth caring for her son who was gravely ill in hospital with meningitis. During rehearsal, Dwan was fastidious about training herself to the speed of recitation that would have surpassed even Beckett's wildest expectations, stopping herself and starting from the beginning each time that she made even the slightest mistake in the details of Mouth's tirade.

The benefit of slow and steady practice working up to the intense Beckettian role of Mouth would seem to have sustained Dwan in the Asmus production for more than three runs, and counting. As Anthony Lane, reviewing the New York stint of the Asmus production, observes, Dwan exudes "the cheerful assurance of one who is set on a calmer path" (*The New Yorker*) than her predecessors Tandy and Whitelaw. The actress indicated, in an interview with Lane, that the role even affords her liberation from material and bodily matters: "When you lock into place, the whole thing sings; move your body around too much, and everything leaks away" (qtd. in Lane).

The latter comments may usefully be harnessed for a theory of the spectator's enigmatic void. The idea of the weight of the world "leak[ing] away", as Dwan describes, echoes the psychotic's capacity to rid him- or herself of the weight of ideology by casting it into the Real via an experience of the enigmatic void. Dwan evidently considers this as positive and emancipatory ("the whole thing sings"). This bears the potential to precipitate an ethically fortuitous situation in which the actress who plays Mouth accesses the emancipatory effects of the "inner scream" and, if Mouth's worldview becomes that of spectators as I argued earlier, the spectator gains equal opening onto the enigmatic void where they too can let the world and its dominant ideologies "lea[k] away" (Dwan).

However, the enigmatic void, which de-naturalizes ideologies and casts them into the Real, has little chance to target the contemporary ideology of gender exceptionalism, which holds that the West "knows best" when it comes to the emancipation of Muslim women. My reason for this statement may be attributed to the absence of the character of Auditor, who is a marker of racial and religious difference in *Not I*. Indeed, an interpretation of *Not I* that remains attentive to racial difference among women is severely inhibited in the one-woman Asmus production. Auditor and the racial and gendered difference that she evokes are not present in the Asmus production to remind spectators of the whiteness of Mouth's position.

Lane, in contrast to my assertion, considers that racial and religious difference *was* connoted in Asmus's production. Dwan was able, in his account, to embody non-Western alterity herself. This view would lead us to surmise that Auditor's absence may not pose a barrier to the reading that I am hypothesizing in this chapter. Dwan, in Lane's account, cannot fail to call to mind "the leaked images of prisoners at Abu Ghraib, and of the humiliation that was meted out there" as she performs this piece in full sensory deprivation, in a "mask of black makeup [...] and a pair of black tights [that] serves as a balaclava" (*The New Yorker*). Lane's reading is that Dwan's one-woman performance of *Not I* evokes the tortured Iraqi prisoners at the Abu Ghraib prison between 2003 and 2004, who were subject to physical and sexual abuse on the part of the United States army. Lane's reading is a hopeful one for a form of viewing that critiques racial and religious injustices, and clearly demonstrates the potential of the Theatre of the Absurd to resonate with spectators in contemporary times as I am arguing in this book.

However, it must not be forgotten that Dwan is white. Any reminder to the audiences of the horrors of Abu Ghraib that Dwan was able to conjure must therefore be read as a white appropriation of Muslim body. Contemporary feminists of color have written on the pernicious effects of "cultural appropriation" particularly when dominant social categories such as white individuals borrow or flagrantly steal aspects and elements from minority cultures. As Law scholar and author of *Who Owns Culture? Appropriation and Authenticity in American Law* (2005) Susan Scafidi argues, "cultural appropriation is most likely to be harmful when the source community is a minority group that has been oppressed or exploited in other ways" (qtd. in Taylor, "How you can fight cultural appropriation"). The minority group evoked in Lane's account of *Not I*, the Iraqi prisoners of Abu Ghraib, has been subjected to other forms of oppression and exploitation as Scafidi describes, as the victims of American military torture. Indeed, they fit into the wider Muslim community that, in the wake of 9/11, has been susceptible to blanket typecasting as a fundamentalist and hyper-violent threat. This threat needs to be kept in check by the West according to post-9/11 ideology – hence the West's "War on Terror". Given contemporary Western Islamophobia, the conditions are apt for a situation in which Dwan's evocation of an Abu Ghraib prisoner may well turn into harmful cultural appropriation that reinforces the oppression of Islamic communities similar to the way in which Scafidi describes.

Indeed, white appropriation of racial difference seems to be risked in more ways than one in the Asmus production. Aside from evoking Abu Ghraib, Dwan's face was covered in black paint. This is no neutral theatrical technique, given the history of white performers enacting black stereotypes in blackface minstrelsy, an art form that became popular in nineteenth-century Britain where the Asmus production was staged and the United States where it stopped on its world tour.[5] Ideally, the enigmatic void, which this production is apt to conjure because of its intense impact on spectators, would act to reduce patterns of white appropriation of

---

[5]   On the history of blackface, see, for instance: Anthony Gerard, Barthelemy. *Black Face, Maligned Race: The Representation of Blacks in English Drama from Shakespeare to Southerne*. Baton Rouge: Louisiana State University Press, 1987; Eric, Lott. *Love & Theft: Blackface Minstrelsy and the American Working Class*. Oxford: Oxford University Press, 1993.

racialized bodies to bare signifiers and symbolic impossibility, by throwing them into the Real. But it is hard to see how a rejection of whiteness can be encouraged among spectators when Dwan remains alone onstage with no Auditor to call attention to her privileged racial identity. With Auditor absent from proceedings, the specificities of the differences and power differentials between minorities groups are lost.

In this chapter, I have proposed that *Not I* presents spectators with a picture of the racial and religious differences between two women grappling with the diminishment of their selfhood in Western patriarchy. I suggested that the play's recourse to these differences potentially contests the gender exceptionalism of our post-9/11 world, which holds that Western women are emancipated and in a position to "rescue" their Muslim sisters from disempowerment. The spectator's experience of an "enigmatic void" permits a reduction of the codes circulating around the idea of the global West's gender exceptionalism to meaninglessness. Various techniques in performance and production bolster my reading. Granting the actress who plays Mouth the retention of her selfhood while still encouraging her to the point of "inner scream" (*Beckett at the BBC*) counters the hypocrisy of audiences leveraging the actress's radically divested personhood for their own liberation from restrictive social codes. Restoring the actress behind Mouth to her selfhood may also work to lessen the risk of this character overwhelming proceedings and occupying the center of the dramatic action at the expense of Auditor.

I have, however, mainly pointed out what productions of *Not I* should *not* do. I argued that an imbalance that foments a view of Auditor "towering" over the protagonist (as in the case of the Lincoln Center production) or the protagonist's "mesmerizing" effect on spectators (Whitelaw's) is antithetical to a rejection of gender exceptionalism into the Real. Balance between the two characters is required to evoke the powerful message about the differences between Western and non-Western women's oppression that are contained within this play.

The question remains: What are the concrete techniques that will enable a psychotic rejection of gender exceptionalism? It seems obvious to state that the character of Auditor should be re-integrated into the dramatic action, contrary to the most recent Asmus production, and that she should be played by a woman of color to set in motion a reflection on the racial differences between her and her loquacious white counterpart.

To my knowledge, no woman of color has ever played the role of Auditor. A production that made the different social positioning of both female characters evident would facilitate the reading that I have proposed.

Starting from this basis, perhaps then what is of most potential for undermining gender exceptionalism can be found by turning back to the Asmus production – specifically by concentrating on the age of Lisa Dwan who played Mouth. Dwan performs the role of Mouth as a woman in her thirties, in contrast to Whitelaw, who was in her forties, and Tandy, who was in her sixties. Breaking away from Beckett's original reflection that Mouth recalled the "old crones" (Brater 24) of rural Ireland, a younger version of the protagonist carries the advantage of furthering the reading that would question the power imbalances between women based along racial lines in the post-9/11 era in which we live. The ideology of the West's superiority over the non-Western world in matters of gender, as Mohanty describes, relies on the myth that "Western women *are* secular, liberated and have control over their own lives" (emphasis in the original) (353). As a number of scholars who have studied the theme of contemporary "third-wave" or "postfeminism" in popular culture observe, young, white women tend to be exemplified as liberated Western subjects.[6] Series such as *Sex and the City* and *Ally McBeal*, magazines such as *Vogue* and *Cosmopolitan*, and "chick flicks" such as *13 Going on 30* are awash with white women in their thirties who have come of age in a world where the feminist ideals of autonomy and independence are standard fare. These young women are "able to exercise their 'empowerment' through consumption" (34) as media studies scholar Anna Gough-Yates observes.

Alongside a female Auditor of color, a younger Mouth battling to liberate herself would directly speak to and trouble the idealized youth of the Western woman of gender exceptionalism. Provided that there is balance in the depiction of the two characters Mouth and Auditor, a youthful, white Mouth might even demonstrate how these idealized women are complicit in the oppression of their non-Western counterparts.

---

[6]   For more on racism in third-wave or postfeminism in Western culture, see Abby, Ferber. "The Culture of Privilege: Color-blindness, Postfeminism, and Christonormativity," *Journal of Social Issues* 68 (2012), 63-77. For more on contemporary forms of feminism in "postfeminism" or the "third wave", see Stephanie, Genz and Benjamin, Brabon. *Postfeminism: Cultural Texts and Theories*. Edinburgh: Edinburgh UP, 2009; Angela, McRobbie. *The Aftermath of Feminism: Gender, Culture, and Social Change*. London: SAGE, 2009; Yvonne, Tasker and Diane, Negra (eds.). *Interrogating Postfeminism: Gender and the Politics of Popular Culture*. Durham: Duke University Press, 2007.

One strategy to instigate visual balance would take inspiration from the alterations that Beckett himself made to Auditor's gestures in the 1978 production of *Not I* in Paris. After the 1975 excision of the character in the first Parisian production, the playwright felt something fundamental had been lost. He decided not only to bring Auditor back into the dramatic action but also to accord greater visual prominence to the character. At the four signal moments in which Mouth takes a pause and breaks her mile-a-minute monologue, Auditor (who was played by a man in this production) would cup his head in his hands "in a gesture of increased helplessness and despair, as if unable to bear any longer the torrent of sound" (Brater 34) emitting from the voluble protagonist. This counteracts a depiction of Auditor as a monolithically oppressive, "towering" force, and it distances the play from currying favor with re-scripted terrorist masculinities which we saw was the case in its Lincoln Center world debut. Modifying this further so that the character is played by a woman of color would draw attention to how racial and religious others may become victims of white people, including white women, as represented by the character of Mouth. This would disturb a Western worldview that has integrated feminist ideals in such a way that it is falsely assumed, as Mohanty asserts, that all "[m]en exploit, [and] [all] women are exploited" (344). A female Auditor of color who cups her head in powerless desperation gives increased visibility to the plight of this character in conjunction with that of the main character, Mouth. This would offset Mouth's tendency toward holding the audience spellbound and fixated on her orifice alone. Perhaps in this way, too, the inner scream might be finally be targeted directly at a rejection of Mouth's power over Auditor, and the gender exceptionalist ideologies of a post-9/11 world that Mouth embodies in her vocal force over her silent playing partner Auditor.

Genet's *The Blacks*: Remixed at the Intersection of Gender and Race

This chapter proposes that Jean Genet's *The Blacks* (1958) – a play about a black community's emancipation from white hegemony – conjures a viewing reaction guided by the unconscious formation of "supplementary enjoyment". Situated between pain and pleasure, supplementary enjoyment falls outside of discourse as a method to "unlearn" ideological scripts. In the case of Genet's *The Blacks*, it is proposed that gendered racism, the form of discrimination that black women face doubly for their gender and race, is unlearned. Deconstructing gendered racism is a key project for the post-millennial age, because while public awareness of racism is at an all-time high, sufficient attention has not been paid, in mainstream society and the media, to black women. The absence of black women from the social conversation about racism is highlighted, for instance, in the United States. Liberal and mainstream media have reported on anti-racist movements such as Black Lives Matter and given full coverage to protesting state-sanctioned police shootings of black men, but they have tended to neglect the violence that black women face (Winfrey Harris, "Ain't I A Woman"). The destabilization of gendered racism is the fourth way explored in this book, in which the Theatre of the Absurd could be subversive in our post-millennial age.

Genet published *The Blacks* in 1958, in an era of French decolonization and the Algerian War of Independence (1954-1962). The play came prior to the playwright's outspoken support for the black revolutionary movement in the US, the Black Panthers. While his sympathies for the struggles against racism informed *The Blacks*, Genet in fact wrote the play at the behest of director Raymond Rouleau, who asked the playwright to compose a stage piece for an all-black theatre troupe that Rouleau wished to found (Finburgh and Bradby 1242).

The Blacks stages a black community's revolution against a "white" court. Black actors in white masks play the members of the court, as an inversion of the racist performance tradition of "blackface", where white actors would blacken their skin and perform crudely reduced versions of black people, in the nineteenth and early twentieth centuries in

Europe and the United States. The play progressively exposes numerous plotlines as fictive, a theme that can also be found in Genet's other plays such as *The Balcony* (1957) and *The Maids* (1947). In *The Blacks*, at the center of the action, a black man Village has murdered a white woman. The function of the murder victim as a symbol of white female purity is indicated in her virginal nomenclature Marie. Marie's funeral rites function as the centerpiece of the play, as her catafalque is covered over by a white pall. This catafalque is placed center-stage. While the black community (the "Negroes") enact their ceremony of emancipation from white power around her catafalque, it emerges that offstage an unnamed black man is in the process of being tried and sentenced for betraying his race. When this is discovered toward the end, the members of the "white" court remove their masks. At the moment of unmasking it transpires that the play's actual ceremony consists in the entire black troupe's staging of the court's demise. Indeed, their basis for being there, to mourn the victim Marie, is exposed as fictive. The murder of the white woman never took place at all, a fact driven home by the court's uncovering of the catafalque where she is supposed to have lain to reveal two empty chairs. The Queen, who is the leader of the court, utters her parting words, which reveal a parodic rejoicing in the destruction of the white identity that she had assumed throughout the play: "As for us, we've lived a long time. We're now going to rest at last [...] we shall lie torpid in the earth like larvae or moles" (96).[1] Her words typify the play's, and more broadly Genet's, lyrical style. The play then ends with Village and his girlfriend Virtue (also a member of the "Negros") who turn their backs to the stage. Virtue, who was also forced into prostitution, implores her lover to separate his preconceived notions of female beauty from whiteness. This is symbolized in her self-professed refusal in *The Blacks* to cater to a category in which she must bear the "long golden hair" (96) commonly associated with Caucasian women.

While I focus on the spectator's chance for the deconstruction of gendered racism in this chapter, the majority of critics have focused on *The Blacks'* racial politics and the fact that the play charts the destruction of white hegemony. Critics of *The Blacks* have absented the question of gender from the way racism manifests itself. For example, drama scholar

---

[1]   References to the play in the text will be to this edition: Jean, Genet. *The Blacks*, translated by Bernard Frechtman. London: Faber and Faber, 1960.

Una Chaudhuri, who has analyzed the function of semiotics in Genet's work, propounds:

> [T]h[e] [play's] fluid version of identity [...] is a comment on the semiotic (conventional) nature of both 'character' and 'race': roles are constructed out of a dramatic system; blacks and whites are constructed out of a cultural system. (Chaudhuri 102-103)[2]

As we recall, black characters perform in white masks, which are removed and replaced. This fact enables Chaudhuri to argue that *The Blacks* exposes the racial categories of black and white as signs or constructions, as opposed to biological phenomena that reinforce racist ideas on the "natural" superiority of whites. While Chaudhuri concentrates on *The Blacks'* deconstruction of the racial markers "white" and "black", it is possible to argue that Genet's play does not separate the social construction of race from gender. Spectators are confronted with the ways gender inflects and informs racism by means of its central premise: the murder of a white woman (Marie) by a black man (Village). Indeed, the play is concentrated just as much on how the category of gender is constructed, since the linchpin of the action consists in the revelation that the murder of a white woman is fictive. Moreover, the play ends with the empowered words of black prostitute Virtue who implores her lover (and would-be murderer of fictive victim Marie) Village, to "invent something else" (96) separate from a standard of white feminine "long golden hair" (96). Attention shifts in other words from an apocryphal white female victimization to an urgent call to think about black female selfhood, a fact overlooked by a large number of critics. This chapter takes this fact, therefore, as a point of departure to concentrate on what the play reveals about the discrimination facing black women at the intersection of racism and sexism.

The study of multiple forms of discrimination facing individuals, such as the aforementioned convergence of racism and sexism, has been named by feminist scholars as "intersectionality". It is an intersectional approach that I follow in this chapter. Legal scholar Kimberlé Crenshaw coined the term "intersectionality" in her article "Mapping the Margins: Intersectionality, Identity Politics, and Violence Against Women of Color" (1989). Here, Crenshaw studied the lack of public awareness

---

[2]   See also Payal, Nagpal. *Shifting Paradigms in Culture: A Study of Three Plays by Jean Genet – The Maids, The Balcony, and The Blacks.* Cambridge: Cambridge Scholars, 2015, 56.

of the violence facing black women. The cases of violence against black women tend to go under-examined in the feminist movement, which has historically concentrated on white women, and in the civil rights and anti-racist struggles in the US, whose activism has tended to focus on black men. Black women, because of the intersectional discrimination that they face at the crossroads of racism and sexism, are made invisible in both feminist and anti-racist struggles. My analysis of *The Blacks* uncovers ways in which the play promotes black women's selfhood and visibility in order to reverse what Crenshaw describes as the invisibility of intersectionally oppressed women. While Crenshaw's notion of intersectionality implicitly informs my reading, it is the work of black feminist sociologist Patricia Hill Collins, who wrote *Black Feminist Thought* (1990), that allows me to specify ways in which black female selfhood is promoted. For instance, I detect in *The Blacks* a destabilization of what Hill Collins names as a stereotype of black female sexual deviancy. I also assert that *The Blacks* puts forth a vision of what Hill Collins describes as an empowered "othermother" – a figure who enables the growth and evolution of black communities.

The chapter insists that intersectional oppression, specifically the gendered racism facing black women, is "unlearned" by spectators with the help of the Lacanian psychical condition of "supplementary enjoyment". Enjoyment, like psychosis, divests ideologies of their weight and casts them into the unnamable Real. *The Blacks'* elaborate intrigue, in which plotlines are hard to follow and constantly collapse in on themselves, forms a baroque mechanism that is also a feature of supplementary enjoyment, as I shall explain in the first part of the chapter. Yet the play does not simply call on spectators to unlearn gendered racism; it also builds on these ruins to covey an empowered form of selfhood for black women, as I shall explore in the second part of the chapter. Throughout the chapter various production and performance techniques that encourage the unlearning of gendered racism are identified. These techniques include the use of lighting, musicality, rhythm, and rap.

Unlearning Gendered Racism

This section explains why supplementary enjoyment, which unlearns gendered racism, could be conjured by *The Blacks*. In order to do this, it is helpful to go back to accounts of the play's début *mise-en-scène*, which was directed by Roger Blin and first performed at the Théâtre de Lutèce in 1959 before moving to the Royal Court production in London two years later. The début production began a tradition in which *The Blacks* created a paradoxical experience of simultaneous pleasure and pain in audience members, which mirrors the Lacanian state of supplementary enjoyment. Genet Scholar Gene Plunka, who wrote on the role of ritual and rite in the French playwright's oeuvre, confirms that in *The Blacks* "we are enthralled by a play that stimulates and surprises us yet at the same time makes us feel uncomfortable" (Plunka 240). A paradoxical mix of pain and pleasure stimulated by *The Blacks* shall be studied first before connecting it to a notion of supplementary enjoyment theorized by Lacan.

In performances of *The Blacks*, pain issued from confusion and a direct visual and verbal assault on the white audience members. Director Blin hired a cast of Francophone black actors who articulated *The Blacks'* lines while refusing to tailor their accents to bourgeois Parisian audience members' expectations. The debut production stressed black historical authenticity, with Blin's hired troupe, "Les Griottes", being named after the singing, dancing, and poetic bards "les griots" hailing from West Africa. Spectators confessed to having difficulty understanding the characters, bringing into relief the colonialism inherent in the notion of language itself. Their incomprehension illustrated the feeling of being targeted and challenged for racist expectations of what constitutes "correct" and "incorrect" ways to speak in the process. The linguistic assault on the white audience carries through to a textual level as well, as Village's girlfriend and prostitute Virtue spits out a "Litany of the Livid" (46) to her white oppressors onstage and by extension to the audience.

An affront to linguistic expectations reflects the sense of attack inherent in *The Blacks*. Genet declared outright that his play was intended to assault white spectators, specifying that in the event that the audience should be composed of black people or people of color, then a white individual robed in ceremonial garb must be seated, spotlighted, and objectified in the front stalls or failing this a white dummy must be installed somewhere in the auditorium in plain sight of the audience. This situation reversed white objectification of black bodies and added to the animosity felt in the auditorium by white audience members. As Genet scholars Clare Finburgh and David Bradby (2012) describe in their book aiming to introduce the playwright to the English-speaking world, Genet's fellow Absurdist playwright, Eugène Ionesco, whose *The*

Bald Soprano we saw in the first chapter, walked out of the debut Blin production, fuming that "he was not going to sit there and be insulted" (Bradby and Finburgh 1313).

The audience's sense of being attacked, conjured in Blin's début *mise-en-scène*, is symptomatic of what Genet critic Carl Lavery terms an affective "wound" pervading the playwright's work. Genet rejects "positive solutions" (Lavery 234) and seeks spectators' emotional injury. Genet's theatrical strategy of wounding consists in the refusal to placate audience members in an Aristotelian resolution of drama in a final, cathartic ending. Rather than the resolution of Marie's funeral rites or the sentencing of her supposed murderer Village – actions that would bring the play's central plot mechanism to a successful, cathartic, conclusion as Aristotle's model of theatre would have it – spectators are exposed to a *mise-en-abyme* of the intrigue. The "white" court remove and then replace their masks, derailing the plot of Marie's funeral rites in order to commit their final act of self-sacrifice – an act that also symbolizes the killing of the white characters that they had played. This disallowing of cathartic relief echoes Genet's earlier plays. For instance, *The Balcony* (1956) explores a counter-revolution inside a brothel as an allegory of power in the wider world. Like the denial of Marie's murder in *The Blacks*, *The Balcony* ends by revealing to spectators that the outside revolution against which the characters mobilize does not exist.

Audience "wound[ing]" (Lavery 234) indicates *The Blacks'* creation of spectatorial pain and unease. The 2003 production of *The Blacks* by black director Christopher McElroen in the Classical Theatre of Harlem took this desire to wound spectators further, as hard white swivel chairs on which spectators sat made for very uncomfortable viewing. The color-coded chairs hinted that aggression was turned towards white spectators in particular. The mobile chairs also echoed avant-garde dramaturge Antonin Artaud's "Theatre of Cruelty", a model expounded on in his *Theatre and its Double*. Artaud wished to shock audiences and draw out from them the most visceral of emotions, such as fear. Theatre must enact the panic of a "plague" on audience members for Artaud. Swivel chairs were an Artaudian device that aimed to place spectators at the center of the dramatic action, rather than safely removed from it in immobile, plush seats, in order to create this immersive, plague-like fear. McElroen's use of the technique would seem to have created the same sense of fear in white spectators as Artaud first designed. Writing for African-American arts and cultural site *Africina.com*, one commentator on McElroen's production cited a black teenager who indicated the erosion of the dividing line between theatre and reality ("Is this still theatre?") and a direct attack on the white spectators (Anon., "The Blacks: A Clown Show"). This teenager "wondered if white people might be too afraid to come to Harlem after the experience" (Anon., "The Blacks: A Clown Show") of seeing *The Blacks*.

Yet watching *The Blacks* is not simply a painful or frightening experience. The unease and pain of watching *The Blacks* is matched by an equal and opposite emotion of excitement and enthrallment. The aforementioned teenage spectator of McElroen's production not only wondered about white fear but also had a "racing" heartbeart (Anon., "The Blacks: A Clown Show"). Pleasure and excitement were also reflected in *The Blacks'* début in Paris. Genet biographer Edmund White described audiences' contradictory experience of disturbance and fulfillment during *The Blacks'* first runs in Paris under the direction of Roger Blin. Spectators did not know whether to "hiss at the hostility or walk out in cold disapproval" or, alternatively, to "applaud [its] beauty" (499) according to White.

Pleasure, in part, seemed to have derived from the baroque nature of the spectacle that Genet lays before spectators' eyes. As Bradby and Finburgh put it, Blin's production evoked "musicality" and rhythm while "words and syllables [were] freed from their strictly semantic function, their acoustic sonority becoming palpable" (Bradby and Finburgh 2625). Words outstripped their meaning to acquire added aesthetic dimensions. One way in which they did this was via a baroque aesthetic strategy involving the proliferation of plotlines, motion, and speed.[3] Baroque or rococo artwork, originating in sixteenth-century Italy, revolves around intricacy, elaborate ornamentation, and the implication of speed in the proliferation of signs. *The Blacks* demonstrates elaborate ornamentation on a theatrical level: the constant manufacture and uncovering of layers of reality creates a sense of shunting-motion and contributes to the speed that characterizes this principle of the baroque. *The Blacks* moves from Marie's murder to her complete inexistence; it oscillates between the roles of the performers and references to their real-life jobs as seamstresses; the

---

[3]   For more on how the baroque inflects Genet's work, see Mary Ann, Frese Witt. *Metatheater and Modernity: Baroque and Neo-baroque.* Plymouth: Rowman & Little, 2013, 19-52.

"white" court unmask and reveal their blackness at the end of the play, before promptly re-masking for their final self-sacrifice.

American director Robert Wilson's production of *The Blacks* in the prestigious Parisan Théâtre de l'Odéon in 2014 (a production which I saw) created baroque speed principally by means of multi-colored lights that he flashed before the spectators' eyes. The "white" court, played by masked black actors, stood on a platform visible via a single, thin, white strip of light. This contrasted with the rest of the stage where the black cast of characters enacted a ceremony of emancipation bathed in resplendent spirals of yellow and multi-hued outfits. Wilson, who asserts that he works with visuals, space, sound and music before he considers the text, infused the play's complex lyricism with the lightshow and this made for a whirlwind spectacle (Loayza and Wilson, "Pour moi tout théâtre est danse"). The result was a sense of excitement echoing the baroque motion of the play's first productions.

Image of the Robert Wilson production in the Théâtre de l'Odéon in 2014

Copyright © Lucie Jansch.

Elsewhere, music and visuals have given motion to *The Blacks* and contributed to a sense of aesthetic pleasure derived by audiences. Michael Levinas's production in the Opéra de Lyon in January 2004 stressed the musicality of Genet's discourse quite literally by adapting the piece to operatic overtures. Elsewhere, costuming and masks have precipitated aesthetic pleasure on the part of audiences. Cristèle Alves-Meira's production in Vincennes (just outside of Paris) in 2006 and reprisal in the French capital's Théâtre l'Athénée-Louis Jouvet the following year had some of the "white" court's masks made of latex. These resembled professional prostheses evoking the commedia-dell'arte. Meanwhile, there were other members of the court who wore masks giving the impression that they had been made by children. The mixture made for a ludic atmosphere. Interviewing Alves-Meira in a recorded academic conference on black theatre in France in 2007, Francophone studies scholar Sylvie Chalaye confirmed, "we are swept up by a kind of very ludic whirlwind and much pleasure" (*on est emporté par une espèce de tourbillon très ludique et plein de plaisir*) (Chalaye *et al.*, "Les représentations du Noir au théâtre"). A woman in the audience of this recorded event likewise opined, "we laugh a lot" (*on rit beaucoup*) ("Les représentations du Noir au théâtre").

The Blacks gives rise in spectators to a simultaneous experience of pain and pleasure, created by a mixture of attack against the audience, and baroque motion and playfulness. Audience response seems to hinge on paradoxical affect – "hiss[ing] at the hostility" and "applaud[ing] beauty" (499) to recall White's words – over and above a response that seeks reason, meaning, and comprehension from the plot of *The Blacks*. The lightshow extravaganza of Robert Wilson's production that I watched in the Théâtre de l'Odéon in October 2014 ended with the spectators around me commenting on their bafflement at what exactly was at stake in this play. It is this admixture of pleasure, pain, and incomprehension that resembles the psychoanalytic concept explored in this chapter: supplementary enjoyment.

Supplementary enjoyment is an affect that blurs a dichotomization or separation of pleasure and pain at the same time as pushing beyond meaning and signification. As Lacanian cultural theorist Jane Gallop confirms, enjoyment is not "beyond pleasure" "but [rather] […] it is beyond principle" (113), beyond efforts to capture it in language or in descriptions of the known feelings of pain and pleasure. Bradby and Finburgh's description of Blin's production of *The Blacks* as separating "words and syllables […] from their strictly semantic function" echoes enjoyment's nature as "beyond principle" (Gallop 113) or meaning. This reaction, taken more positively than simple incomprehension on the part of the audience, also indicates the departure of language (whether visual or spoken) from strict and stable meaning. The evacuation of meaning, and the paradoxical mix of pleasure in equal parts to pain signal that productions of *The Blacks* evince on an affective level something akin to supplementary enjoyment in audience members.

As Lacan described in his twentieth seminar on the subject of supplementary enjoyment between 1972 and 1973 (which was entitled "Encore" or "More"), enjoyment "doesn't signify anything" (*On Feminine Sexuality* 74). It is a state where the "Other", a Lacanian term to describe the locus of dominant ideologies, is "barred" and thrown into the Real, deemed radically lacking and inconsistent. It is my contention that *The Blacks* uses audience enjoyment – their experience of pleasure, pain, and incomprehension – as a means to overturn the ideologies that structure white subjectivity by casting them into the Real. The denial of various plotlines – Marie's murder, the existence of the "white court" and so on – positions *The Blacks* as pivoting more specifically on something similar to the "apophatic" (Hollywood 16-17) knowledge that Lacan observed in supplementary enjoyment. Apophatic knowledge in the *OED* is defined as the knowledge "obtained through *negating* concepts that might be applied to [God]" (my emphasis). Lacan was inspired by the female Christian mystics of the Middle Ages in tracing the historical existence of supplementary enjoyment as religious historian Amy Hollywood notes in her account *Sensible Ecstasy: Mysticism, Sexual Difference and the Demands of History* (2002). Women such as St Teresa of Avila claimed a connection with the highest state of authority, God. However, because patriarchal religious dogma proscribed such an affinity, the mystics had to use apophatic knowledge, a form of negative knowledge of God, which as Lacan clarified in his twentieth seminar "consists in saying that they experience it, but know nothing about it" (*On Feminine Sexuality* 76). "[K]now[ing] nothing about it" encapsulates the apophatic nature of the knowledge that the mystics obtained, beyond the patriarchal language of religious scripture. For the female mystics, apophatic knowledge was a way of embracing and refuting God's mastery at the same time.

Similar to the female mystical experience of negative knowledge, as theatre historian Christopher Innes observes, all Genet's work functions as a "ceremony of negation" that enables "spiritual transcendence" (113-114). Such negative transcendence reflects the broader drive in much avant-garde theatre of the twentieth century to seek an expiation of the unconscious by means of quasi-religious and carnivalesque ritual (Innes

113-114). Genet's plays, from *The Balcony* to *The Screens* and *The Maids*, exemplify a shift where social revolution is implemented only via "the violent exorcism of an alien presence" (Innes 113-114) or power. In *The Maids*, for instance, two sister-servants enact nightly a ritualistic murder of their mistress before audiences discover at the end of the play that "Madame" is alive and that the sisters are trapped in their ritual of staging a fake murder *ad infinitum*. The "ceremony of negation" (Innes 113-114) in *The Maids* echoes *The Blacks'* denial of Marie's murder at the end of the play. Like *The Maids'* sisters, *The Blacks'* cast of characters enact the funeral rites to audiences every night and it is Marie, the white murder victim, who is "violent[ly] exorcised" (113-114), to borrow Innes's formulation, via the play's end denial that she ever existed. *The Blacks* invites spectator transcendence through the negation of the very existence of Marie, the white "murder" victim.

Since many have interpreted *The Blacks* as a play about race, Marie's funeral rites may be perceived as a ceremonial conduit to the expiation and transcendence of white domination. *The Blacks*, in this view, is targeted at white spectators and their confrontation, followed by relinquishment, of their racist conceits. However, scratching beneath the surface, the nexus of the play's apophatic knowledge, the negative knowledge that supplementary enjoyment propels, lies in the denial of the murder of a white *woman*. In other words, it is not simply white domination but a form of white domination that props itself up by white supremacist ideologies at the intersection of gender and race. It is via the consideration of Marie's gender as well as her race that we may assert that apophatic or negative knowledge is targeted at gendered racism.

A number of black feminist sociologists and historians (e.g. Crenshaw 1989; Hill Collins 1990; McGuire 2010) have argued that white female victimhood, such as can be seen in the "murder" of Marie in *The Blacks*, functions to obscure the gendered racism facing black women. Looking to the US context, historian Danielle McGuire's *At The Dark End of the Street: Black Women, Rape, and Resistance – a New History of the Civil Rights Movement from Rosa Parks to the Rise of Black Power* examines, among other subjects, the way white female victimhood has reinforced the intersectional oppression facing black women. As McGuire describes, since the post-bellum period of the nineteenth century, false or overblown accusations of assaults on white women were used to legitimate the mass lynching of black men, while cases of black women being raped and aggressed went under-reported and often under-punished. A comparison of the case of Emmett Till with that of the little-known rape of black woman Betty Jean Owens reveals this double standard. Till was a black teenager who was murdered and thrown into the Tallahatchie River in Mississippi by white supremacists J.W. Milan and Roy Bryant in 1955 for purportedly flirting with Bryant's white wife (McGuire 147). Till's case involved a white female victim, and it became one of the most famous examples in the history of US racial segregation. Till's case, falsely construed by racists as evidence of the vulnerability of white women around black men, functioned as a smokescreen covering the sexual and physical violence visited on black women at the hands of white men. McGuire names the case of Betty Jean Owens, a young black woman who was brutally raped by four white men on June 12, 1959. After a dramatic trial replete with the white prosecution's attempts to de-legitimize Owens' testimony, the white rapists were finally sent to jail but with a "mercy ruling" (McGuire 175). The attackers avoided the death penalty – an eventuality not available to black men accused of raping white women. As McGuire makes the point, "[u]nlike white women, who were often able to play the role of 'fair maiden' before a lynch mob worked its will on their alleged [black] attackers, Betty Jean Owens had to tell her story in front of hundreds of white people in a segregated institution" (McGuire 175) of the court room, all the while knowing "that the four white men who raped her might go unpunished" (175). Narratives of white female victimhood, such as can be seen in the case of Emmett Till, work to obscure, underestimate, or make invisible cases of rape of black women, such as Betty Jean Owens.

The construction of white female victimhood relies, in short, on the invisibilization of the oppression facing black women. Spectators of *The Blacks*, by being made to confront the reality that the white female murder victim "Marie" never existed, are encouraged to transcend the ideologies of white female victimhood. This exposes the oppression that black women face. I make this claim more specifically about *The Blacks* not only with reference to the history of gendered racism in the United States, but also because the end actions of *The Blacks* seek to intertwine its undermining of white female victimhood with the revelation of the oppression facing black women. *The Blacks* reveals the falsity of the narrative of the rape and murder of white women by black men in the cast's gesture of uncovering two empty chairs where Marie's body was supposed to have lain. At the same time, the character of Virtue launches parting words that insist on the recognition of black women in all their beauty. Virtue, who had played the role of the "murderer" Village's girlfriend, calls upon her boyfriend to leave behind white beauty standards in order to love her fully. She reminds Village that he "won't be able to wind [his] fingers in [her] long golden hair" (96). As Debby Thompson, who has written extensively on race in avant-garde drama, confirms, the ending of *The Blacks* demonstrates "how deeply entwined sex/gender and race systems are" (Thompson 421). But it is also possible to see Virtue's words as *refusing* this deeply entwined system of sexism and racism. Her words demand a recognition of black women's beauty outside of white standards; they call for a place for black women's subjectivity in all its specificity and fullness.

I argue that *The Blacks* destabilizes white female victimhood in demonstrating Marie's inexistence in order to maneuver spectators to a point where gendered racism, to return to a theory of supplementary enjoyment, "doesn't exist and doesn't signify anything" (Lacan, *On Feminine Sexuality* 74). This reading has resonance in the current US context in particular, where black women's victimization is still underplayed even in contemporary movements for racial justice, such as Black Lives Matter. As author of *The Sisters Are Alright: Changing the Broken Narrative of Black Women in America* (2015) Tamara Winfrey Harris points out in her commentary on gendered racism in the contemporary setting of the United States, black "women like Rekia Boyd, Yvette Smith, Pearlie Smith and Tyisha Miller, all victims of police violence, have not become the rallying points that [black men] Eric Garner, Mike Brown, Tamir Rice and Freddie Gray have" ("Ain't I A Woman"). *The Blacks*' destabilization of gendered racism – its drive to replace white female victimhood (Marie's) with black female beauty (Virtue's) – bears the capacity to challenge this contemporary American context. This is especially since the play has demonstrated an extraordinary capacity to rattle American spectators. As Loren Glass, a cultural historian who has written on the Theatre of the Absurd's importation into the United States, states, *The Blacks* was the first of Genet's plays to be understood by American audiences because of its echoes with the struggle against racism in the Civil Rights era. The role of publication and the play's American debut production off-Broadway at St. Mark's Playhouse, which was directed by Gene Frankel, were both significant in popularizing Genet's play in the United States. Grove Press published *The Blacks*, printing Bernard Frechtman's translation of the text from the French *Les Nègres*. As Glass explains, "[m]ore than any other play Grove published, *The Blacks* was inextricably yoked to a specific

American performance" and "photos [from the Frankel production] [...] were generously distributed throughout the paperback reissue of the play, which sold more than 80,000 copies over the course of the 1960s" (*Counterculture Colophon* 80). Reflecting the play's popularity not only with American readers but also American audiences, *The Blacks* had a stint of 1,408 performances between 1961 and 1964 with the Frankel production, and was the longest running non-musical production of the 1960s (Plunka 219).

With its popularity in the United States already proven, *The Blacks* could resonate with contemporary American audiences to destabilize modern-day forms of gendered racism. Indeed, the deconstruction of contemporary gendered racism potentiated by the text was partially exploited by Christopher McElroen's production of *The Blacks*, mentioned earlier, in Harlem in 2003. McElroen confronted white spectators with their racist conceits via attack and Artaudian cruelty-like hard swivel chairs. Confrontation was verbal in form at one point. Notably one actor of the production, J. Kyle Manzay, focused on the exposure of conceits held by white women in the post-9/11 era of racial and religious intolerance. As reviewer of McElroen's production Jenny Sandman recalls:

> At one point, Village (J. Kyle Manzay) pulled a woman out of the audience and broke character to harangue her for close to fifteen minutes – until she admitted that yes, she did clutch her purse tighter when black men passed by, and yes, this was the same sort of racism that George Bush was currently displaying. (Sandman, "The Blacks")

Manzay's intervention recalls Genet's stage direction that a white person be isolated from the audience of *The Blacks*. A strategy of ostracizing this audience member would deconstruct the white supremacist ideologies that they embodied. In the McElroen production, the ostracized audience member was a white woman, which could be significant for our reading since, as I have pointed out, the gendered racism facing black women is obscured by means of the exaggeration of white women's victimization by black men. Manzay challenged the ideology of white female victimization via his selection of a white female spectator whom he "harangued" until he exposed her fear of black men as unjustified and unfounded. He was careful to connect this to a racist social structure ("until she admitted that [...] yes, this was the same sort of racism that George Bush was currently displaying").

Manzay's selection of a white woman could turn spectators to focus not only on racist ideologies but also how gender plays into prejudice too. While spectator-actor interaction in McElroen's *The Blacks* concentrated on the convergence of gender and race in its attack on a white female spectator, the reaction of the latter also reveals one of the greatest challenges to our reading of the destabilization of gendered racism in Genet's play. Through admission and shaming, the white woman's response was nonetheless reverted to spotlighting racism against black men ("until she admitted that yes, she did clutch her purse tighter when black men passed by"). Nothing was said of black women, whose oppression remained invisible or, at least, not vocalized in this instance.

One of the greatest challenges, therefore, to instigating audience enjoyment that would evacuate gendered racism of meaning lies in the play's overdetermination as purely about racial politics. This is the case for the critical literature surrounding *The Blacks* too. For instance, Thompson, who I quoted earlier, considers ultimately that *The Blacks* is most useful for a deconstruction of "whiteness studies" (421), even though she reads intersectional oppression and "how deeply entwined sex/gender and race systems are" (421) in the play's ending. Making the deconstruction of intersectional oppression facing black women emerge in performance is therefore a formidable task. However, there are performance techniques and moments earlier in the text of *The Blacks* that may give added momentum to a deconstruction of gendered racism. We turn to these elements now.

Making Sense of the Incomprehensible

Black feminist scholar Gina Dent, in a chapter entitled "Black Joy, Black Pleasure: An Introduction" in the 1992 anthology *Black Popular Culture*, discusses the need for an authentically black women's reclaiming of psychoanalytic theories of pleasure such as the supplementary enjoyment I have been discussing here. For Dent, "Black joy" must "revis[e] the discussion of women's pleasure inherited from feminism and psychoanalysis and plac[e] it within a black progressive context" (Dent 2). Applying Dent's argument to a black feminist recuperation of *The Blacks*, then, must involve the discussion of how Genet's play is to act in the service of a progressive black context – more specifically a progressive black women's context. In other words, a black feminist reading of Genet's play cannot rely solely on the idea that supplementary enjoyment is derived from the denial of white woman Marie's murder and the devaluation of white hegemony that this act represents. Destabilizations of white dominance would only seem to go halfway to a cause that recuperates *The Blacks* for black women's pleasure. They must be accompanied by a renunciation of the stereotypes surrounding black women and a language of empowered black female pleasure and self-actualization to conjure the "Black joy" that Dent posits.

Both in performance and at a textual level, *The Blacks* contains the seeds of black women's self-actualization. I discussed in the previous part of the chapter how the ending was crucial to a strategy of supplementary enjoyment that unlearns gendered racism. But this ending also goes much further than this in its creation of an empowered language for black women. Virtue implores to would-be murderer and lover Village: "All men are like you: they imitate. Can't you invent something else?" (96). Because of the hammy romanticism of Village's response, many critics have qualified this ending as just as contrived as the rest of the play. As Village concludes, "For you I could invent anything: fruits, brighter words, a two-wheelbarrow, cherries without pits, a bed for three, a needle that doesn't prick" (96). Mary Ann Frese Witt states that the ending of *The Blacks* reflects "mimesis rather than diegesis", presenting itself as an imitation of reality rather than the successful conclusion of a dramatic play, since "the actor-characters seem to be struggling toward breaking through the theatrical wall to 'really' falling in love with each other" (Frese Witt 41). However, as Michael Bennett reminds us, this is the one moment in the play when layer upon layer of illusion unfolds to reveal the dramatic reality of the play's characters. "Virtue and Village have literally turned their backs to illusion at the very end of the play" (*Reassessing the Theatre of the Absurd* 71), argues Bennett, since the rest of the characters exit right and left having finished their ceremonial slaughter of white supremacy for the evening.

The ending calls for spectators to embrace reality outside of theatrical illusion. More specifically, the reality that they are impelled to confront is one of black female empowerment outside of the illusion of gendered racism that I have argued that the play lays waste to. This is not least of all because Virtue quickly undercuts Village's lofty overtures, as she responds: "I'll help you. At least, there's one sure thing: you won't be able to wind your fingers in my long golden hair..." (96). Virtue reinforces the play's rejection of pure white womanhood by envisioning a world in which women may be loved outside of a standard of "long golden hair", a qualifier privileged in our culture for its association with women's beauty – most often Caucasian women's beauty. Virtue is given the authority to articulate the play's parting words. Not merely a rejection of this discourse of white feminine standards of beauty involving "long golden hair", Virtue also gestures toward a new knowledge and language of black female beauty and empowerment in her first-person, embodied articulation of the play's final words.

As Thompson notes, the character conveys a picture of "mutuality and re-birth" (421) in one of the only hopeful moments of the play. However, I disagree with this critic that this represents a "Utopian" outcome and that *The Blacks* "ultimately fails to imagine racial identities outside of white hegemony and white mythology" (421). Virtue's allusion to love and beauty outside of a blonde-haired, white paradigm may be brief but it connects to and builds on earlier moments in the play when such an eventuality is deemed impossible. Fellow member of the play's black community, Snow, reprimands Village for killing the white woman Marie out of desire, and she ridicules Virtue when the latter steps in to defend the would-be murderer: "So you think he loves you, you, the submissive negress? [...] To turn pink, to blush with emotion, with confusion – tender expressions that will never apply to us" (24). Snow implies that love will never be the preserve of black women because of white constructions of female innocence, associated with the white-skinned blushing of cheeks. Village confirms the inextricability of love and white supremacist notions of beauty, saying to Virtue: "I began to hate you when everything about you would have kindled my love" (29). He attributes this to his marginalized status in a racist world where "mov[ing] along the edges of the world, out of bounds" (29) he is unable to feel amorously for Virtue.

The ending and Virtue's insistence on "invent[ing] something else" where Village does not "wind [his] fingers in [...] long golden hair" thus recant earlier propositions that love and beauty are impossibilities for black women. In contrast to Thompson's assertion that *The Blacks* cannot imagine "racial identities outside of white hegemony" (421), the ending may be seen as a refusal of white patriarchy. More specifically, Virtue refuses what queer black feminist Audre Lorde in the American context names as "the master's tools", a reference dating back to the period of white slave-masters. It is worth quoting Lorde's essay "The Master's tools will never destroy the master's house," published in her book *Sister Outsider* (1984), in detail here:

Those of us who stand outside the circle of this society's definition of acceptable women; [...] those of us who are poor, who are lesbians, who are Black, who are older, know that survival is not an academic skill [...] It is learning how to stand alone, unpopular and sometimes reviled [...]. It is learning how to take our differences and make them strengths. *For the master's tools will never dismantle the master's house.* They may allow us temporarily to beat him at his own game, but they will never enable us to bring about genuine change. (Lorde 112)

Black women are among the outcast and "[un]acceptable" women in American society, but they must find "strength" in this outside position as Lorde counsels. Returning to *The Blacks*, Virtue's insistence to Village that he cannot love through a white-centered prism of "wind[ing] [his] fingers in [her] long golden hair" takes up this exterior position to white patriarchal beauty standards – the "master's tools" in this context. In walking hand-in-hand with Village as the two characters turn their backs to the audience, Virtue also disproves Snow's earlier accusation that Village cannot authentically love her as a black woman. Virtue, in her ending, therefore enacts a refutation of the "master's tools" that constitute a starting point in the black feminist project that Lorde outlines.

In this ending, *The Blacks* also breaks the endless circularity that other examples from the Theatre of the Absurd demonstrate. As we saw in the cases of *The Bald Soprano* and *Not I*, the dramatic action never in fact comes to a successful conclusion; spectators are merely reverted to the beginning of the play with the roles of the two married couples reversed in *The Bald Soprano* and Mouth continuing to babble behind a curtain as she did at the start of *Not I*, having resolved nothing from her monologue. In *The Blacks*, the white catafalque – representing where the murder victim lies – resumes its position center-stage implying that the ceremony will start again soon. Nevertheless, the plot has advanced by the play's end. Advancement comes in the audience's final image of the empowered, self-affirmed black couple of Virtue and Village. In this couple, both members are equal partners, something that was not present at the beginning of the play. Albeit briefly, spectators are left with a visual language that is radically different from the start of the play. As the play's master of ceremony Archibald declares at the beginning of *The Blacks*, the sole purpose of the characters' actions is "to round out [the white court's] grief" (12) through Marie's funeral rites. But by the end of the play, armed with a picture of the empowered Virtue and Village seeking a new form of authentic black love and beauty, audiences are presented with a language of black self-actualization, which differs drastically from the white hegemony of Marie's funeral rites at the play's start.

Virtue's end request to think black female beauty outside of a white paradigm accords the character a sense of selfhood outside of white paradigms. Certain productions of *The Blacks* have chosen to break down white paradigms of black women via a different strategy of exaggeration. This was the case with Peter Stein's production in Berlin in 1984 and reprisal at the Autumn festival in the Parisian Théâtre de la Ville. The playing time was a grueling three-and-a-half hours, and before the start spectators were invited to occupy what would later become the stage. This strategy inversed audience's normal role and made them active actors in, rather than passive viewers of, *The Blacks*. During this preparatory time, spectators witnessed the white cast's "blackening up" of the cast, as they painted their faces and bodies, a choice that Stein made in order to stress the constructed nature of race-based stereotypes. The time that the production took to make spectators actively take account of white constructions of the characters meant that they were primed to view the end scene just described with an active will to interrogate and deconstruct the stereotyping surrounding Virtue. Describing the final love scene, reviewer Georg Hensel notes the highly stylized gestures used to convey black femininity – finger clicking, hip popping, breast swaying, and more – on the part of Virtue ("La beauté de la haine"). It was evident that Virtue, played by a white woman in blackface, was the product of white hegemonic perception and a centuries-long objectification of black women. Such objectification is exemplified by the history of Saartjie Baartman or the "Hottentot Venus" who was brought to nineteenth-century London to be shown to the leering visitors to the "human zoos" because she was deemed to have abnormally large buttocks. By drawing attention to the white manufacturing of Virtue's gestures of finger clicking and so on, Stein's production invited the spectator's deconstruction of white stereotypes of black women's corporeality. This worked in conjunction with the end words to Village to think of black beauty separate from white standards in order to convey a sense of black women's empowerment to spectators.

There are a number of other elements in the text of *The Blacks* that create a language of black female self-actualization. For instance, the text repeatedly prioritizes black woman Virtue over white woman Marie. While the murder of Marie is revealed as false, spectators are given to understand Virtue's real-life victimization at the hands of white patriarchy. Dismissing

Marie's funeral, Virtue quips, "let me tell you that this evening's ceremony will affect me less than the one I perform ten times a day. I'm the only one who experiences shame to the bitter end" (31). Virtue alludes to the debasing sexual favors that she must perform daily, as she is a prostitute by profession. Master of ceremony Archibald reprimands Virtue for drawing attention to her profession, since it stands outside of the constructed narrative about Marie's murder that he wishes spectators to see: "Don't allude to your life" (31). Virtue, no shrinking violet, retorts "*ironically*": "You've been infected by the squeamishness you've picked up from the Whites. A whore shocks you" (31). Much like the ending, Virtue insists with rightful anger on spectators' acknowledgement of black female selfhood.

Virtue's simultaneous denial of Marie's victimization and acknowledgement of her own brutalization in this brief interlude spotlight and reverse a system in which, as black feminist sociologist Patricia Hill Collins describes, "Black 'whores' make White 'virgins' possible" (145). As Hill Collins elaborates, "[n]ormal female heterosexuality is expressed via the cult of true White womanhood whereas deviant female heterosexuality is typified by the 'hot mommas' of Black womanhood" (Hill Collins 83) in contemporary US society. Black women have been deemed animals and inviolable since the time of slavery when white slave masters would rape them with impunity and without consequence. This inability to see black women's victimization continues today with, for instance, the occlusion of black women from the Black Lives Matter movement. Black women, in other words, have never been cast as innocent or pure like white women. Virtue's insistence that she is much more of a victim than Marie ever was deconstructs the relegation of black women to deviancy, something that is reinforced by her virginal name, which may be read as a wresting of the "cult of true [...] Womanhood" (Hill Collins 145) from her fictive white counterpart.

A subsequent exchange between the white court's Queen and Virtue sees the latter triumph over the former. This builds a language of black female empowerment on the disparaged ideologies of white female victimization and black female deviancy; it also avoids the sedimentation of black women as inevitable victims of a racist and sexist society, which the previous reference to Virtue's work as a prostitute risks. Taking advantage of the Queen's state of heavy sleep, Virtue persuades the Queen to take part in a recital. She disarms the sovereign of her power by parodying a white feminine purity: "I am the lily-white Queen of the West [...] Whether in excellent health, pink and gleaming, or consumed with languor, I am white" (36). The Queen awakens from a snoring that overturns preconceptions of the white feminine "delicacy" to which Virtue refers, adding to the irony of the latter's statements about a "noble pallor" and "delicately-shaded iris, bluish iris" (36). In this moment, the Queen falls under the prostitute's spell: *"in a dazed state...[she] recites along"* (36). Together they utter the words "innocence and morning" (37). Their conjoining up to this point takes up and subverts a stereotype that privileges white women as pure in white patriarchal ideology. However, just as they are aligned in a stereotype of white femininity, the Queen and Virtue are made to coalesce in the controlling image of black sexual deviancy when they describe an exoticized "bit of shade [that] remained in my armpits" (37) separate from the "innocence and morning" that is contained in them (37). Virtue enraptures the "white" Queen with her role as a promiscuous seductress, persuading her to follow suit and hinting to spectators that she has reclaimed this stereotype as an empowering strategy. She is in control of both stereotypes of white female innocence and black female lubriciousness, so much so that she persuades the racist Queen to declare in unison with her "I love you" (37) to Village. These proclamations of love blur the racist and sexist ideologies previously alluded to, which implied that "beautiful" white women were the sole beneficiaries, but only as objects, of such an emotion. This moment shows a black woman as the empowered *agent* of love, since Virtue controls the "white" Queen and is in fact the mouthpiece behind the latter's amorous declaration to Village.

From liquidated stereotypes of black female sexual deviancy, then, *The Blacks* steadily builds a language of black female power based on love. Elsewhere in the play, protection and maternalism figure at the forefront of a language of black women's empowerment. An oratorical contest between the character of Felicity, who is part of the community of "Negroes", and the already-weakened "white" Queen, who is played by a black woman in a white mask, demonstrates black women's empowered appropriation of protection and maternalism. Felicity champions the black community's cause: "(*suddenly standing up straight*) [...] Are you there, Africa with the bulging chest and oblong thigh? [...] I call you back this evening to attend a secret revel" (59-60). In response to Felicity's verbal conjuring of Africa, the "white" Queen avails herself of patriarchal rule, relying on her male subordinates – the Missionary, the Valet, the Judge, and the Governor – for support in her attempted suppression of the black community. Felicity labels the Queen "a ruin"; the Queen retorts with a joyful indulgence in this insult. She connects it with a white-dominated gravitas of heritage and legacy, thereby subverting the slur: "I haven't finished sculpting myself, haven't finished carving and jagging and fashioning myself in the form of a ruin. An eternal ruin" (79). The Queen further boasts of her white supremacy, willfully and jubilantly allying herself with "the white man's burden" (80). This is a reference to British writer Rudyard Kipling's 1899 poem of the same name in which the author defends the legitimacy of the British Empire with claims of a "white man's burden" to civilize colonized peoples. The Queen allies herself with this white imperialist "burden" and, additionally, white patriarchal constructions of beauty: "I was more beautiful than you! [...] Clouds of heroes, young and old, have died for me [...]. At the Emperor's ball, an African slave bore my train [...]. You were still in darkness" (80). The implication is that the Queen basks in her servants' worship of her beauty. Felicity, meanwhile, remains out of sight and invisible ("You were still in darkness"), and is denied access to the beauty that the Queen boasts of. But in response to the Queen's insults, Felicity rejoices in the accusations of her "darkness", re-appropriating the slur as a powerful force. Hers is "[n]ot the darkness which is absence of light, but the kindly and terrible Mother who contains light and deeds" (80). Felicity's re-appropriation of darkness mirrors the Queen's earlier reclaiming of Felicity's insult that she is a "ruin" (79), which instead becomes a cipher for the Queen's heritage and legacy.

The Queen and Felicity verbally lock horns, with each woman taking her opponent's insult, divesting it of derogatory force, and reclaiming it. I disagree with Comparative literature scholar Loren Kruger who posits that both women evidence the regulatory impositions of white patriarchal discourse. As Kruger writes, "If the refuge available to the Queen is limited to Kipling and the White Man's Burden, then the black alternative becomes nothing more than a self-reflecting inverse of white culture" (66). While the Queen boasts of her white beauty and shields herself with white men's discourses of dominance, Felicity vaunts a stoic black motherhood that displays much more agency in a system that wishes to disempower women of color doubly for their race and gender. The image of the strong black mother that Felicity invokes has been used to stigmatize black women as unfeminine as the stereotype of the emasculating "sapphire" confirms (Abagond, "The Sapphire Stereotype"). It has also been used to cast black mothers as drains on social resources as the preconception of the single-mother "welfare queen" demonstrates. However, when framed appropriately, black motherhood offsets and disturbs white patriarchal expectations that women must be passive. Hill Collins observes that "bloodmothers" and "othermothers" are often "invoked as a symbol" in African-American communities, encouraging an "ethics of caring and personal accountability [which] move[s] communities forward" (191). It is this transformative image of black motherhood that Felicity's description of the "kindly and terrible Mother who contains light and deeds" (80) approximates. Motherhood is understood on a figurative rather than literal level, and it incubates and foments the community's passage to action, as Felicity's later words confirm: "Our merciful mother will keep us in her house huddled, between her walls! Twelve hours of day, so that these fragments of darkness can perform for the sun ceremonies like those of this evening" (81). Protective motherhood will enable the black community to keep "huddled" together and grow. Indeed, community growth is brought into being shortly after as "*a firecracker explodes off-stage*" (84), the "white" court remove their masks, and we discover that the real motivation for the dramatic action is the sentencing of the man who betrayed the cast's project of black emancipation. Felicity, armed with a re-signified notion of black motherhood, is the verbal victor of the oratorical contest as the Queen goes willfully to her own slaughter exclaiming that the white court's "massacre will be lyrical" (87).

The London-based production of *The Blacks* in 2007, renamed *The Blacks Remixed*, maximized the potential of Felicity's redefinition of black maternalism separate from stereotypes of "welfare queens" and "sapphires". Black directors Excalibah and Ultz produced their version of Genet's play in a heartland of black London, Stratford East. The production's location emphasized the need for the audience to view the characters through a lens of black authenticity rather than through whitewashed eyes. A sense of a racially authentic reclaiming of *The Blacks* also came in the adaptation of text to rap lyrics, which were articulated, as Bradby and Finburgh describe, "by some of the UK's leading rappers, singers and performance poets" (2720). The choice to adapt the play to rap also gave *The Blacks* a new vitality and demonstrated the potential of the Theatre of the Absurd to signify in subversive ways, using the pop cultural technique of rap, in the post-millennial age.

Rap also meant that musicality and rhythm were stressed when Felicity engaged in her oratorical contest with the Queen. She was depicted as an "African 'earth mother', in her batik dress and headscarf" (Bradby and

Finburgh 2747). Her role as an "earthmother" hints at a metaphorical form of "othermother" (Hill Collins 191) as the harbinger of black communal self-development that I described before. In traditional dress, Felicity emphasized a form of black maternalism that refuses to tailor itself to white Western stereotypes of black "welfare queens".

The rap-poetic form of the oratorical contest between Felicity and the Queen also potentially brought about a contemporary black feminist reclaiming of *The Blacks* in performance, and not only because Felicity was seen to be using a black cultural form of expression to defy the "white" Queen. As numerous critics have noted rap and music more generally – as the history of blues, soul, and disco divas indicates – are resources that black women have always commissioned for the purposes of creating agency (Hill Collins 16). Hip-Hop specialist and African-American feminist Gwendolyn Pough states that "[r]ap music provides a new direction from Black feminist criticism" (94-95). Female rappers such as Salt-n-Pepa and Queen Latifah, who rose to stardom in the 1990s and 2000s, and contemporary acts such as Angel Haze demonstrate how women's rap can combat misogyny. The strategy of using rap to talk about the realities confronting black women avoids alienation of black male rappers and creates a sense of inclusive and empowered community building for black women, as Pough continues:

> It is not just about counting the bitches and hoes in each rap song. It is about exploring the nature of Black male and female relationships [...] looking for ways to speak out against sexism and racism while starting a dialogue with Black men right on the front lines of the battlefield against oppression. (Pough 94-95)

The potential of black women's rap may be mapped onto productions such as the Excalibah and Ultz 2007 production of *The Blacks*. White female hegemony could be destabilized with a rapping Felicity lyrically trumping the "white" Queen in their exchange.

As this part of the chapter has discussed, *The Blacks* deconstructs certain stereotypes surrounding black women – as sexually deviant and incapable of being beautiful or of being loved, for instance. Deconstructed stereotypes are replaced by a steady increase in the power and agency of black women as they articulate a language of selfhood, love, and maternalism outside of the white patriarchal stereotypes that constrain them. In this way, the play's supplementary enjoyment may be targeted at not only unlearning the gendered racism facing black women, as we explored in the first part of the chapter, but also in creating a sense of "Black joy" (to recall Gina Dent's description cited at the start of this part) focused on black women's self-actualization more specifically.

This chapter proposed that *The Blacks* deconstructs the centuries-long oppression of black women, turning gendered racism into a meaningless abyss of "supplementary enjoyment". What is particularly prescient about this play is that it operates according to a double gesture of destroying gendered racism while promoting the visibility of empowered black womanhood. Empowered black womanhood has the potential to subvert power imbalances in our post-millennial era that, though increasingly willing to discuss the crimes committed on black male bodies as evidenced in the Black Lives Matter movement, has failed to discuss black female vulnerability and forms of resistance with the same attention. As we discovered, *The Blacks* occasions a switch where over-determined social scripts of white female vulnerability and beauty, embodied by murder victim Marie, are radically divested of value in order to be supplanted by codes of black women's agency and self-actualization. This switch demonstrates the potential of a well-targeted and channeled implementation of meaninglessness of Lacanian supplementary enjoyment. We saw in performance that rhythm and musicality (highlighted by rap for instance) could aid the play's dissolution of racist and sexist language. It was also shown that extra-theatrical interactions such as those seen between the white female spectator and the black cast member in Christopher McElroen's production may enable us to identify the continued existence of the ideological narrative of white female victimhood at the hands of black men in a modern-day setting – a social script that keeps white hegemony in place and occludes the gendered racism that black women experience.

Although the moments discussed in this chapter where black women find agency and voice are immersed in descriptions in *The Blacks* that do not directly pertain to gendered racism or the empowerment of black femininity, spotlighting these moments in performance will serve to transform *The Blacks* from one in a long line of Genet's works that, to return to Carl Lavery's argument, constitutes a rejection of "positive solutions" enacted via an affective "wound" (234) to the audience. Instead, Genet's "wound[ing] [of] the audience with an affective experience" (Lavery 234) will be accompanied by joyful images of black women's self-actualization, enabling a black feminist recuperation of the play.

Queering the Carceral and Assaulting America's Prison Industrial Complex: Arrabal's *And They Put Handcuffs on the Flowers* (1969)

In this chapter, on Fernando Arrabal's *And They Put Handcuffs on the Flowers*, supplementary enjoyment as a viewing position that unlearns dominant ideologies is examined once more. By taking as its premise the idea that spectators of Arrabal's play experience supplementary enjoyment, the chapter argues that the ideologies idealizing the institution of the prison in our post-millennial society are undermined. A subversion of the prison is relevant for current-day America, which has the highest rate of incarceration in the world despite falling crime levels. America has made a business out of incarceration with a large number of prisons being owned by the private sector. These profit-driven businesses aim to maximize internment in the name of making money. Queer theorists have dubbed America's profit-driven prison system the "Prison Industrial Complex" (PIC) and have sought to denounce this system for its disproportionate incarceration of sexual and racial minorities.[1] The chapter proposes that the spectator of *And They Put Handcuffs on the Flowers* is positioned to unlearn the modern-day valorization of the Prison Industrial Complex via supplementary enjoyment. Undermining the Prison Industrial Complex is the final way explored by this book in which an avant-garde play from the past can assume subversive meaning for today's setting.

And They Put Handcuffs on the Flowers tells of the atrocities undergone by the political prisoners of an unnamed dictatorship. The play was inspired by Arrabal's internment at Carabanchel penitentiary in 1967 under Spanish tyrant General Francisco Franco's regime. Arrabal was sentenced for dissent from the Fascist regime, which was expressed in

---

[1]   For a synthesis of queer theory's work on the Prison Industrial Complex, see Elias Walker Vitulli's review article "Queering the Carceral: Intersecting Queer/Trans Studies and Critical Prison Studies", from which the title of this chapter is inspired. Elias Walker, Vitulli. "Queering the Carceral: Intersecting Queer/Trans Studies and Critical Prison Studies," *GLQ* 19 (2012), 111-123.

his oeuvre. The theatrical adaptation of the playwright's experience in prison, *And They Put Handcuffs on the Flowers*, does not anchor itself in a specific timeframe. Instead it constitutes a cross-historical snapshot, from Ancient Greece onwards, of the cruelty that prison has exacted on inmates. The play committed itself to furnishing spectators with a cross-historical and cross-geographical snapshot of the "witch hunts and intolerance that put[s] [prisoners] away" (185) as one of the characters, Amiel, articulates.[2] The play's spatio-temporal looseness reflects the Theatre of the Absurd's self-separation from a paradigm of unified time and space, as in Aristotle's model of theatre. This looseness also allows us to analyze the ways in which it might make an intervention in a post-millennial setting of America's Prison Industrial Complex.

Prison is often conceived as the harbinger of society's wellbeing, protecting the general public from dangerous criminality. From the nineteenth century creation of the penitentiary to the post-millennial Prison Industrial Complex, prison relies on the "false logic that criminal punishment produces safety" (90) as queer theorist Dean Spade describes. *And They Put Handcuffs* denounces this narrative, instead suggesting that penitentiaries perpetuate violence and injustice rather than solving it. The play depicts four prisoners (Tosan, Pronos, Katar, and Amiel) who endure brutal torture at the hands of overzealous servants of state fascism. The four inmates act out eroticized fantasies. These are non-normative in form, for instance coprophilia and homoerotic sex. These non-normative acts allow them reprieve from the daily grind of carceral life. The play concludes with the murder of prisoner Tosan, who is sent to the gallows for attempting a counter-fascist "revolution of man" (207). The character's execution positions him as a Christ-like martyr. Tosan demands nothing less than the wholesale abolition of the prison system: "We must open the prisons and disband the army. The emancipation of man must be total" (207). Heralding the eradication of prisons, Tosan is the implied savior of humanity.

I propose in this chapter that the play stimulates supplementary enjoyment in order to destroy the ideology that insists that the Prison Industrial Complex is a necessary institution for the wellbeing and safety of society. In asserting this, my approach draws doubly on the work

---

2   References to the play in the text, unless otherwise indicated, will be to the following edition: Fernando, Arrrabal. "And They Put Handcuffs on the Flowers," in *Guernica and Other Plays*, translated by Charles Marowitz. New York: Grove Press, 1974.

of queer theorists who have written on the subject of injustice of the prison system, and cultural historians who have used historical analysis to denounce incarceration as indissociable from the strict imposition and reinforcement of social norms, notably Christian ones. Queer legal theorist Dean Spade has written extensively on the subject of prison as "a site of enormous violence" (Spade 90), particularly against the racial, sexual, and gender minorities that are statistically speaking most vulnerable to incarceration in the US, notably in his work *Normal Life: Administrative Violence, Critical Trans Politics, and the Limits of Law* (2015). The authors of *Queer (In)Justice: The Criminalization of LGBT People in the United States* (2011) Joey Mogul, Andrea Ritchie, and Kay Whitlock argue a similar point, and add that normative society has sought to "queer", in the sense of rendering abnormal and depraved, those who are incarcerated: "[u]ltimately, prisons and jails have always served as a breeding ground for a raced, gendered and classed archetypal amalgam of criminality, disease, predation, and out-of-control sexuality" (Mogul *et al.* 2059). In the arena of American cultural history, Regina Kunzel's *Criminal Intimacy: Prison and the Uneven History of Modern American Sexuality* (2008) and Caleb Smith's *The Prison and the American Imagination* (2009) have, too, documented the construction of the prisoner as aberrantly sexual. Christian ideology heavily influenced the establishment of the prison during the Jacksonian era (the 1830s) of US history. Prison acted at a crucial time, between the American Revolution and the Civil War, in the formation of American national identity to separate "normal" citizens from "non-normal" ones. The latter group was cordoned off and its threat to social norms was extinguished via the construction of the penitentiary.[3]

As these works in queer theory and cultural history indicate, my theoretical framework in this chapter is focused on the US context of the Prison Industrial Complex. This is partly for the purposes of narrowing my critical scope and partly because Arrabal's *And They Put Handcuffs* chimes with the Christian history of the US prison system in its re-appropriation of the parable of the Crucifixion. Tosan's final

---

[3] Indeed, entrapment, bondage, and servitude are as central to the US cultural landscape as the American dream itself, as those such as Orlando Patterson observe. Patterson argues that the American ideal of individual freedom was defined in contradistinction to the institution of slavery. American liberal values in fact permitted the country to amass its wealth and reign as a super-power today. See Orlando, Patterson. *Freedom in the Making of Western Culture*. London: I.B. Tauris, 1991.

execution, in other words, contains a peculiar ability to resonate with and subvert the quasi-religiosity of the US penitential system. Aiding the case for the play's resonance in a United States context is the fact that *And They Put Handcuffs* debuted on the New York theatre scene – at the Mercer Arts Center in 1972 – to critical praise and excitement. This was in sharp contrast to the world debut at the Théâtre de l'Épée de Bois in 1969 on the outskirts of Paris, which garnered a lukewarm reception and a lawsuit for grievous bodily harm (more on that below). Many considered Arrabal, who directed the production, ill-equipped to convert his text to the stage. Conversely, the play was deemed the event of the season once it hit American soil by the *New York Times* and *Cue* magazine. Eric Bentley, who was commissioned by the *NY Times* to review the American production, recalls discomfiture and fluster from audience members at suggestions that "the Lord was being 'molested'" (Bentley 226). Simultaneous audience unease and praise implies the successful exportation of the play's sacrilegious assaults on the prison from Catholic Europe to Christian America. It strengthens the case for an analysis of the subversions made possible by Arrabal's play in the context of America's love affair with the Prison Industrial Complex.

The chapter begins with an explanation of how supplementary enjoyment, the psychoanalytic concept analyzed in spectatorship, is conjured in viewing *And They Put Handcuffs*. I focus on the play's quasi-religious mysticism, its baroque display of images told at high speed, its dialectic of veiling and unveiling of the hidden violence behind bars, and its call for the spectator's metaphorical re-birth in the end scene. These elements impugn the ideology of the prison as a social safety net and stir a supplementary enjoyment that transcends this ideology. The play does not simply compel spectators to unlearn the idealization of the prison via supplementary enjoyment; it also promotes a discourse of abolition and alternative modes of practicing justice in the non-normative erotic fantasies that the prisoners enact, a subject that will be explored in the second part of the chapter.

Arrabal has been roundly condemned by critics (e.g. Donahue 1980; Innes 1993; Podol 1998) as immature and sensationalist for the sexually explicit nature of his theatre, which he termed "Panic" theatre after the Greek god of fertility Pan. For instance, avant-garde theatre critic Christopher Innes pathologizes "the so-called innocence of Arrabal's retarded characters, whose incest and murder, sadism and suicide are performed with child-like unconsciousness of the consequences, [which] appears as a further perversion" (Innes 120).[4] The second part of the chapter distances itself from Arrabal's critical condemnation to demonstrate that *And They Put Handcuffs'* sexual dissidence transforms – queers – the norms of social and moral propriety that prison relies on to assert its power.

The potential of Arrabal's play to connect with the post-millennial Prison Industrial Complex is mentioned throughout the chapter, but it is particularly in this second part that it is discussed. I connect the play's non-normative erotic aesthetic to what legal theorist Sarah Lamble describes as the need to dismantle the Prison Industrial Complex via a queer politics that "questions, disrupts, and transforms dominant ideas about what is normal" (Lamble 237), which are the very ideas that help to put sexual and racial minorities away in disproportionate numbers in the first place. Throughout the chapter, performance and production methods that aid the reading of supplementary enjoyment's deconstruction of the Prison Industrial Complex are pinpointed. These techniques include the racialization of the cast of characters and Japanese masked performances in the Kubuki tradition.

Destruction of the Myth of the Prison as Protector

This part of the chapter explores how the unconscious affect of supplementary enjoyment may be conjured in *And They Put Handcuffs on the Flowers*. I also explore how enjoyment enables spectators to transcend social valorization of the prison system, in particular the "false logic that criminal punishment produces safety" (Spade 90). First it is important to remind ourselves of a definition of supplementary enjoyment, which we saw in the last chapter. Enjoyment is experienced as both pleasure and pain. It exists in the Lacanian dimension of the Real. This is a realm of the psyche that lies beyond language and the social meanings and ideologies that structure our society. Various aspects of *And They*

---

[4]   Also see David, Bradby. *Modern French Drama: 1940-1980*, 2nd edn. Cambridge: Cambridge UP, 1991; Thomas John, Donahue. *The Theater of the Fernando Arrabal: A Garden of Earthly Delights*. New York: New York UP, 1980, 87-88; Peter, Podol. "Spanish Sources of Fernando Arrabal's Theatre of the Grotesque: Goya, Valle-Inclán and Buñuel," *Contemporary Theatre Review* 7 (1998), 104. The work of Frédéric Aranzueque-Arrieta is one of the only examples to champion the politics of eroticism (deemed utopian and sacred) in Arrabal's work in a non-pathologizing manner. See Frédéric, Aranzueque-Arrieta. *Arrabal: la perversion et le sacré*. Paris: L'Harmattan, 2006.

Put Handcuffs on the Flowers call forth the spectator's supplementary enjoyment. The Christian mystical dimension of *And They Put Handcuffs*, the play's baroque speed, its dialectic of veiling and unveiling, and the play's final scene permitting the spectator's metaphorical re-birth away from the violence of the prison all serve to position spectators in the Real. This position lies beyond the ideologies which secure prison as a central institution in our social imaginary.

First let us explore the Christian mysticism of *And They Put Handcuffs*, which may be connected to the psychoanalytic theory of supplementary enjoyment. More so than any of the other Absurdist playwrights studied in this book, the Catholic Church and Biblical scripture heavily influenced Arrabal. A glance at some of the titles of Arrabal's plays illustrates the religiosity of his theatre: *Great Ceremony* (1965), *Ceremony for an Assassinated Black Man* (1965), *The First Communion* (1968), and *The Tower of Babel* (1978). Arrabal grew up in Fascist Spain. Franco's regime (1939-1975) allied itself with the Church to demand that Spaniards lead a lifestyle that was highly pious, conservative, and moral. Arrabal was a dissenter from the regime as well as a product of it. He extensively referenced Catholicism in his theatre at the same time as he repurposed it for the liberation of his characters. For instance, in *The Tower of Babel* (1978) Arrabal rewrites the Biblical myth of God's division of people after their failure to construct the tower of Babel designed to unify humanity. In Arrabal's version of Babel, the tower is successfully completed. Its completion was a metaphor for the possibility of social unity after the fall of Franco's regime in 1975. *And They Put Handcuffs on the Flowers* demonstrates a similar re-appropriation of a Biblical story. Christ's crucifixion is retold and enacted by the character and prisoner Tosan who becomes a twentieth-century Messiah. Tosan is placed in a position of saving humanity by calling for an abolition of the prison system.

Critics have acknowledged Arrabal's sacrilegious rewriting of Biblical mythology, such as the parable of the Tower of Babel or the Crucifixion, but they have rarely explored in-depth the influence of women's Christian mysticism on the playwright. This influence helps us to align his oeuvre with the Lacanian concept of supplementary enjoyment. The story of the sixteenth-century mystic Saint Teresa of Avila (1515-1582) influenced Arrabal as he openly admitted. Arrabal described being "very flattered" (Knapp 87) by the comparison of his theatre to the mystic. He stated in an interview with theatre specialist Bettina Knapp that "Saint Teresa said she felt the Lord driving himself into her deeply; she spoke of the fire which invaded her being at those moments, of the extreme *pain and pleasure* she knew during those experiences" (my emphasis) (87). The paradoxical "pain and pleasure" noted by Arrabal in his admiration for Saint Teresa is also a mix that is taken up by psychoanalytic accounts of supplementary enjoyment. Indeed, it was the feeling of ecstasy, mid-way between pain and pleasure, recounted by mystics such as Saint Teresa that informed Lacan's theory of supplementary enjoyment, as religious historian Amy Hollywood describes in her book *Sensible Ecstasy: Mysticism, Sexual Difference and the Demands of History* (2002), as I mentioned in the last chapter on Genet's *The Blacks*.

Lacan secularized the testimonies of female Christian mystics of medieval times and early modern Europe as Hollywood argues. He was as fascinated with the case of Saint Teresa of Avila as was Arrabal. Saint Teresa claimed a divine connection to God. In making this claim, she defied the dictates of the medieval Church, which was male dominated and denied women transcendental communion with God. Saint Teresa's transcendental experience emblematized Lacan's concept of supplementary enjoyment, because she claimed to feel an ecstasy that could not be circumscribed by the paternalism of religious scripture. Standing outside of religious norms, Saint Teresa felt an ecstasy that was both painful and joyful. Enjoyment could be not be captured by conventional distinctions between pain and pleasure. Indeed, it couldn't be described by language *tout court*. In his twentieth seminar, Lacan stated that the female mystics writings "consis[t] in saying that they experience [enjoyment], but know nothing about it" (*On Feminine Sexuality* 76). The ignorance of the female mystics (they "know nothing") is not regarded negatively in Lacanian theory. Ignorance indicates enjoyment's existence in a realm beyond language. Enjoyment falls into the meaningless Real dimension of the psyche, showing a realm of "symbolic impossibility" (Dean 50-51) beyond dominant ideologies.

An ecstatic connection to a higher state beyond conventional social meanings in the realm of the Real is enabled by supplementary enjoyment. One way in which supplementary enjoyment transports individuals to the meaningless Real is by way of baroque profusion, and this is a notable feature of Arrabal's *And They Put Handcuffs on the Flowers* too. In *Sensible Ecstasy*, Hollywood takes the example of Gian Lorenzo Bernini's baroque sculpture of Saint Teresa of Avila, whose ecstasy inspired both Lacan and Arrabal, to explain how enjoyment works through the "engulfing of representation by the materiality of the sign" (166). Bernini's "The Ecstasy of Saint Teresa" (1647-1652) features "the folds of Teresa's gown [which] overtake her figure" (Hollywood 166), indicating an aesthetic ornateness that also defines the baroque and enjoyment's push to deprive signs of meaning. *And They Put Handcuffs* works according to the same mechanism in order to deprive the prison of meaning or ideological significance.[5] The play displays images that are all related to the violence that prisoners experience, as we shall see, in order to undermine the prison. These images "burst forth, fuse, cross over each other" and in their quantity "destroy themselves" (*les images jaillissent, fusent, s'entrecroisent, se détruisent entre elles*), as theatre reviewer Jean-Jacques Olivier recounted after watching the debut production of the play at the Théâtre de l'Épée de Bois in 1969 (*Combat*). *And They Put Handcuffs* is technically a one-scene play but has no less than twenty-two switches where characters change roles or enact an event unrelated to the previous sketch. The switches oscillate between realism and fantasy, detailing the prisoners' back-stories of how they came to be in prison in the first place and their dreams for escape and nightmares as a result of the trauma that they have endured. Change in the dramatic action is denoted by either the lighting or blackout, contributing luminal velocity to the viewing experience. Spectators are thus witness to the display of multiplicity and speed, an "engulfing of representation by the materiality of the sign" (Hollywood 166).

Similar to Saint Teresa's transcendence of religious patriarchy to a higher realm beyond meaning, it is a call for transcendence of the institution of the prison that is solicited from spectators from the very start of *And They Put Handcuffs*. Even before the dramatic action begins, as the stage directions read, spectators enter a space of complete darkness, and are manhandled by actors who guide them to their seat in the auditorium. The spectator must be *"gripp[ed] as forcefully as possible"* (Arrabal 131-132). The same sense of entrapment that the play's prisoners feel is replicated in spectatorship by the act of being violently handled as if by prison guards, reflecting what Michael Bennett names as audiences' tendency to "experienc[e] the same emotions as the characters on stage" (*The Cambridge Introduction* 117) in plays of the Theatre of the Absurd.

---

5   For scholarship on Arrabal's inspiration from the baroque, see Peter, Podol. *Fernando Arrabal.* Boston: Twayne Publishers, 1978, 63; Raymond Steven, Bevitt. *Fernando Arrabal: Towards A Theatre of Images.* Berkeley: University of California Press, 1974, 23.

This allows them to attain a visceral understanding of the senselessness and absurdity of the world presented to them, argues Bennett. Some spectators felt so completely the same state of constraint as the prisoners in the play's debut production at the Parisian Théâtre de l'Épée de Bois in 1969 (directed by Arrabal himself) that a lawsuit was brought against the playwright for the grievous bodily harm that actors caused spectators (Anon., *La Tribune de Genève*).[6] Yet violence is interspersed with caresses in the tactile preamble to *And They Put Handcuffs*, recalling the "extreme pain and pleasure" (Knapp 87) that Arrabal admired in Saint Teresa. Spectators were not simply instructed to feel constraint but also to seek comfort, pleasure, and most importantly a sense of liberation. Actors would *"gently murmur to"* and *"reassure"* spectators (131-132), inviting them to imagine a cosmic realm beyond the material violence of the dramatic action that they would subsequently see. *"You are dust and to dust you will return"* (131), actors promise spectators in the preamble. Such a promise emulates Saint Teresa's transcendence of the earthly constraints of religious patriarchy to a higher state.

Buffalo-based (NY) group Subversive Theatre created, in their production of *And They Put Handcuffs on the Flowers*, a dialectic between a cosmic state and the entrapment of the prison at the city's counter-cultural Infringement festival in 2008 by means of costuming and space choice. The production had actresses clad "in shimmering white robes and neutral white masks" (Binder *Buffalo News*) ushering spectators into their seats as *Buffalo News* theatre reviewer Galia Binder describes. The "shimmering" costumes denoted ethereality, and an almost angel-like, otherworldly, quality to proceedings. Meanwhile, the setting recalled the grimness of the prison in which the characters and audience members find themselves entrapped. Spectators were led "down rickety wooden steps into the shadowy bowls of this massive Turn-of-the-Century warehouse to sit on rotting crates, pallets, and barrelheads" (*Buffalo News*), according to Binder. The dank setting stressed the sense of entrapment, while the ethereality of the cast's "shimmering" costumes invited spectators to transport themselves to an otherworldly realm transcending the space of the theatre-prison.

Returning to the text, the play repeatedly moves to divest the institution of the prison of ideological weight by exposing the violent truth behind

---

[6] Indeed, the playwright was ordered to pay twenty thousand francs in compensation. (Anon., *La Tribune de Genève*).

the carceral space. It does this by a dialectic of veiling and unveiling, which also mirrors the mechanism of supplementary enjoyment. As Hollywood notes in *Sensible Ecstasy*, mysticism, as a non-canonical form of knowledge about God, etymologically means "to close (the eyes)" in order to "designate the hidden reality underlying scripture or liturgy" (146). Similarly, the tactile preamble of *And They Put Handcuffs* created an unconscious economy of blindness, or veiling, before an exposure to hidden truths. In the tactile preamble *"the spectator has the impression of being blind"* (131) as the stage directions read, before they are opened onto a "hidden reality" (Hollywood) of enormous violence committed against the play's prisoners at the hands of overzealous and officious wardens, bankers, priests, wives, and other servants of a tyrannical state. We are told, for instance, of a man who is locked up in solitary without food or water until he starved to death for replacing the holy wafer in Mass with a slice of sausage, and who is driven to eat his own arm out of hunger and desperation. Another anecdote involves the character Pronos narrowly escaping death-by-shooting by prison henchmen. The character remains mute thereafter because of the muzzle the executioners placed on his mouth immediately before the near-fatal punishment. The play also reveals joke-trials that last six minutes before condemning prisoners to serving life sentences so that "[j]ustice must be seen to be done" (191) even if it is not practiced in reality. These examples of violence follow the metaphorical blinding of spectators in the tactile preamble. Blinding followed by the unveiling of hidden violence behind bars conjures the logic of mysticism and, by extension, the unconscious economy of supplementary enjoyment.

A number of symbols that are tangential to the prison system are divested of similar authority in a dialectic of veiling and unveiling. These symbols are, in turn, directed at transcending the social idealization of the penitentiary. The first of these tangential symbols is Neil Armstrong's moon landing, an emblem of social progress in the 1960s when the play was first published. The play's refrain is that the moon landing, judged the only form of colonization that has not been violent in the history of humanity, willingly leaves behind those who are imprisoned. This undermines the claim to a better, more egalitarian world that Armstrong's inimitable words "One small step for man, one giant leap for mankind" were meant to presage. Yet, "[e]ven the first men on the moon have forgotten us…", the prisoner Katar laments (136), an idea that he expands on later in greater detail:

AMIEL: Do you remember what he said when he first set foot on the moon?

THE LOUDSPEAKER: One small step for man…a giant leap for mankind.

AMIEL: It was a peaceful conquest – the first in history. The first victory in which other men weren't the losers.

KATAR: But we're still in prison, right?

AMIEL: This success will force people to come together and forget the witch hunts and intolerance that put us away.

KATAR: Tell that to the tyrants, to the dictators. (185)

At best, technological progress symbolized by the moon landing is reframed as utterly indifferent to and independent of imprisonment ("we're still in prison, right?"). At worst, the play implies that the moon landing is complicit in carceral injustice, functioning as a smokescreen of social progress that maintains authority. Armstrong's memorable words are articulated over the prison's loudspeaker, fusing this mantra of hope with a mechanism of control of the penitentiary.

Gay marriage is likewise aligned with the prison and positioned as a smokescreen of progress that harbors atrocity. This again reflects *And They Put Handcuffs'* dialectic of display and unveiling of hidden truths, which invites the transcendence of supplementary enjoyment. Gay marriage is first associated with the moon landing, which as we just saw is exposed as a smokescreen of social progress that hides the violence of the penal system. Amiel, playing German Renaissance artist Alberto Durero, deems the moon landing to be redolent of a "country wedding", continuing:

AMIEL (*Durero*): Well, the astronauts are getting married on the moon. They were wearing white.

DRIMA (*Roupa*): Two men, married?

AMIEL (*Durero*): Shape of things to come. In the future you'll be able to marry several people at a time – a woman, the moon, and two men. Or even homosexual marriages.

DRIMA (*Roupa*): Homosexuals *married?* (142)

The scene refracts gay marriage through a prism of the moon landing, since it envisages two male "astronauts […] getting married on the moon". The incredulity of Drima, playing Durero's prostitute Roupa, at the thought of two men getting married ("Homosexuals *married?*") may appear dated in today's world, where the US supreme court made gay marriage a federal right across all fifty states. However, carceral violence lurks behind the question of marriage equality. Amiel, still playing Durero, deploys equal access to marriage to declare, "We're leaving the age of fanaticism [...] entering a new age of tolerance – a time when penitentiaries and prisons will remain only as outdated relics of the past" (143). The irony of the hopeful claim that prisons are soon to be a thing of the past is hardly lost on spectators who are privy, throughout the dramatic action, to the stories of violence recounted in the play. Supplementary enjoyment is conjured through this display of gay marriage as a symbol of hope (the "Shape of things to come" as Amiel wistfully declares) and the unveiling of the violent reality behind it. Enjoyment's capacity to transcend social symbols to reach the meaningless Real could divest both gay marriage and the prison of authority.

The palpable falseness of the claim that prison will become extinct with the advent of gay marriage may also be recuperated for the post-millennial moment. Queer theorists have pointed out that the LGBT community's focus on gaining the right to marry comes at the expense of deconstructing the prison as a site of immense violence against queer people, especially queer people of color. As Equal Justice specialist Asher Waite-Jones (2015) observes in his discussion of the disproportionate incarceration of racial and sexual minorities, institutions such as gay marriage have allowed "[w]hite, cisgender, rich and middle class gays and lesbians" to buy themselves "acceptance" in society but this has been at the expense of "distancing themselves from the poor, from people of color, and from transgender folk" (183) who are disproportionately incarcerated. "Bad" unmarried, often criminal, LGBT individuals are pegged against "good", marriageable ones in this schema. The play's association of gay marriage with the violence of the prison may presciently bespeak the reality that gay marriage favors only the most privileged queer individuals in society at the expense of the most vulnerable – gender non-conforming people of color – who are left to rot in prison.

The ending makes good on the play's claim to spectators in the preamble, "*You are dust and to dust you will return*" (131) and brings to a climax supplementary enjoyment's transcendence of the prison system. Tosan's execution functions as a Christ-like site of re-birth for the spectator. The character wishes to implement a revolution that would open the gates of the prisons and abolish the penal system, but is instead sentenced to death by beheading by the penal authorities. The play's final moment stages Tosan's execution:

> *[Two executioners] put straps around [Tosan's] neck, arms, and legs. The executioner works the handle. Drum roll. A sharp crack. Tosan's head falls to one side and hangs. At this moment Tosan, who is naked, urinates. A woman, Falidia, catches the liquid in a bowl. Two women take the bowl from Falidia and hold it before her. She dips her hands into the bowl. When she removes them they are covered with blood. The urine is really blood. She washes her face in this blood. There is a very slow fade to black.* (212)

Falidia's ablutions in urine-cum-blood ape and refigure the codes of the Eucharist, the last supper before Christ's sacrifice in which wine was denoted to represent, even transform into, his blood. Falidia derives a sacrilegious form of transcendence from the refigured Eucharist. Tosan's blood, evoking that of Christ in the Eucharist, signals to spectators that the scene is to be interpreted as a sacrilegious Crucifixion. Tosan becomes a secular Messiah in this interpretation who functions as a conduit for the metaphorical re-birth of the spectator.

The end scene, indeed, plays with and subverts the very codes of Christian re-birth that have secured the penitentiary's hegemony in the American social imaginary. From its inception in the nineteenth century, prison was dubbed a matrix of re-birth, a place where "the inmate was divested of rights, social connections, and identity, stripped down to a bare life no longer recognizable as human" (Smith 22). This was so that "through the rituals and disciplines of the prison, this bare life [would be] ennobled with citizenship, a Christian soul, and the powers of reflection and self-governance" (Smith 22) in accordance with post-Enlightenment constructions of selfhood as social historian Caleb Smith describes in his book *Prison and the American Imagination* (2009). The ending of *And They Put Handcuffs* both conjures this fantasy and refutes it. It implies the "Christian soul" (as Smith describes) that the fantasy of the prison pivots on for the legitimation of its existence in the Biblical-like execution of Tosan. "[B]are life" (Smith 22), which is embodied by Tosan, however, is not "ennobled" but brutally bloodied and decapitated. This undermines the notion that the penitentiary is invested in the social rehabilitation of criminals.

The first production of *And They Put Handcuffs*, directed by Arrabal in 1969, chose black actor Mabussoo Lo, from Martinique, to play Tosan in this final crucifixion scene. Lo was sent to the gallows naked in a scene that was as challenging theatrically to enact as it was to watch. Re-contextualizing the casting choice in the post-millennial moment, this enactment of the play's martyr by a black actor could challenge racial biases of the Prison Industrial Complex, which as civil rights advocate Michelle Alexander contends is the "new Jim Crow". In *The New Jim Crow: Mass Incarceration in an Age of Colorblindness* (2010), Alexander argues, "mass incarceration in the United States [has], in fact, emerged as a stunningly comprehensive and well-disguised system of racialized social control that functions in a manner strikingly similar to Jim Crow" (1). An astonishing one in eight African American men will find themselves placed in prison during at least one point in their lives, with mechanisms such as a "school-to-prison pipeline" funneling members of the black American community into jail at a young age through disproportionate surveillance and control of their activities. In addition, the sight of a black man being executed in *And They Put Handcuffs*, when placed in the American setting, cannot help but recall the history of lynching. Lynching was a key mechanism that enabled the continuation of racist discrimination, violence, and segregation in the century following the American Civil War up until the civil rights movement of the 1960s. The execution of a black Tosan thus readily brings forth the implication that prison functions as a new form of Jim Crow segregation as Alexander suggests. Since Tosan is also transformed into a sacrilegious Messiah, the racialization of the play's martyr could also accord black people the power to arrest the ideology of the penitentiary and re-appropriate it for the purposes of black transcendence of white power structures, according the figure of the prisoner and those suffering at the hands of state-endorsed carceral violence the dignity that they have historically been disallowed.

However, the performance technique of casting a black Tosan is not without risk, especially for the US setting. African American suffering could be fetishized by means of the religious and lyrical qualities of *And They Put Handcuffs*' ending. Reviewer of the Arrabal's 1969 production of *And They Put Handcuffs* Mathieu Galey clearly warns us of this risk. Galey took offense to the final execution scene, describing it as an act of gratuitous torture in which "a poor man from Martinique undergoes the test of an electric chain while urinating in a copper basin" (Galey *Les Nouvelles littéraires*).[7] Galey considered the urination irrelevant and

---

7   My translation. Original: "un pauvre Martiniquais subit l'épreuve d'une chaise de torture tout en urinant dans une bassine en cuivre".

confined to the realm of fantasy as "a physiological reaction that [he] had never heard of".[8] He advised that the end sacrifice be lifted from the production so as to preclude understandings of Arrabal's work as "exploiting the misfortunes of suffering minorities" (*se pencher sur les malheurs des minorités souffrantes*).

This part of the chapter has discussed the creation of the spectator's supplementary enjoyment via *And They Put Handcuffs'* mystical dimension, its baroque speed, and its dialectic of optimistic surface displays of social progress and the unveiling of the violent, hidden truths behind them. Supplementary enjoyment permits a transcendence of the commonplace social associations of the space of the prison as securing the safety and freedom of society at large, especially in the final scene where the figure of Tosan functions as a cipher for the metaphorical re-birth of the spectator who casts free of the violence of the prison. The spectator is given the chance to reach a state of zero-degree of meaning or a blank slate cast free of the ideology of the prison in this final scene. The sacrilegious Crucifixion of Tosan makes good on the play's prefatory promise that spectators will return to a pre-social state of dust, emulating Saint Teresa of Avila's transcendence of earthly ideologies to reach a state of the Real in supplementary enjoyment. But blank slates of meaning are futile unless they are generative of social change as well. Indeed, from a zero-degree of meaning, the play simultaneously conjures new more egalitarian codes beyond the stereotypes accruing to prisoners. It does so via its non-normative erotic politics. I turn to the details of these alternative codes now.

Alternative Queerness

In *And They Put Handcuffs* a sexually dissident aesthetic builds on the destruction of the social fantasy of the prison as a space that secures society's wellbeing. We recall from earlier in this chapter and in the previous chapter on *The Blacks* that supplementary enjoyment occasions a lack of knowledge, a call to unknowing that can obliterate hegemonic social fantasies. Genet's *The Blacks* fashioned a language of black women's empowerment to replace the state of unlearning gendered racism. *And They Put Handcuffs on the Flowers*, similarly, does not just leave its spectators in ignorance in the experience of enjoyment. The play is characterized

---

[8] My translation. Original: "réaction physiologique des suppliciés dont je n'avais jamais entendu parler".

by a maneuver that constructs an alternative set of sexual discourses at the same time as rupturing the social fantasy of prison as a necessary tool for the correction of criminal wrongdoing and the protection of the law-abiding masses in society. Non-normative sexual acts in Arrabal's play accord prisoners a transformative dignity that disrupt their historical construction as aberrant and depraved individuals as I shall explain shortly. Transformative eroticism enables us to re-position *And They Put Handcuffs* as subversive of the post-millennial Prison Industrial Complex. The play's non-normative erotic aesthetic connects to what legal theorist Sarah Lamble describes as the need for a queer politics that "questions, disrupts, and transforms dominant ideas about what is normal" (237). A pressure to be "normal" in our society – or in other words, *normative* – is the very mechanism that puts sexual and racial minorities away in disproportionate numbers.

The richness of Arrabal's theatre lies not only in the sacrilegious transformation of Christian norms but also in its sexual dissidence. This erotic dissidence provides another means to spectators' liberation from social norms. Arrabal's theatre, in general terms, contains scenes in which primarily heterosexual couples enact non-normative scenes of necrophilia, cannibalism, S/M, and so on, which may be deemed "hetero-dissident". Arrabal named the eroticization of his theatre a "Panic" aesthetic, inspired by the Greek god of fertility, the faun-like Pan. In the context of *And They Put Handcuffs on the Flowers* Arrabal's Panic theatre may be considered as transforming the historical framing of the prison as containing aberrant and depraved sexuality in order to keep the latter from tainting the outside world. The prisoners commit acts of non-normative sexual practice, but they are accorded dignity in so doing. The very title of the play indicates dignity in queerness, as it pays homage to Spain's much-loved poet Federico García Lorca (1898-1936), shot dead by henchmen of Franco's regime not only for his literary dissidence but also for his homosexuality. As theatre scholar R.L. Farmer (1971) points out, the words "And they put handcuffs on the flowers" plays on a line from Lorca's poem "Vuelta a la ciudad" (Return to the City), which laments the violence of urban expansion and the "manacled roses" (*rosas maniatadas*) that lie in its wake (Farmer 158). The image of chaining something as harmless and beautiful as a rose brings forth the idea of unjust forms of imprisonment.

Arrabal's play demands that the spectator take note of the reference to Lorca but it also seeks to re-appropriate the Lorcan tragedy of brutalized flowers for transformative ends. As Amiel states, "[i]t's over – or nearly over – the time when they put handcuffs on the flowers" (185). This reflects a broader will of the plot to move from prison-based atrocity to the transformative possibilities that attend the subversion and abolition of the carceral institution. The choice of Lorca as inspiration for the title casts transformation in a sexually non-normative, queer, light. Amiel also re-tells the story of Lorca being shot dead, making explicit the play's sympathies with the queer plight:

> He wasn't trying to be a poet. He just wanted to innocently express what he felt. […] And because when he was alive he had the reputation of being a homosexual, as a little joke the commanding officer finished him off with a bullet up the ass. And this frail little man who foretold the tyranny we live under today, foretold freedom and justice for tomorrow. (186)

These lines reflect the play's call to the abolition of the prison system, which forms part of the "tyranny we live under today" as Amiel describes. Amiel seeks inspiration from a queer Spanish literary legend who "foretold freedom and justice for tomorrow" in order to imagine a social setting where the prison does not exist. Queer sexuality is deemed the victim of gratuitous violence at the hands of the penal system: "because he was a homosexual […] the commanding officer finished him off with a bullet up the ass".

The play's title and this excerpt indicate a narrative arc that sympathizes with rather than condemns the incarceration of queer individuals. This is important because it corrects the construction, pointed out by cultural historians and queer theorists, of prisoners as depraved sexual beings who merit being locked up for the good of society, particularly in the Americas. The indigenous people of Quaraca, in what would now be modern-day Panamá, were thrown to the dogs of conquistador Vasco Núñez de Balboa in 1513 as punishment for their cross-dressing habits, as just one early example of the fusion of "actual or projected 'deviant' sexualities and gender expressions" and the project of "colonization, genocide, and enslavement" (Mogul *et al.* 251) as the authors of *Queer (In)justice: The Criminalization of LGBT People in the United States* (2011), Joey Mogul, Andrea Ritchie, and Kay Whitlock point out. Building on early constructions of prisoners as deviantly sexual, twentieth-century American prison specialists or "penologists", such as Joseph Wikson, Michael Pescor, and Louis Berg, took inspiration from European nineteenth century sexology (notably Havelock Ellis, Richard von Krafft-Ebing, and Magnus Hirschfeld) to catalogue the "deviant" sexual habits of prisoners (Kunzel 48). They did so in order to assert the idea of in-born sexual differences between criminals and the law-abiding as cultural historian Regina Kunzel points out in her work *Criminal Intimacy: Prison and the Uneven History of Modern American Sexuality* (2008). *And They Put Handcuffs'* accordance of dignity to prisoners' sexual non-normativity, such as its reference to Lorca "who wanted to innocently express what he felt" and received the inhumane punishment of a "bullet up his ass" for doing so (186), debunks the historical denigration of prisoners. The play's privileging of the queer intellectual Lorca, indeed, corrects the idea that prisoners are "promiscuous, dangerous, dependent, lazy, violent, foreign, and unintelligent" (Spade 113) as trans legal theorist Dean Spade puts it.

Another of the play's central figures, the martyr Tosan who heralds a subversion of the prison's social weight in the play's final act of execution, also reflects the valorization of queer practices. He is no all-round heterosexual hero. While he has a wife and family, and is most emphatic on this point (imploring his wife Falidia several times to "Take care of the children" (174)), he is caught literally with his pants down *"fucking"* (179) (as the stage directions read) fellow inmate Katar. He only stops when the warden threatens "six months on bread and water" and this he does only reluctantly ("Yes sir, but let me finish here first" (179-80)). The exchange is presented in a matter-of-fact way. This disrupts traditional denigrations of prison-based queerness; homoeroticism is an implied act of intimacy between prisoners without any added negative value. Indeed, as with the allusion to Lorca, it is the prison authorities' reaction to queerness, suffused with vitriol and unnecessary cruelty, that is cast negatively and not the notion of carceral queerness itself. The prison warden condemns both Katar and Tosan to solitary confinement ("Throw 'em in the hole" (179)) after catching them having sex ("I can hardly believe my eyes... two prisoners..." (179)).

The juxtaposition of Tosan's heterosexual life choices on the outside with his homoerotic proclivities on the inside also suggests the spatial contingency of sexuality. In other words, sexuality is not a permanent identity but is susceptible to change depending on one's surroundings. The spatial contingency of sexuality confounds the project of labeling criminals as inherently deviant and in need of caging from the "normal" world – a project that has its origins in the sexologists' theory of the "congenital" nature of homosexual (and by extension criminal) identity in the nineteenth century. The mutability of Tosan's sexual identity, cases of which were hardly rare in penologists' and sexologists' records as Kunzel uncovers, "exposed the impossibilities inherent in [the] taxonomical project" of identifying the in-born sexual depravity of prisoners "from the outset" (Kunzel 48-49).

The play's prison space also becomes the site of hyperbolic sexual fantasy – fusing parody, humor, and critique – in order to interrogate gender and sexual norms, notably norms that reinforce the institution of marriage. In an extension of its prescient critique of gay marriage (described earlier), the institution of matrimony is more broadly exposed for bolstering the ideologies of heterosexuality and patriarchy in one such hyperbolically sexual fantasy. The same character to conflate gay marriage with carceral injustice, Amiel, later has a dream containing baroque Flemish painter Peter Paul Rubens, the biblical prophet Elijah, the maligned character of Shakespeare's *Othello* who is falsely accused of adultery, Desdemona, and one of the play's female characters Imis (who does not play a literary or historical figure). Bringing together this improbable band of historical and literary figures, Amiel (playing Rubens) declares, "We'll get married, all four of us" (164). The line recalls his earlier musing that several people at a time will be able to marry ("In the future you'll be able to marry several people at a time – a woman, the moon, and two men" (142)). This destabilizes, or queers, the principal of heterosexual monogamy that marriage, deemed a holy union between man and woman, has historically been premised on. Arrabal's queered vision of marriage also pinpoints the underlying ideological force that supports marriage: patriarchy. Katar and Amiel, playing Elijah and Rubens respectively, continuously enjoin their "angels" Imis and Lelia ("Desdemona") to "lick", "rub", and "brush off" (162-64) stains from their crotches. The dream sequence evidently aims at bawdy innuendo in the repeated allusion by the men to their crotches that are in need of servicing, bringing into relief the female servitude that marriage pivots on via parody and humor.

Sacrilegious undercurrents are also enjoined to the project of a humorous reconfiguration of marriage. The "chariot of fire" that allowed the prophet Elijah to ascend to Heaven in the original Biblical passage becomes synonymous with Katar's penis as he responds to his admirers Lelia-Desdemona and Imis: "Of course I'll show [my chariot of fire] to you and if you like I'll take you up to heaven – or we'll go for a ride down underground passages of hot blood" (163). The line intermixes Heaven with Hell (hence the allusion to "underground passages"), and it sexualizes both realms as Katar-Elijah promises to take his female admirers for a "ride" on his "chariot of fire". The innuendo pokes fun at the male member grossly exaggerated in its fire-powered proportions, contributing to the culmination of the sequence in a "*[g]rotesque marriage*" (165) between the supposedly wayward Desdemona (played by Lelia) and Rubens, played by Amiel. Amiel-Rubens promises Lelia-Desdemona that they will "get married with a broom up [their] ass and go on [their] honeymoon in a chariot of fire" (165). This recalls earlier references to Elijah's eroticized ascendency to Heaven (since his "chariot of fire" is his penis). Meanwhile the reference to getting married via anal impalement on a broom mocks the institution of matrimony deemed untouchable in its solemnity. Conjuring anal sexual practices most readily associated with male homoeroticism, the description of marriage via a "broom up [the characters'] asses" also connotes an assault on solemnity via queerness. This humorously re-appropriates the homophobic punishment meted out to Lorca who died via a "bullet up the ass" (186).

A queer re-definition of the prison takes place in *And They Put Handcuffs*, re-appropriating the image of inmates as aberrantly sexual to demonstrate that there is dignity, transformative power, and light-hearted humor in such queerness. As such, the play reflects what legal theorist Sarah Lamble describes as the need to dismantle the Prison Industrial Complex via a queer politics that "questions, disrupts, and transforms dominant ideas about what is normal" (237), which are the very ideas that help to put sexual and racial minorities away in disproportionate numbers in the first place.

Aside from the dramatic content of *And They Put Handcuffs on the Flowers*, various performance strategies have also played a part in re-purposing queer sexual praxis for a re-definition of inmates as victims of the pernicious institution of the prison. Recalling the practices of sadomasochism, the play's torturers derive erotic pleasure from punishing inmates. They are, in addition, interchangeable with prisoners. No dividing line exists between torturers (priests, presidents of multinational companies, executioners, and so on) and the prisoners, with all actors playing both roles with the arbitrary signifier of headgear separating them. Oppressors wear hoods and prisoners remain hatless, as the stage directions indicate ("*When the actors play the part of oppressors they are to wear hoods*" (133)). In this process of de-individualizing prisoners and torturers, the play erodes the dividing parameter between a deviant sexual economy inside the prison and a sexually normative one outside, which the Prison Industrial Complex relies on for its ideological force. Torturers are deemed just as queer and derive as much non-normative erotic pleasure from their roles as do the prisoners. Inmate-turned-executioner Amiel, for instance, instigates a punishment on Katar that is evocative of the practices of sadism and coprophilia. He *"violently seizes* KATAR *and whips him"* while crying out "Shit on him, madam" to Katar's wife and informant to the authorities, Drima (172), who takes equal erotic pleasure in proceedings. As Amiel beats him with *"a thick chain"*, Drima *"continues, slowly, with relish, her eyes shut"* and *"rides him like a horse"* while luxuriating in her husband's blood (187).

The fluidity of roles undermines a powerful ideology that queer theorist Dean Spade dubs the "perpetrator/victim model" (Spade 102), which the post-millennial Prison Industrial Complex relies on for explanatory force. The perpetrator/victim model fixes only certain people as the principal cause of discrimination in our current era. These individuals, deemed a minority of ignorant bigots, constitute "perpetrators" who are considered to deserve or merit incarceration. The perpetrator/victim model "[t]hink[s] about violence and oppression as the work of 'a few bad apples' [which] undermines our ability to analyze our conditions *systemically* [...] and to therefore organize for system change" (Bassichis *et al.* 23) as Spade states, in conjunction with Morgan Bassichis and Alexander Lee. The "perpetrator/victim model" obscures the fact that those who are most vulnerable to incarceration in American society tend to be the racial, sexual, and gendered minorities who have been socially outcast. These minorities have less access to a social safety net of welfare, housing, and health care that keeps people from crime and incarceration. Complex administrative processes to sign up to these bodies of housing, welfare, and health care requires a certain level of educational and economic privilege that these individuals do not have. *And They Put Handcuffs'* interchangeability of prisoners and torturers overturns the idea that only a "few bad apples" (Bassichis *et al.* 23) commit crimes. The fluidity of torturers and prisoners, distinguished only by those who wear a hood (the torturers) and those who don't, queers or destabilizes the "perpetrator/victim" (102) model that Spade condemns as reinforcing the Prison Industrial Complex.

The Buffalo-based Subversive Theatre production of *And They Put Handcuffs on the Flowers*, mentioned earlier, deployed de-personalized, white masks that were redolent of Japanese Kabuki in order to drive the point home about the interchangeability of the roles of prisoner and torturer. All actors in the production were dressed in white, to emphasize homogeneity of the characters. Kabuki is a classical form of dance-drama in Japan hailing from seventeenth-century Kyoto, and it involves the painting of actors' faces in heavy white make-up. Originally women would play both men and women in humorous sketches of quotidian occurrence. Subversive Theatre harnessed the Kubuki tradition's plasticity of roles, as both men and women periodically played prison torturers, who were signaled not via a hood (as per Arrabal's original instructions) but by donning a solid white facial prosthesis with only the natural color of their chin exposed. Black detailing in these masks had the effect of hollowing out the actors' eyes, which depersonalized them. Reviewer Galia Binder confirms that Kabuki-like masks made the prison guards anonymous as if they "they were simply playing a role anyone could fill; they represented the system of fascism, not particular individuals" (*Buffalo News*). This speaks to the deconstruction of the contemporary "perpetrator/victim" (102) model highlighted by Spade, evoking the faceless administrative and structural forces that constitute the most prominent and potent causes of disadvantage in today's world. The blanched masks also help to characterize this structural discrimination as stemming from a de-personalized but all-powerful *white* hegemony specifically, which is all too pertinent for challenging the Prison Industrial Complex, which has been characterized as the "new Jim Crow" as we saw earlier (Alexander). Meanwhile, Subversive Theatre maintained the non-normative erotic charge of the play by the simultaneous caressing, handcuffing, and gagging of prisoners on the part of torturers, helping to redefine the space of the prison as one that accords queer sexual practices the freedom and dignity to experiment.

If a criticism may be lodged against Arrabal's queer aesthetic in *And They Put Handcuffs*, it is that it accords more agency and complexity to the men of the play than it does to the women, who are often objectified. The projection of erotic non-normativity onto the non-incarcerated Drima (who takes sadistic and coprophilic pleasure in torturing her husband) may displace the notion that queerness is the exclusive preserve of prisoners but it also reinforces the image of the "castrating [...] woman" (Miller 92) that Arrabal scholar Judith Miller identifies as recurring figure throughout Arrabal's oeuvre. Don Hall, a reviewer of the Right Brain Project's production in Chicago in 2009, complained of the sexual stereotyping of the play's women. Like Subversive Theatre, the entire cast was clad in white to connote homogeneity of the characters. The presence or absence of white caps separated the prisoners from the torturers in this production. Character homogenization, however, did little to mitigate what Hall describes as a pornographic form of humor that came at the expense of women:

> Nothing feels as hollow as when you know Arrabal was presenting what he thought was a very funny sacrilege that just falls flat or has a character randomly discuss pissing on someone, sticking something in someone's ass or an extended musical scene featuring a woman shitting on a man in mime accompanied by fart noises on the soundtrack. I'm certain that in 1969 Arrabal's use of perverse language was rather shocking but in the Age of 2 Girls, 1 Cup it just feels juvenile and extraneous. (Hall, "Theatre Review")

According to Hall, the play's bawdy-sacrilegious humor fell flat because it aped clichéd pornographic videos circulating on the Internet as Hall recounts in his comparison of the play's defecatory bits to the infamous scatological skit "2 Girls, 1 Cup" that went viral in 2007. Hall's comparison of *And They Put Handcuffs* to "2 Girls, 1 cup" evokes the misogyny that Arrabal's play risks, which comes at the expense of the transformative queerness that I have pointed out in this section. The play is in fact replete with this trade-off between patriarchal stereotyping and queer transformation. For instance, the myth of the Our Lady of Fátima, where the Virgin Mary appeared to three shepherd children in Portugal in 1917, is re-appropriated so that Amiel figures as the Madonna while the three women of the play become the "shepherdesses" who drink chocolate milk from his penis in an implied act of fellatio. This exemplifies Arrabal's use of the misogynistic binary opposition between masculine potency and feminine sexual servitude. Another sequence sees queer fluidity and gender experimentation being accorded only to the male character of Pronos, who cross-dresses in a ballerina's tutu while dancing to the tune of Saint-Saëns's *The Death of the Swan*. Meanwhile the female character Drima is encouraged to defecate on her husband Katar's head in order to punish him for his treachery to the nation. Drima appears confined to the role of the "castrating", overly pious woman signaled by feminist theatre critic Judith Miller. Drima admonishes her husband in castrating overtures: "Quiet. Suffer. You must pay for your sins" (171). During this same scene, another inmate Pronos engages in an "*effeminate*" ballet while simultaneously "*dancing like Frank Sinatra*" (171-172). It is only the men who are given full freedom to experiment with gender and queerness.

The stigmatization of women as castrators may act as a counterweight to the play's reconfiguration of prisoners as practitioners of a queer politics that can transform the norms of society. Stereotypes of castrating women must be corrected if this play is to queer the gender norms surrounding women, which also help to put gender, sexual, racial and other minorities away in disproportionate numbers (Lamble).

But, provided that current practitioners are attentive to Arrabal's sexism in the recuperation of this play, *And They Put Handcuffs* reflects queer theorists' calls to abolish the Prison Industrial Complex and find alternative forms of practicing justice. Let us recall that prison abolitionism is at the heart of the play as the martyr Tosan's words indicate, "We must open the prisons and disband the army. The emancipation of man must be total" (207). Queer practices that transform norms are aligned with alternative justice in an under-explored detail in the original French text, which was elided in the English translation of *And They Put Handcuffs*. *Et Ils passèrent des menottes aux fleurs* (the original French title) in fact did not conclude with the execution of Tosan, but with a sadomasochistic rite that was accessible to consenting individuals who wished to stay behind after the conclusion of the dramatic action. Spectators were, as the text instructed, to be blindfolded, holding the hands of their playing partner, and would choose the role of either torturer or victim. The actors stimulate the spectator's senses of taste and touch, giving them oranges and imploring them to rub hands with one another. The rite was designed to grant absolute autonomy to spectators: "Finally, the actors let [spectators] act alone, without guidance from the 'professionalism' of the theatre" (106).[9]

Such actions reflect this play's position in a canon of short-lived "guerrilla" theatre flourishing in the late 1960s and early 1970s, which aimed, as R.L. Farmer observes commenting on Arrabal's presence in the movement, to inspire spectators out of a state of passive viewing to direct action, "purport[ing] to dynamite the subject-object dialectic and rearrange the fragments resulting from the explosion" (Farmer 156). The guerrilla energies of the final rite of *And They Put Handcuffs* may be applied to exploding the prison-like qualities of the enclosed space of the theatre itself, which reinforces the passivity of spectators as if they were inmates.

---

[9]   Fernando, Arrabal. "Et Ils Passèrent des menottes aux fleurs," in *Théâtre de guerrilla.* Paris: Christian Bourgois, 1969. My translation. Original: "*Enfin, ils* [les acteurs] *les laisseront agir seuls, hors de la présence de tout 'professionnel' du théâtre*".

The prison-like passivity of spectators of the medium of theatre was first described by the English-American poet W.H. Auden in his speech "The Future of English Poetic Drama" (1938). As Auden wrote, "the stage is a box, it is a prison. We are in this prison with the audience, and the actors are in it too" (Auden 517). Going beyond the constraints of the theatre in the final rite of *And They Put Handcuffs* may serve to demolish the symbolic power of the penitentiary if we take Auden's analogy between the prison and the theatre to its logical conclusion.

Specifically, the commissioning of spectators to play torturers and victims strikes up an affinity with new methods of "transformative justice" that Spade describes being practiced as an alternative to prison. Initiatives such as Critical Resistance, the Audre Lorde Project, INCITE!, Communities Against Violence, and generationFIVE are challenging "[t]he framing of harm as a problem of bad individuals who need to be exiled" (Spade 2466), which merely reinforces structural iniquities based on race, class, gender, and sexuality. Instead these grass-roots organizations "seek healing and transformation for both people experiencing and people responsible for harm" (Spade 2471) outside of the prison. Abolitionism, in other words, is not a utopian vision of a post-criminal world but an ongoing project where accountability and reparations are implemented locally, remaining within the communities affected by the crime and violence in question. By enabling spectators of *And They Put Handcuffs* to play the role of torturer or victim, they are permitted the same access to localized justice as an alternative to the Prison Industrial Complex.

With its torturers and victims, the rite enables spectators to use sadomasochistic practices to transcend the violence meted out to victims of crime. As queer theorists have noted, S/M practices can act as a means for working through past trauma. Elizabeth Freeman, for instance, describes a form of S/M practice that potentially "holds sensuality and historical accountability in productive tension", where traumatic memories "can be burned into the body through pleasure as well as pain" (Freeman 2441). In this view, the weight of trauma is lessened, challenged, and its inevitability is reversed in the suffusion of pain with erotic pleasure so that a different future may be conceived. Spectators of *And They Put Handcuffs* may enlist the final rite to seek similar post-carceral reparations. Those who have found themselves the brunt of criminal violence may be empowered by choosing to play either torturer or victim, taking command of past pain by assuming the former role or repeating and working through trauma in the latter.

The rite, in the few times that it has been implemented, has already proven successful in facilitating the admission of criminal guilt and implementing alternative forms of justice. *France Soir* theatre reviewer Guy Dupont, who attended Arrabal's debut production of *And They Put Handcuffs on the Flowers* at the Théâtre de l'Epée de Bois, recounted that a man who participated in the rite confessed to raping a twelve-year girl (Dupont *France Soir*). The rite proved powerful enough to occasion an admission of guilt on the part of this spectator. If alternative justice is to work in the theatre setting, however, admissions like this must be carefully handled to hold people such as this man to account for his crime. While the practical possibilities and limitations of this rite need to be examined in greater detail, the confession of this man demonstrates that avant-garde theatre can elicit confessions, which form the starting point for seeking alternative justice outside of the Prison Industrial Complex.

I have argued in this chapter that *And They Put Handcuffs on the Flowers* is premised on a double call. Firstly the play abolishes faith in the prison system as protector of social wellbeing via supplementary enjoyment. Secondly the play destabilizes received discourses of inherent criminal deviancy by means of transformative queer practices such as S/M, alternative views of marriage, and re-appropriations of lines from the queer victims of Spanish tyranny. Supplementary enjoyment is conjured through a spectatorial experience of transcendence, which is inflected with a mystical pain and pleasure, baroque aesthetics, and the metaphorical unveiling of the violence that lies behind the smokescreen of prison as the protector of social wellbeing. Supplementary enjoyment strips the carceral system of its ideological weight. The queerness that supplants this is characterized as transforming the sexual, racial, and gender norms that put minorities away in disproportionate numbers. In performance, I proposed that the racialization of prisoners and the guards would help to make the play's relevance in today's age of a neo-segregationist Prison Industrial Complex more obvious. Racialized prisoners, such as Mabussoo Lo who played Tosan in Arrabal's debut production of *And They Put Handcuffs*, and white prison guards, such as the actors who donned the blanched Kabuki masks in the Subversive Theatre production in Buffalo, help emphasize the white hegemony of the American Prison Industrial Complex, where sixty percent of inmates are people of color (Mogul *et al.* 76). The final rite, suffused with sadomasochistic interchange and in which spectators break their role as observers and become either torturers or victims, provides one way of transcending the injustice of the prison system. A setting that would encourage spectators' admission of crime and that would hold them to account has emerged in this chapter as one way in which the alternative justice pointed out by queer theorists might be enacted.

Conclusion

"As I watched [*The Blacks*], I found myself drawn into Genet's inspiring demonstration of the workings of racism through an aesthetic formalism that turns "real-world" institutions such as the law into the aestheticized figure of the Court on stage – until I suddenly realized the rest of the audience – all Mexican – was staring at me. Nudging each other, they looked at me whispering "¡Mira! ¡La Negrita!" ("Look! The Negress!"). […] It dawned on me that I was the only black person – and a black woman, at that – in the audience. The staring continued, putting me ill at ease, and the hubbub grew to a distracting level. […] The audience could not quite believe a black person was sitting among them who (was not) part of the audience – it would be ridiculous to assume that, like them, I was simply there to enjoy the play. I suddenly felt very small and frail, as though I wanted to collapse into nothingness – but I could not because I was chained to an apparition created by the color of my skin."

Frieda Ekotto on *The Blacks* (*Race and Sex Across the Atlantic* ix-x)

"'You mean you didn't understand it.' All of a sudden he was angry and he began to shout at me. He said *The Blacks* was not only a good play, it was a great play. […] Genet understood the nature of imperialism and colonialism and how those two evils erode the natural good in people. […] [A]s a black woman married to a South African and raising a black boy, [he said] I should damn well understand the play before I started laughing at it. […] I got up and gathered my purse. I wanted at least to reach the door before the tears fell."

Maya Angelou on reading *The Blacks* for the first time
(*The Heart of a Woman* 201)

The aim of this book has been to resurrect the social politics of the Theatre of the Absurd and to re-locate this social politics in a post-millennial context. In so doing, I have aimed to make the broader point that past avant-garde theatrical movements are capable of making social subversions in the now. Avant-garde movements are presumed to be short-lived, and their capacity for social subversion is locked into a time-specific model of the aesthetic innovation of prevailing artistic norms. True to this trend in avant-garde studies, the Theatre of the Absurd quickly became the victim of the aesthetic innovations that were said to be the sole determinant of its radical gesture. Absurdist theatre's aesthetic eviscerations of drama to the bare minimum of coordinates (often lacking a plot, psychological complexity to its characters, and an ending) overdetermined understandings of the subversive value of the movement. Linking aesthetic minimalism to philosophical currents circulating in post-war Europe, Martin Esslin (1961) defined Absurdism's subversions in terms of the "absurdity of the human condition" and "metaphysical anguish" of "Man" (*The Theatre of the Absurd* 25). As I stated in the introduction, the "Man" who was victim of this so-called metaphysical or existential anguish is synonymous with the dominant qualifiers of identity: white, male, middle-class, and heterosexual. Esslin's highly influential reading caused the plays that belonged to the Theatre of the Absurd to petrify and appear out-of-date *vis-à-vis* the rising tide of gender-, sexuality-, race-, and class-conscious identity politics of the latter half of the twentieth century. Such identity politics was championed in social movements such as second-wave feminism, civil rights, post-colonialism, and queer liberation. The Theatre of the Absurd's universalist "Man" appeared out of sync with these movements.

What I show in these pages is that while criticism clung tenaciously to outdated universalisms (under-acknowledging the dominant social position which universalism bespeaks), the plays within the Absurdist movement debunk and *displace* the universal or the white, straight, middle-class male perspective that the category of the universal connotes. It is shown that heteronormativity is called into question in Ionesco's *The Bald Soprano*; racism and the way it shapes representations of war in the middle decades of American history is destabilized in Adamov's *Off Limits*; the way that race, religion, and ethnicity play into the differences between women is brought up in Beckett's *Not I*; the invisibility of black women in Western patriarchy is put on display and destabilized in Genet's *The Blacks*; and the prison's violence against sexual and racial minorities is highlighted in Arrabal's *And They Put Handcuffs on the Flowers*. These themes, in turn, are compatible with battles against the post-millennial ideologies of heteronormativity (chapter one), docile patriotism (chapter two), gender exceptionalism (chapter three), white patriarchy (chapter four), and the Prison Industrial Complex (chapter five).

However, this is not to say that the argument of my book – that an avant-garde of the past connects to the politics of the present moment – should be over-egged. I have provided the above quotes by Genet scholar Frieda Ekotto and the late author and *The Blacks'* performer

Maya Angelou (1928-2014) as epigraphs to this conclusion in order to prevent us from getting carried away with the claim that the Theatre of the Absurd betokens a social politics of the marginalized. To write from a white male point of view about the displacement of the white male point of view in society is emphatically not the same as saying that the individuals oppressed for their gender, race, class, sexuality or any other perceived form of "difference" from the white male norm need look no further than the Theatre of the Absurd. Both Ekotto and Angelou describe their experience of disempowerment in their interactions with Genet's *The Blacks*. Two real-life black women, in other words, found themselves targeted because of a play that, as I suggested in chapter four, theoretically destabilizes the interaction of sexism and racism, or gendered racism, that disempowers black women. Their comments are pertinent reminders that lived reality often contradicts theory.

Ekotto, as the only black person in the audience at a Mexican production of *The Blacks*, found herself the center of scrutiny among the Latin American spectators surrounding her. She opens her book *Race and Sex Across the French Atlantic: The Color of Black in Literary, Philosophical, and Theatre Discourse* (2011) with a memory of becoming a hyper-visible member of the audience because of the blackness of her skin. This turn of events was informed by the Mexican cultural context in which she saw the production. Ekotto's anecdote demonstrates that Absurdist plays can and do miss the mark in practice when it comes to the social politics that I have suggested in these pages. Her account of feeling "small and frail" and of wanting to "collapse into nothingness" hints not only at the racial discrimination that she recounts when describing being "chained to an apparition created by the color of [her] skin" (Ekotti ix-x); it also echoes the centuries-long objectification of black *women* specifically ("I was the only black person – and a black woman, at that" (ix-x)). Black women's objectification is most saliently exemplified by the case of Saartjie Baartman, or the "Hottentot Venus", who was animalized as an exhibit in the "human zoos" of nineteenth-century London.

Likewise, Maya Angelou remembers the reaction of reproval that she met with when in conversation with Max Glanville, the stage manager of the first off-Broadway version of *The Blacks*, about Genet's play at the beginning of the 1960s. Angelou recalls the first time that she read the script. She subsequently played the white-masked Queen in Gene Frankel's phenomenally successful production of *The Blacks* at St. Mark's Playhouse (also starring Roscoe Lee Browne, Cicely Tyson, and James Earl Jones), which ran for three years and nearly one and a half thousand shows. Yet on reading the script for the first time, Angelou's response was one of hysterical laughter at the pressed-for-time self-importance of the producers, most of whom were white, and at what she described as the "extremely complex" structure and "convoluted" (Angelou 200) language of *The Blacks*. Glanville reprimanded Angelou for what he deemed a facile reaction, reminding her of her obligations as a symbol of strength as a wife and mother in the black community: "as a black woman married to a South African and raising a black boy, [he said] I should damn well understand the play before I started laughing at it" (Angelou 201). Similar to Ekotto's objectification by the Mexican audience members surrounding her, Angelou was brought down to stereotyped size as a "super-strength" black mother who is not permitted selfhood outside of a self-sacrificing responsibility to her community. This is not much different from a controlling image of the "mammy" figure that is pervasive throughout American history. Since the time of Reconstruction, the "mammy" stereotype has cast black women as the caretakers of others', usually whites', needs at the expense of attending to their own.[1]

I do not wish to position either Ekotto or Angelou as victims of *The Blacks*. That would do an injustice to both women. Ekotto's *Race and Sex Across the French Atlantic*, following its opening anecdote, illustrates cogently that *The Blacks* aligned Genet with the Négritude movement that swept the French Atlantic; with its origins in continental philosophy and Négritude, Genet's play, asserts Ekotto, is insightful for the US context. Ekotto posits that *The Blacks* reclaims black identity and imagines it outside of racist reality, which she argues is contrary to the often realpolitik-like stakes of the anti-racism struggle in United States history from the post-bellum period of Reconstruction to the Civil Rights era. Similar to Ekotto, Angelou "began to see through the tortuous and mythical language" (Angelou 202) and gain clarity on Genet's intentions as she came to perform the play for the first time. As Angelou described, Genet demonstrated that "colonialism would crumble from the weight of its ignorance [...] [while] the oppressed would take over the positions of their former masters" (202). In fact, Angelou stated her disagreement with Genet about black usurpation of white hegemony, citing black spirituality and compassion as power counterforces that would break the cycle of domination and oppression. Despite her intellectual difference of

---

[1]   On the figure of the mammy see Patricia Hill Collins. *Black Sexual Politics: African Americans, Gender, and the New Racism*. New York: Routledge, 2004, 140-147.

opinion from Genet, Angelou was no less blocked from connecting with *The Blacks* than was Ekotto.

The point I wish to make is that Ekotto's and Angelou's accounts demonstrate the very real workings of sexism and racism that were perpetuated by *The Blacks*. Deconstructive of gendered racism or not, the play was unable to aid the cause of fighting black women's oppression in these instances of audience and public reception. Indeed, the play fueled and facilitated gendered racism here. Developing on this, it is important to keep in mind that what I have proposed in the foregoing chapters are theories. Theory has its potential but it also has its limitations. Though theoretical spectatorship is a paradigm that has allowed me to revive the texts and discern the sexual, racial, and gender-based politics that they may elicit today, it cannot be de-coupled from the need to experiment with these plays so that they may fulfill their socio-political potential in practice. I have suggested some production and performance techniques that might aid the social politics I have covered in this book. However, it is up to practitioners of the future to explore and adapt accordingly.

The Theatre of the Absurd was characterized by its "nothingness" – its reduction of drama to the bare minimum, its oftentimes-strained language, and its circularity of plot. Such nothingness has proven to gel especially well with a Lacanian politics of the Real, which pivots on meaninglessness as an impetus to social change. However, I have demonstrated that this is not where the story stops. Exploring the possibilities of a women's Theatre of the Absurd, theatre critic and professor Toby Zinman (1991) asserts, the "theatre of the absurd assumes the Beckettian premise [uttered by Estragon in *Waiting for Godot*] 'Nothing to be done'" (Zinman 205). Women, oppressed for their gender, cannot afford to live with this resolution to follow the status quo ("Nothing to be done") to the same extent as men, Zinman argues. In contrast to Zinman, I have argued that Absurdism does not simply resign itself to a "Nothing to be done". Instead, many Absurdist plays envisage alternative realities cast free of gender, racial, and sexual injustice once they have thrown such injustice into the realm of the meaningless Real. Sometimes I demonstrated this textually. In the case of *Off Limits*, Sally and Molly enjoin spectators to consider the truth of what happened in Vietnam outside of the racist and sexist accounts given by the cast of characters. In *The Blacks* a language of black female empowerment replaces the play's reduction of gendered racism to meaninglessness. In *And They Put Handcuffs*, inmates are emboldened by queer sexual practices after the play unsettles the fantasy of the prison as the arbiter of social peace and security. Other times, I used pre-existing or potential future production and performance methods to point out Absurdism's envisioning of a different world. For instance, Jean-Claude Berutti produced an otherworldly *The Bald Soprano* where female characters resisted objectification through masks and drag costume. As I proposed in chapter four, having characters such as Felicity rap their way to victory against the "white" (be-masked) Queen would be a way for the language of black women's empowerment to be implemented on the stage.

The Theatre of the Absurd's repeated gesture of divesting ideologies of their meaning – whether we are discussing the devaluation of heteronormativity, docile patriotism, gender exceptionalism, gendered racism, or the Prison Industrial Complex – implicitly points to the constructed nature of ideology itself. By showing the constructedness of dominant ideologies, the Theatre of the Absurd aligns itself with trends in social constructionism, which holds that reality is produced by society through visual codes, discursive language, and other social mechanisms.[2] Once we can identify ideology as constructed, we can also change it. However, to call attention to the social constructionist undercurrent of the Theatre of the Absurd is not to say that it is beyond scrutiny. Ekotto's and Angelou's anecdotes bring to mind black feminist Kimberlé Crenshaw's comments on "vulgar constructionism": "To say that a category such as race or gender is socially constructed is not to say that that category has no significance in our world" (Crenshaw 1296). Racism and sexism do not simply vanish with an identification that they are socially constructed. They have material, real-life "significance in our world" (Crenshaw). Absurdism may be accused of vulgar constructionism, displaying ideologies as constructed and stripping them of authority all the while evading its own part in real-life discriminatory practices. Its role in real-life discrimination is demonstrated by Angelou's and Ekotto's experiences of temporary disempowerment at the hands of *The Blacks*. The drive to reach beyond post-millennial ways of viewing the world that may be drawn out of the Theatre of the Absurd should not, in other words, entail unchecked escapism.

It is instructive to turn to African-American playwright Lorraine Hansberry's critique of *The Blacks* in order to understand this limit point

---

[2]   See for instance Vivien, Burr. *Social Constructionism*, 3rd edn. New York: Routledge, 2015 (1995).

of the Theatre of the Absurd better. Hansberry criticizes Genet's self-extraction from the practice of racism divulged by his play. Calling Genet part of a brigade of "New Paternalists" (which also included Norman Mailer and Nelson Algren) (*To Be Young, Gifted, and Black* 211), she continued:

> The problem in the world is the oppression of man by *man*; it is this which threatens existence. And it is this which Genet evades with an abstraction: an elaborate legend used to affirm, indeed, entrench the quite *different* nature of pain, lust, cruelty, ambition presumed to exist in the blacks ... [...] To have had to deal with *human beings*... would have been to confront Guilt with a greater imperative: the necessity for action – that is, to *do* something about it. The too easy purgation of the Whites – self-condemning and self-absolving – the untouched remoteness of the Blacks – would be nullified by a drama wherein we were *all* forced to confrontation and awareness. (qtd. in Wilkerson 32)

Academic ideas on the constructed nature of racial discrimination let whites off too easily, Hansberry suggests. It absents the second, emphasized "*man*" who does the oppressing in her above description of the "problem in the world is the oppression of man by *man*". At the same time that the "New Paternalists" cloak racism in truisms about the socially constructed nature of racism, such authors evade the implication that they are inevitably involved (whether they like it or not) in racist practices and that they benefit from white privilege. This limits *The Blacks* to "a conversation between white men about themselves" and "an empty if seductive piece of poetry" (qtd. in Wilkerson 32).

Hansberry was already drafting a play about racial revolution before she saw Frankel's off-Broadway production of *The Blacks* in May 1961, which starred Angelou, but her decision to name her play *Les Blancs* came "in immediate visceral response to Jean Genet's celebrated drama" (qtd. in Wilkerson 32) and a tongue-in-cheek dig at her French contemporary. *Les Blancs* literally translates as "The Whites" and it alliteratively plays off the similar sounding title of Genet's drama at the same time as positioning itself as the monochromatic inverse of the French author's work. Hansberry's drama enacts the revolution of the black community against the white colonialists in an African nation, in a similar way to *The Blacks*. However unlike her French predecessor, Hansberry insists on the real-life weight of racist prejudice that theories of vulgar constructionism simply cannot account for. Conversing with white liberal journalist Charlie, *Les Blancs'* protagonist Tshembe admits that "racism is a device that, of itself, explains nothing [...] [a]n invention to justify the rule of some men over others" (*Les Blancs* 67). However he continues to his interlocutor that a device "also has consequences", and while "you and I may recognize the fraudulence of the device [...] the fact remains that a man who has a sword run through him because he refuses to become a Moslem or a Christian – or who is shot in Zatembe or Mississippi because he is black – is suffering the utter *reality* of the device" (67). Warning of the escapism inherent in theories of social constructionism, Tshembe concludes, "it is pointless to pretend that it doesn't *exist* – merely because it is a *lie!*" (67).

Hansberry's criticism of Genet's self-abstraction from the history of discrimination recounted in *The Blacks* applies to all the Absurdist offerings explored here. The destabilized authority of the white male perspective in the Theatre of the Absurd may, in short, be a significant discovery of this book, but it would be spurious to suggest that white male authorship (however much it is displaced) made no difference at all to the possibilities of realizing the subversive ways of viewing that I have proposed in these pages. Hansberry's argument indicates that the experience of the material reality of discrimination counts in representation. Being cognizant of "the utter *reality* of the device" (Tshembe) through personal experience aids a complex and nuanced representation of prejudiced practices in our society. Prejudice must be shown to be both constructed *and* holding real-life disempowering weight. This is where the white male-authored social politics in the Theatre of the Absurd might find its biggest flaw. Indeed, the author is never as dead as semiologist Roland Barthes would have us believe.

However, the beauty of theatre performance's perpetual "life [...] in the present" (Phelan 146), to borrow performance studies critic Peggy Phelan's phrase, helps us counteract the problem. Absurdist texts can be made to minimize the damage they enact upon spectators living with the real-life consequences of prejudice. With attention to detail and sensitivity in production and performance, Absurdist plays might avoid the situations of disempowerment that Angelou and Ekotto recount. I have laid emphasis on exploration through performance and production method throughout all five of the book's chapters. Directors of color, women producers, performers who have to face religious prejudice, and so on will be powerful agents in reviving the plays in the ways I have described in the foregoing chapters.

Past, Present, Future Absurdist Avant-gardes

I presented this book as a challenge to the unwritten rule of avant-garde studies that past vanguards bear little potential for current-day social subversions. The Theatre of the Absurd provided an apt case study allowing me to take up this challenge. The ways that my contention may be extended to the recuperation of other past avant-gardes is a subject for future scholarship to explore. But in order to demonstrate briefly how the material in this book might aid the detection of contemporary social subversions in other past avant-gardes, I would like to return to the subject of the post-millennial Prison Industrial Complex and the twentieth-century avant-garde's interaction with the institution of the pentientiary which I explored in chapter five with reference to Arrabal's *And They Put Handcuffs on the Flowers*. There are, in fact, a wealth of other "prison plays" in the history of avant-garde theatre of the twentieth century.

Throughout the twentieth century, the avant-garde deployed, almost to the degree of obsession, the theatre as a "symbol of the captivity of the human mind or imprisonment of the body, or indeed a conglomeration of the two" (Warden 75-76) as scholar Claire Warden explains, tracing the theme of the penitentiary in British, European, and American avant-gardes in her book *British Avant-garde Theatre* (2012). Alfred Jarry, whose *Ubu Roi* (1896) Martin Esslin dubbed one of the founding precursors of the Theatre of the Absurd, depicts the eponymous tyrant throwing those who deign to oppose him into prison. Swedish playwright August Strindberg's *A Dream Play* (1901), which belonged to the avant-garde movement of Expressionism, was originally titled *Prisoners*. As a sign of the influence of Freudian psychoanalytic theories of the unconscious circulating in Europe at the turn of the century, the play cast humans as incarcerated within their own bodies, and this is confirmed scenographically in one scene as a palace transforms into a prison (Innes 34). Ernst Toller's *Masses and Man* (1934) stages a similar metaphorical entrapment of the human psyche (Innes 39). Jean Genet's *Deathwatch* (1947) theatricalized a hierarchy of male superiority in a prison cell, culminating in the strangling of one character (LeFranc) by another (Maurice) in order to win the affections and respect of the hardest worn of outcasts and criminals "Green Eyes". Into the 1960s, the Living Theatre's *The Brig* (mentioned in the introduction) depicted the harsh conditions of a Marine prison. Three years after *The Brig*, Living Theatre's 1965 *mise-en-scène* of Mary Shelley's *Frankenstein* (1818) conjured a multi-leveled jail and the automaton-like movement of prisoners from one cell to another in an infernal cycle. The carceral set was designed to reflect the deadening effect of social conditioning (Innes 182).

This inexhaustive snapshot gives an idea of how the institution of the prison provided a locus to reflect the themes of personal and political entrapment. But this is intimately connected, in the twentieth-century history of the avant-garde, with the theme of character and spectatorial liberation. In *Ubu Roi*, the eponymous hero in the end *voluntarily* enters jail in an effort to find the purest form of freedom as an outcast of society with nothing left to lose. Ubu's subjects, loyal to him, follow him to the penitentiary too (Innes 25). Similarly, Toller's *Masses and Man* aimed to provide therapeutic liberation for spectators (Innes 39). Prison often functioned, for the avant-gardists, as a means of instating Antonin Artaud's idea of a "Theatre of Cruelty". Artaud insisted that revolutionary theatre must provide a means for liberating spectators, by creating a sense of public chaos similar to that seen in historical instances of plagues (for instance, the Great Plague of London in 1665, and the plague of Marseille in 1720). The prison, as the site of extreme entrapment, could be a similar conduit to unleash a public frenzy that creates the conditions for the characters' and spectators' liberation. We saw a similar dialectic between entrapment and liberation in chapter five, where I argued that *And They Put Handcuffs on the Flowers* pushed spectators to feel that they were inmates in order to transcend the violence of the institution of the prison. The prison plays that I have just named, by grappling with a similar dialectic of entrapment and liberation, might too subvert the post-millennial Prison Industrial Complex. They may, similar to the argument proposed in chapter five, invite spectators to transcend the powerful ideology that prison exists for the good of society, an ideology that obscures the wide-scale violence that this institution in fact commits against racial and sexual minorities. In short, these prison plays may, too, present themselves, as avant-garde critic James Harding explains, as candidates for "the stealing of one historical moment for the purposes of another" (*The Ghosts of the Avant-garde* 26). This is a contention that Harding in fact makes in relation to a prison play, Living Theatre's *The Brig*.

In *Avant-garde Performance and the Limits of Criticism*, Mike Sell explores vanguard movements such as the happenings, which flourished as a result of post-war economic expansion but also as a form of resistance to it. Sell states,

[I]f revolution is indeed a complex process of borrowing, appropriation, destruction, and reconstruction, then it may behoove the next vanguard to study those that have been left hanging on the horns of transformative capitalism. (204)

Exploring the French context, my book has been in a certain sense about studying a similar avant-garde "left hanging on the horns of transformative capitalism". The Theatre of the Absurd was quickly commodified as I stated in the introduction, which is something that Martin Esslin even confirmed and bemoaned when he compared the movement to a "branded product of the detergent industry" ("The Theatre of the Absurd Reconsidered" 179) ten years after his milestone publication. But the Theatre of the Absurd's commodification is not to say that its social politics became extinct, as I have illustrated throughout this book. Commodification as the index of a dead vanguard prematurely obliterates its radical gesture. Such an index would make it extremely difficult, if not impossible, for there to even be a contemporary avant-garde given the late capitalist times that we live in. Many works in avant-garde studies (including Sell's) contest the theory put forward by Peter Bürger, which aligned a cultural object's marketization with the death of its vanguard potential. My book has contributed a unique perspective in this critical pattern of protest by positing, with the use of the case study of the Theatre of the Absurd, that the social politics of past avant-gardes may change form but can still endure today.

Sell also advocates in the above quote a need to look at the avant-gardes of the past in order to understand those of the future. It is with this comment in mind that I turn finally to examine what *post*-Absurdist theatre might derive from the material studied in this book. In the spirit of dialectical exchange I also reflect on what post-Absurdist theatre brings to our understanding of the Theater of the Absurd. I proposed earlier that authorship plays a role in shaping and even lessening socio-political gestures. Writing about the displacement of the white male from a white male perspective is not as cogent as an individual writing on the same subject who materially experiences oppression for their race, sexuality, gender or class. Turning to post-Absurdist works which undertook "a complex process of borrowing, appropriation, destruction, and reconstruction" (Sell 204) from the Theatre of the Absurd while standing outside of a white male pattern of authorship could be a way to maximize the social politics discovered in these pages.

Since gender has been a main theme of this book, with the Theatre of the Absurd creating more opportunities than previously supposed for viewing regimes that subvert various gender-based hierarchies, I want to turn to feminist post-Absurdist work in particular. The question of a feminist absurd aesthetic is a hotly contested one, and critics such as Celeste Derksen (2002), Toby Zinman (1991), and Neil Cornwell (2006) illustrate that any "borrowing, appropriation, destruction, and reconstruction" (Sell 204) of male-dominated Absurdism by female playwrights has happened in tandem with an at least minimal degree of referencing patriarchal social reality. An illustration of this lies in Derksen's assessment of Canadian playwright Margaret Hollingsworth's *The House that Jack Built* (1988). This play focuses on a couple who have prematurely aged and who spend most of the dramatic action in their rocking chairs discussing the past actions that have led to their current marital misery. The premise is not worlds apart from the conjugal circuitousness of *The Bald Soprano* that we discussed in chapter one. I proposed in this chapter that the leitmotif of conjugal conflict (present also in Pinter's *The Birthday Party* and Albee's *Who's Afraid of Virginia Woolf?* for instance) makes Absurdism ripe for a closer exploration of its assault on heteronormativity. *The House that Jack Built* also recalls the minimal stage of *The Bald Soprano* and it resembles the circularity of the never-ending discursive digressions of the two couples of Ionesco's play. Hollingsworth's play ends more or less where it began with the couple rocking back and forth in their chairs entrapped in an unhappy marriage, despite wife Jenny's attempt at escape by joining a women's group for environmental activism. The only difference is that Jenny is pregnant by the end of playing time, further trapping her in marital obligation.

Details such as the final pregnancy of the heroine inspire Derksen to assert that Hollingsworth "insists that we see the operation of those abstract structures [such as marriage] that control human behaviour as having very real costs" (219). This reflects Lorraine Hansberry's call (cited earlier) for seeing "the utter *reality*" (*Les Blancs* 67) of the social structures that oppress individuals, such as racial and gender hierarchies. Jenny is the victim of the structure of marriage to a much greater degree than her husband because of her gender. Jack entraps Jenny by getting her pregnant even though his "masterful manhood" is, as Derksen continues, "frustrated" (215) because of the alienation that he experiences as a result of an unhappy marriage. "Jack's maleness may be a construct, [but] it is a powerful one, with detrimental effects" (Derksen 223) disproportionately meted out to Jenny.

The House that Jack Built downplays didacticism, ending where it began, which corresponds to the circularity of plot that we have seen in *The Bald Soprano*, *The Blacks*, and *Not I* in this book. *The House that Jack Built* therefore reflects the Theatre of the Absurd's circularity, rather than allowing Jenny the means to liberate herself from the matrimonial structure that encloses her. However, Hollingsworth's play also retains at least some linkage to gender-based reality, and this shows just how disproportionately detrimental Absurdism's circularity can be for women. This is a far cry from *The Bald Soprano*, which is limited in its exploration of the disproportionate cost of hetero-normative ideologies for women specifically. Lines from *The Bald Soprano* such as "Men are all alike! You sit there all day long, a cigarette in your mouth, or you powder your nose and rouge your lips" (*The Bald Soprano* 13-14), apart from playing with gendered expectations, remain textual and abstract. Derksen's contention is that *The House that Jack Built*'s lack of didacticism and Absurdist circularity afford a glimpse into the complexities of asserting women's agency. Feminist theatre has been often unsympathetic towards these complexities, instead preferring didactic displays of women's emancipation from patriarchal forces. Indeed, the fact that Jenny carries on despite the odds is enough for Derksen to espy feminist potential. Derksen concludes, "While [*The House that Jack Built*] suggests that power relations between men and women continue to be unequal, with men invested in maintaining the status quo, the potential for women's resistance and resilience (like Jenny's), continue to exist in subversive expressions" (Derksen 227-228).

Much is to be said of Absurdist calls to derailing social structures of marriage while resisting the heavy-handedness of didacticism – a balance that we see in *The House that Jack Built*, and before that in *The Bald Soprano*, and other "marriage" plays of the Theatre of the Absurd such as Pinter's *The Birthday Party*. Indeed, *The House that Jack Built* might take inspiration from its precursors such as *The Bald Soprano* to heighten "the potential for women's resistance and resilience [...] in subversive expressions" (Derksen 228). I examined the genre's capacity for transformative forms of laughter and comedy in chapter one with reference to *The Bald Soprano*. This capacity could be applied to production method in the case of *The House that Jack Built*. Spectators may for instance be encouraged to experience a subversive form of laughter that acknowledges but also *resists* male dominance depicted in *The House that Jack Built.* We saw drag-inflected parodies of gender norms in the Berutti production of *The Bald Soprano*, as a lithe man played the maid Mary, and in the Lucy Cavendish College *mise-en-scène* where women enacted the male characters Mr. Smith, Mr. Martin, and the Fire Chief. Drag parody in *The House that Jack Built* may invite a similar form of laughter. This laughter would defy gender norms even as the play more seriously seeks to stress the material hold of patriarchal ideologies in the end image of a pregnant Jenny unable to escape her miserable marriage.

Another playwright who has been classified as deriving inspiration from the Theatre of the Absurd is British playwright Sarah Kane (1971-1999). Neil Cornwell (2006) locates Kane, who touches on topics such as rape, sexual abuse, and mental illness, as a "strident exception" to the "women writers [who] are seen as avoiding, or rejecting, the pessimistic and abstract philosophies entailed in absurdism" (Cornwell 292). Kane's work, like Hollingsworth's, has no didactic solution to offer spectators. However, it arguably goes beyond the ambivalence of Hollingsworth's depiction of Jenny's survival and Absurdist negativity by breaking the cycle of repetitiousness that we have seen in plays from *The Bald Soprano* to *Not I.* Kane's last play *4.48 Psychosis* (1999) was written immediately before the author hanged herself at the age of twenty-eight. The play, too, suggests a final suicidal act of its heroine. This goes beyond the playwrights of the Theatre of the Absurd, who found themselves unable to depict their characters following through with the act of suicide that would end their suffering. Esslin referenced Albert Camus's essay on Sisyphus who refuses to escape via suicide the cycle in which he pushes a rock up a hill, only to watch it fall back down again. By contrast, Kane's play, written in 1999 and performed for the first time in the Royal Court Jerwood Theatre Upstairs a year later, tells of the life of a character, or set of characters depending on how it is performed, suffering at the hands of the psychiatric establishment's medical gaze after having been diagnosed with psychosis. Like Sisyphus, who endlessly pushes a rock up a hill only to watch it roll down again, Kane's protagonist contemplates daily the act of suicide that she will commit at 4.48 in the afternoon. However, unlike Sisyphus, it is implied that the tortured protagonist of *4.48 Psychosis* fulfills her fantasy of suicide in the last moments of the play. She declares to the audience "watch me vanish" and "please open the curtains" (42-43) letting in a flood of light that often symbolizes the moment of death in Western culture.[3]

4.48 Psychosis and its theme of feminine psychosis are evocative of Beckett's *Not I*, which I analyzed in chapter three. I am not the first to draw attention to the parallels between Beckett's and Kane's work. Cornwell compares her previous play *Crave*, which depicts four voices discussing their experience prior to rape and sexual abuse, to the negativity of Beckett's *Play* and *Waiting for Godot* (Cornwell 297-298). I build on this by stating that *4.48 Psychosis* demonstrates the real-life consequences of women's experience of psychosis in a way that *Not I* does not. Mouth of *Not I* is only able to voice the fact that she is suffering, and she only anchors her torment implicitly in her gender. Kane's protagonist, by contrast, explicitly speaks of the oppression she must endure at the hands of a male psychiatric establishment:

> Dr This and Dr That and Dr Whatsit who's just passing and thought he'd pop in to take the piss as well. Burning in a hotel tunnel of dismay, my humiliation complete as I shake without reason and stumble over words and have nothing to say about my "illness" which anyway amounts only to knowing that there's no point in anything because I'm going to die. And I am deadlocked by that smooth psychiatric voice of reason which tells me there is an objective reality in which my body and mind are one. But I am not here and never have been. Dr This writes it down and Dr That attempts a sympathetic murmur. Watching me, judging me, smelling the crippling failure oozing from my skin, my desperation clawing and all-consuming panic drenching me […]. (7)

The protagonist evokes the male hegemony behind the construction of reason, pervasive in Western culture since the Age of Enlightenment, which "deadlock[s]" her. She inhabits a place of irrationality that has been gendered as female since the same time period. She demonstrates concrete patriarchal power divides as a corollary of the binary opposition between male reason and female unreason. She experiences a "crippling" sense of failure. Beckett's Mouth, meanwhile, is only able to communicate a sense of alienation – a leitmotif of Absurdism – and it is up to spectators to actively work to deduce that such alienation is disproportionately punitive because she is a woman. Taking Mouth's rejection of feminine vulnerability implicit in *Not I*'s refrain "what?…who?…no!…she!…" to

---

[3]   References to the play in the text will be to the following edition: Sarah Kane. *4.48 Psychosis*. London: Methuen Drama, 2002.

a much more explicit level for the spectator, Kane's protagonist dreams of "resist[ing] coercion and constriction" (21) of the three male nurses "twice her size" (21) who restrain her. She envisions casting free of her gender as a "broken hermaphrodite who trusted hermself" (3).

Kane also articulates the all-too-feminine nature of self-destruction. While Mouth is unable to do anything but labor on in auto-destructive failure, Kane's protagonist laments her habitual experience of self-sacrifice, describing: "I have been dead for a long time" (12). The character confesses to never having "had a problem giving another person what they want. But no one's ever been able to do that for [her]" (13). She also quips that the only way for her to live in this world is through the act of being deadened in medicalization: "Okay, let's do it, let's do the drugs, let's do the chemical lobotomy, let's shut down the higher functions of my brain and perhaps I'll be a bit more fucking capable of living" (19). *4.48 Psychosis*'s final act of suicide, however ethically fraught, is framed in this need for liberation from the gendered norms that restrict the protagonist. She needs an act of self-destruction more radical than the gender-normative self-sacrifice expected of her in life. But Kane does not demonstrate this in any sense that abstracts her voice and identity from proceedings. Contrary to her Absurdist forebears, Kane's protagonist promises to take "abstraction to the point of / unpleasant / unacceptable / uninspiring" (19).

This "unpleasant[ness]" is made all too real if we consider the authorial voice that haunts this piece. In many ways, *4.48 Psychosis* may be considered a protracted, theatrical suicide note penned by Kane before she killed herself, particularly if we reflect on the circumstances behind the publication of the play. After writing the first draft of *4.48 Psychosis* Kane sent the manuscript to her editor Mel Kenyon asking the latter to read and correct it as soon as she could. They spent an afternoon together revising it days before Kenyon learned of Kane's hospitalization for attempted suicide. Two days later, Kenyon went to visit Kane in hospital where she learned that the author had hanged herself. Kenyon received the revised manuscript of *4.48 Psychosis* that same day (Pousseur "*4.48 Psychose*, Sarah Kane"). Kane's text is also littered with allusions to the author's real-life plan to kill herself. Her protagonist reflects, "[t]hey will love me for that which destroys me / [...] the sickness that breeds in the folds of my mind" (11). These words hint at an awareness on the part of the author that she would be remembered for her text, romanticized in death for what made her most suffer in life. The protagonist in fact adamantly refuses theatrical abstraction. In response to a voice telling her that the idea that her "mind wants to die" is nothing but a metaphor, she retorts: "It's not a metaphor, it's a simile, but even if it were, *the defining feature of a metaphor is that it's real*" (my emphasis) (9). A further inflection of the author's subsequent actions insinuates itself as one of the voices in *4.48 Psychosis* states, "Nothing will interfere with your work like suicide" (19). This conveys, via a rather macabre sense of humor, an acknowledgement that this would be Kane's last work.

Kane's play, understood as a suicide note, might be deemed to rescue Absurdism from the charge of white male abstractions on the real-life suffering of those around them. *4.48 Psychosis* constantly reminds spectators of the heroine's and author's pain at the hands of a male-dominated world. Read as a suicide note, Kane's text resembles James Harding's interpretation of second-wave radical Valerie Solanas and her decision to shoot pop art darling Andy Warhol in 1968. Harding posits that Solanas's act, committed in the aftermath of Warhol callously losing Solanas's play *Up Your Ass*, literally "makes good" on the premise of her *S.C.U.M. Manifesto*, published one year prior (Harding, "The Simplest Surrealist Act" 144). *S.C.U.M. Manifesto* agitates for women's violent, even murderous, overthrow of male rule: "Life in this society being, at best, an utter bore and no aspect of society being at all relevant to women, there remains to civic-minded, responsible, thrill-seeking females only to [...] destroy the male sex" (Solanas 35). Connecting the attempted murder of Warhol to *S.C.U.M. Manifesto* allows Harding to interpret the shooting as a performance, restoring Solanas to her rightful place in a history of American experimental performance. This is instead of dismissing the shooting as nothing more than the act of a crazed woman as critics have been wont to do. Kane, similarly, may be understood as making good on the premise of *4.48 Psychosis*, turning her subsequent suicide into an aesthetic act itself. This is another way of reading Peter Bürger's theory that the avant-garde fused art and the "praxis of life" (Bürger 54). In fulfilling the premise of *4.48 Psychosis* in real-life, Kane enacted the ultimate vanguard coup in which the barrier between theatre and reality is eroded.

But this has been a book that has added its voice to critiquing, not supplementing, Peter Bürger's theory of the avant-garde. Aesthetic experimentalism has overdetermined the social politics of avant-garde movements, something confirmed by Bürger's theory that vanguard politics lie in the way aesthetic innovation may be fused with "praxis of life". Bürger's theory is most troubling in the context of a discussion of Kane, since the implication is that in order to be political, the vanguard work necessitates someone's violent death.[4] To help us out of this bind, the politics of Absurdism uncovered in this book, which has separated social subversion from aesthetic innovation, can elucidate matters. It enables us to re-read post-Absurdist texts such as *4.48 Psychosis* in a less ethically fraught light where the radical gesture is not contingent on the author's suicide.

A comparison of the French production of *4.48 Psychosis*, starring Isabelle Huppert, with Beckett's *Not I* elucidates ways that a rejection of the discourses on women and psychosis may be stressed in viewing, for instance. Huppert was the first to introduce Kane's play to French audiences when she debuted at the Bouffes du Nord in Paris in 2002. The production was directed by Claude Régy and in many ways resembled Beckett's *Not I*. Although spectators could see the whole of Huppert, unlike Mouth's reduction to a vocal orifice, she was dressed simply in a dark blue t-shirt and dark trousers, hinting that spectators were not supposed to remark greatly on her body except to chalk the performer's small frame up to Kane's protagonist's confession of anorexia. Much like Mouth, Huppert was almost immobile in a "stage of near paralysis" throughout the performance exhibiting a "bravura feat of negative athleticism [that] gives savage expression to her character's unyielding intent to make her body implode" (Baron Turk 159) as American author Edward Baron Turk recalled, watching the New York reprisal at the Harvey Theatre at the Brooklyn Academy of Music (BAM) in October 2005.

Huppert's version of Kane's suffering protagonist further recalled the feverish rate at which Beckett's Mouth spits out words in *Not I*. As Baron Turk remembers,

> At first, Huppert's slow monotone and ultraprecise articulation of discrete syllables suggested a digitally simulated voice. Soon the voice exhibited mounting anger against the ogling, diagnosing shrinks who forever claimed to have "secret knowledge of my aching shame". At the scene's climax it rose to a loud and tormented gooselike honk: as if throwing back judgment on those who dared to judge her, the protagonist repeated, "SHAME, SHAME, SHAME. Drown in your fucking shame". Later in the piece, Huppert

---

4   Bürger's theory of the fusion of aesthetics and the praxis of life in his theory of the avant-garde has been nowhere more contentious than in the classification of 9/11 as an avant-garde act. See Mike Sell. *The Avant-Garde: Race, Religion, War.* Chicago: University of Chicago Press, 2012, 8.

accelerated to an astonishing velocity as her character detailed, fiendishly and caustically, the drugs she received or administered to herself on the sly. (Baron Turk 160)

With Huppert's "acceler[ation] to an astonishing velocity" recalling Mouth's lightening speed of recital in *Not I*, *4.48 Psychosis* may take inspiration from the Beckettian precursor and the social politics discovered in this book. I suggested that fast, intense address in *Not I* occasions spectators' experience of the Lacanian "enigmatic void". This enigmatic void enables spectators' rejection of the play's presentation of the white woman (Mouth) who wields power over a woman of color, Auditor. Audience members of Kane's play may be persuaded to jettison the images presented before them in *4.48 Psychosis* – notably the feminization of mental illness that Kane's protagonist embodies. Kane's protagonist could work up, for instance, to the speed of reigning *Not I* champion Lisa Dwan in the Walter Asmus production. Indeed, a reduction of Kane's protagonist to a mouth, in an emulation of Beckett's *Not I*, may help to stress the torment and terror of the experience of psychosis for audience members without inviting their pity and objectification of the heroine. As Kane's character herself implores to spectators, "Stop judging by appearances" (27). Productions of *4.48 Psychosis* therefore might borrow from the Beckettian capacity to draw the spectator into the same tortured experience as the heroine herself. A reproduction of the enigmatic void in Kane's play could lead spectators to reject the male medical establishment that dismisses women as crazy, which is lamented in the text.

A reproduction of Beckettian visual and acoustic intensity is certainly not something that the text of *4.48 Psychosis* rules out as the text lacks any kind of stage directions. However, productions need to strike a balance. They need to establish *4.48 Psychosis*'s links to real-life suffering and disempowerment, something which *Not I* risks eluding, perhaps even acknowledging openly Kane's suicide. Meanwhile they need to foster the spectator's deconstruction of the misogynist discourses framing women's madness, showing it as a construction that can be denaturalized. The spectator's experience of the enigmatic void furnishes us with one way to denaturalize the ideology of women's madness. Productions that maintain a balance between reminding spectators of women's real-life suffering at the hands of the male medical establishment and denaturalizing the ideology that women are perforce more "crazy" than men would successfully avoid the Theatre of the

Absurd's tendency toward abstractionism. In this way, a conversation between a past avant-garde and the next might successfully be instated, and "borrowing and appropriation" might occur in tandem with "destruction, and reconstruction" (Sell 204). The contents of this book will aid that conversation not only in the case of Sarah Kane, but also Margaret Hollingsworth, Cuban-American Maria Irene Fornés, and others who have or will be recovered as part of the post-Absurdist canon.

Works Cited

Abagond. "The Sapphire Stereotype," March 7, 2008, https://abagond. wordpress.com/2008/03/07/the-sapphire-stereotype/.

Ahmed, Sara. *Queer Phenomenology: Orientations, Objects, Others*. Durham: Duke UP, 2006.

Ahmed, Sara. *The Cultural Politics of Emotion*. Edinburgh: Edinburgh University Press, 2004.

Alexander, Michelle. *The New Jim Crow: Mass Incarceration in the Age of Colorblindness*. New York: New Press, 2010.

Alter, Nora. *Vietnam Protest Theatre: The Television War on Stage*. Bloomington: Indiana University Press, 1996.

Anderson, Andrew Woodruff. "The Violence of Identity Construction in French and Francophone Absurdist Theatre." Ph.D. dissertation, The Ohio State University, 2011.

Angelou, Maya. *The Heart of a Woman*. Grangemouth: Hachette Digital, 2010 (1981).

Anon. "Arrabal ne mordra plus les spectateurs," *La Tribune de Genève*, December 23, 1969.

Anon. "The Blacks: A Clown Show," http://www.christophermcelroen.com/ the-blacks-a-clown-show/.

Artaud, Antonin. *The Theater and its Double*, trans. by Mary Caroline Richards. New York: Grove Press, 1958 (1938).

Auden, W.H. *Plays and Other Dramatic Writings by W.H. Auden and Christopher Isherwood*. Ed. Edward Mendelson. Princeton: Princeton UP, 1988.

Baron Turk, Edward. "Isabelle Huppert; or, The Gallic Valkyrie Who Bewitched Brooklyn," *Camera Obscura* 65: 22 (2007), 158-165.

Barthes, Roland. *Critical Essays*, trans. Richard Howard. Evanston: North Western UP, 1972.

Bassichis, Morgan *et al.* "Building an Abolitionist Trans and Queer Movement with Everything We've Got." Ed. Eric Stanley and Nat Smith.

Captive Genders: Trans Embodiment and the Prison Industrial Complex. Oakland: AK Press, 2011, 15-40.

Bennett, Michael Y. *The Cambridge Introduction to the Theatre and Literature of the Absurd.* Cambridge: Cambridge UP, 2015.

—. *Reassessing the Theatre of the Absurd: Camus, Beckett, Ionesco, Genet and Pinter.* New York: Palgrave, 2011.

Bentley, Eric. *Thinking About the Playwright: Comments From Four Decades.* Evanston: NorthWestern UP, 1987.

Berghaus, Günter. *Avant-garde Performance: Live Events and Electronic Technologies.* Basingstoke: Palgrave Macmillan, 2005.

Bergson, Henri. *Laughter: An Essay on the Meaning of the Comic.* Rockville: Arc Manor, 2008.

Binder, Galia. "*And They Put Handcuffs on the Flowers* by Fernando Arrabal," *Buffalo News*, June 8, 2008, http://www.subversivetheatre.org/productions/handcuffs_flowers/afterward.htm.

Bishop, Tom. "Whatever Happened to the Avant-Garde?," *Yale French Studies* 112 (2007), 7-13.

Brater, Enoch. *Beyond Minimalism: Beckett's Late Style in the Theatre.* Oxford: Oxford UP, 1987.

Bürger, Peter. *The Theory of the Avant-garde.* Manchester: Manchester University Press, 1984 [1974].

Butler, Judith. *Gender Trouble: Feminism and the Subversion of Identity.* London: Routledge, 1990.

Camus, Albert. *The Myth of Sisyphus and Other Essays.* New York: Vintage, 2012 [1942].

Cano Vara, Cristina. "Beckett's *Not I* vs. del Amo's *Yo no*: Some Notes on Cultural Translation," *Studies in Theatre and Performance*, 25 (2005), 23-32.

Chalaye, Sylvie, *et al.* "Les représentations du Noir au théâtre." Conference on October 16, 2007. Recording available via Conférences de la Bibliothèque nationale de France. Paris: Bibliothèque nationale de France, 2007.

Chaudhuri, Una. *No Man's Stage: A Semiotic Study of Jean Genet's Major Plays.* Ann Arbor: UMI Research Press, 1986.

Chong, Denise. *The Girl in the Picture: The Remarkable Story of Vietnam's Most Famous Casualty.* London: Scribner, 2001.

Connell, R.W., and W. Messerschmidt, James. "Hegemonic Masculinity: Rethinking the Concept," *Gender & Society* 19 (2005), 29-59.

Copjec, Joan. *Read My Desire: Lacan Against the Historicists.* Cambridge, MA: MIT Press, 1994.

Cornwell, Neil. *The Absurd in Literature.* Manchester: Manchester UP, 2006.

Cox, Lara. "The Curious Case of *La Cantatrice chauve*: Re-thinking the death of the avant-garde," *French Cultural Studies* 24 (2013), 104-115.

Crenshaw, Kimberlé. "Mapping the Margins: Intersectionality, Identity Politics, and Violence Against Women of Color," *Stanford Law Review* 43 (1989), 1241-1299.

Cummings, Lindsay B. *Empathy as Dialogue in Theatre and Performance.* Basingstoke: Palgrave, 2016.

de Certeau, Michel. *The Writing of History.* New York: Columbia University Press, 1988 [1975].

Dean, Tim. *Beyond Sexuality.* Chicago: University of Chicago Press, 2000.

DeBenedetti, Charles, *An American Ordeal: The Antiwar Movement of the Vietnam Era.* Syracuse: Syracuse University Press, 1990.

Dent, Gina. "Black Pleasure, Black Joy: An Introduction." Ed. Gina Dent. *Black Popular Culture.* Seattle: Bay Press, 1992, 1-19.

Derksen, Celeste. "A Feminist Absurd: Margaret Hollingsworth's *The House that Jack Built*," *Modern Drama* 45 (2002), 209-30.

Dolan, Jill. *The Feminist Spectator as Critic.* Ann Arbor: University of Michigan Press, 1988.

Dupont, Guy. "Pour participer au spectacle d'Arrabal, j'ai dû mettre une cagoule," *France Soir*, September 10, 1969.

Dwan, Lisa. "Beckett's *Not I*: How I became the Ultimate Motormouth," *Guardian*, May 8, 2013, http://www.theguardian.com/culture/2013/may/08/beckett-not-i-lisa-dwan.

Ekotto, Frieda. *Race and Sex Across the French Atlantic: The Color of Black in Literary, Philosophical, and Theatre Discourse.* Plymouth: Lexington Books, 2011.

Esslin, Martin. "The Theatre of the Absurd Reconsidered," in *Reflections: Essays on Modern Theatre.* New York: Anchor Books, 1971, 179-186.

–. *The Theatre of the Absurd.* 3rd edn. London: Penguin, 1980 (1961).

Farmer, R.L. "Fernando Arrabal's Guerrilla Theatre," *Yale French Studies* 46 (1971), 154-166.

Finburgh, Clare and Bradby, David. *Jean Genet.* London: Routledge, 2012. Kindle Edition.

Fischer, Eileen. "The Discourse of The Other in *Not I*: A Confluence of Beckett and Lacan," *Theatre* 10 (1979), 101-03

Franklin, Bruce. "'Vietnam' in the New American Century." Ed. Jon Roper. *The United States and the Legacy of the Vietnam War.* Basingstoke: Palgrave Macmillan, 2007, 33-50.

Freedman, Barbara. "Frame-up: Feminism, Psychoanalysis, Theatre," *Theatre Journal* 40 (1988), 375-397.

Freeman, Elizabeth. *Time Binds: Queer Temporalities, Queer Histories.* Durham: Duke UP, 2010. Kindle edition.

Frese Witt, Mary Ann. *Metatheater and Modernity: Baroque and Neo-baroque.* Plymouth: Rowman & Little, 2013.

Freud, Sigmund. "Splitting of the ego in the process of defense," in *The Standard Edition of the Complete Psychological works of Sigmund Freud.* London: Hogarth Press and the Institute of Psychoanalysis, 1939, Vol. 23.

–. "'Psycho-analytic Notes on an Autobiographical Account of a Case of Paranoia' (Dementia Paranoids)," in *The Standard Edition of the Complete Psychological works of Sigmund Freud.* London: Hogarth Press and the Institute of Psychoanalysis, 1911, Vol. 12.

Galey, Mathieu. "Un Théâtre qu'on porte au nu," *Les Nouvelles littéraires,* October 8, 1969.

–. *"Off Limits* d'Arthur Adamov: Pâteuse Fin de Partie," *Combat,* January 27, 1969.

Gallop, Jane. "Beyond the *Jouissance* Principle," *Representations* 7, Summer (1984), 110-115.

Gamman, Lorraine, and Makinen, Merja. *Female Fetishism: A New Look.* London: Lawrence & Wishart, 1994.

Garde-Hansen, Joanne. *Media and Memory.* Edinburgh: Edinburgh UP, 2011.

Gatten, Brian. "The Posthumous Worlds of *Not I* and *Play,*" *Texas Studies in Literature and Language* 51 (2009), 94-101.

Gaudy, René. "La Pièce d'Arthur Adamov *Off Limits* au Piccolo Teatro de Milan," *L'Humanité*, February 26, 1969.

Gautier, Jean-Jacques. "*Off Limits*," *Le Figaro*, January 27, 1969.

Glass, Loren. *Counterculture Colophon: Grove Press, the Evergreen Review, and the Incorporation of the Avant-garde*. Stanford: Stanford UP, 2013.

—. "Absurd Imprint: Grove Press and the Canonization of the Theatrical Avant-Garde," *Modern Drama* 54 (2011), 534-561.

Gough-Yates, Anna. *Undermining Women's Magazines: Publishing, Markets and Readerships*. London: Routledge, 2003.

Grosz, Elizabeth. *Space, Time, and Perversion: Essays on the Politics of Bodies*. New York: Routledge, 1995.

Halberstam, J. Jack. *Gaga Feminism: Sex, Gender, and the End of Normal*. Boston: Beacon Press, 2012.

—. *The Queer Art of Failure*. Durham: Duke UP, 2011.

—. *Female Masculinity*. Durham: Duke UP, 1998.

Hall, Donald and Jagose, Annamarie (eds.). *The Routledge Queer Studies Reader*. London: Routledge, 2013.

Hall, Don. "Theatre Review: And They Put Handcuffs on the Flowers," February 10, 2009, http://donhall.blogspot.fr/2009/02/theatre-review-and-they-put-handcuffs.html.

Hansberry, Lorraine. *Les Blancs: A Drama in Two Acts*. New York: Samuel French, 1972.

—. *To Be Young, Gifted and Black: An Informal Autobiography of Lorraine Hansberry*. New York: Signet, 1970.

Harding, James. *The Ghosts of the Avant-Garde(s): Exorcising Experimental Theatre and Performance*. Ann Arbor: The University of Michigan Press, 2013.

—. *Cutting Performances: Collage Events, Feminist Artists, and the American Avant-garde*. Ann Arbor: University of Michigan Press, 2010.

—. "The Simplest Surrealist Act: Valerie Solanas and the (Re)Assertion of Avantgarde Priorities," *The Drama Review* 45 (2001), 142-162.

Hayman, Ronald. *Theatre and Anti-Theatre: New Movements since Beckett*. London: Martin Secker & Warburg Ltd, 1979.

Hensel, Georg. "La beauté de la haine," A Press Release for Peter Stein's *Die Nieger*, 1984. Available in the Archives des Arts du Spectacle at the Bibliothèque nationale de France.

Hill Collins, Patricia. *Black Feminist Thought: Knowledge, Consciousness, and the Politics of Empowerment.* New York: Routledge, 2000 [1990].

Hinchliffe, Arnold. *The Absurd.* London: Methuen & Co., 1969.

Hollywood, Amy. *Sensible Ecstasy: Mysticism, Sexual Difference and the Demands of History.* Chicago: University of Chicago Press, 2002.

Innes, Christopher. *Avant-garde Theatre 1892-1992.* London: Routledge, 1993.

Ionesco, Eugène. *Notes & Counter Notes.* London: John Calder, 1964.

Jannarone, Kimberly. *Artaud and His Doubles.* Ann Arbor: University of Michigan Press, 2010.

Jeffers, Jennifer. *Beckett's Masculinity.* New York: Palgrave, 2009.

Kant, Immanuel. "An Answer to the Question: What is Enlightenment," in *An Answer to the Question: What is Enlightenment.* London: Penguin, 2009, 1-11.

Knapp, Bettina. *Off-stage Voices: Interviews with Modern French Dramatists.* Troy: Whitston Publishers, 1975.

Knowlson, James, and Pilling, John. *Frescoes of the Skull: The Later Prose and Drama of Samuel Beckett.* London: J. Calder, 1979.

Kooijman, Jaap. *Fabricating the Absolutely Fake: America in Contemporary Pop Culture.* Amsterdam: Amsterdam UP, 2013.

Kruger, Loren. "Ritual Into Myth: Ceremony and Communication in *The Blacks*," *Critical Arts* 1 (1980), 59-69.

Kubiak, Anthony. *Agitated States: Performance in the American Theatre of Cruelty.* Ann Arbor: University of Michigan, 2002.

Kunzel, Regina. *Criminal Intimacy: Prison and the Uneven History of Modern American Sexuality.* Chicago: University of Chicago Press, 2008.

Lacan, Jacques. *Ecrits.* New York: W.W. Norton & Company, 2006.

–. *On Feminine Sexuality, The Limits of Love and Knowledge: Book XX Encore 1972-1973.* New York: W.W. Norton & Company, 1998.

–. *The Seminar of Jacques Lacan: Seminar II, The Ego in Freud's Theory and in the Technique of Psychoanalysis 1954-1955.* New York: W.W. Norton & Company, 1991.

–. *De la psychoses paranoïaque dans ses rapports avec la personnalité.* Paris: Seuil, 1975.

–. *Desire and its Interpretation 1958-1959: Seminar VI,* http://www.lacaninireland.com/web/?page_id=123, 310.

–. *Séminaire III: Les Psychoses.* Unpublished seminar, 1955-1956.

Lamble, Sarah. "Transforming Carceral Logics: 10 Reasons to Dismantle the Prison Industrial Complex Through Queer/Trans Analysis and Action." Ed. Eric Stanley and Nat Smith. *Captive Genders: Trans Embodiment and the Prison Industrial Complex.* Oakland: AK Press, 2011, 235-265.

LaMont, Hillary Ione. "The Existence of Dualistic Absurdism: Presented by Albert Camus and Generatively Absented by Edward Albee." Ph.D. dissertation, Indiana University of Pennsylvania, 2012.

Lamont, Rosette. "The Nouvelle Vague in French Theatre," *The Massachusetts Review,* 5 (1964), 381-396.

Lane, Anthony. "Chatterbox," *The New Yorker,* September, 2014, http://www.newyorker.com/magazine/2014/09/29/chatterbox.

Lavery, Carl and Finburgh, Clare (eds.). *Rethinking the Theatre of the Absurd: Ecology, the Environment and the Greening of the Modern Stage.* London: Bloomsbury, 2015.

Lavery, Carl. "Between Negativity and Resistance: Jean Genet and Committed Theatre," *Contemporary Theatre Review,* 16, No. 2 (2006), 220-234.

Lewy, Guenter. *America in Vietnam.* Oxford: Oxford UP, 1979.

Loayza, Daniel, and Wilson, Robert. "Pour moi tout théâtre est danse: Entretien avec Robert Wilson," *Odéon: Le Magazine,* March 6, 2014, http://www.theatre-odeon.eu/fr/le-magazine/2014/09/pour-moi-tout-theatre-est-danse.

Lorde, Audre. *Sister Outsider: Essays and Speeches.* Berkeley: Crossing Press, 2007 (1984).

Madral, Philippe. "Un Univers torturé: *Off Limits,* d'Arthur Adamov," *L'Humanité,* January 27, 1969.

Mann, Paul. *The Theory-death of the Avant-garde.* Bloomington: Indiana University Press, 1991.

Mars-Jones, Adam. "Not I," *London Review of Books,* 36: 5 (2014), 22.

McCarthy, Gerry. "On the Meaning of Performance in Samuel Beckett's *Not I,*" *Modern Drama,* 33 (1990), 455-469.

McGuire, Danielle. *At The Dark End of the Street: Black Women, Rape, and Resistance – a New History of the Civil Rights Movement from Rosa Parks to the Rise of Black Power.* New York: Vintage Books, 2010.

McRobbie, Angela. *The Aftermath of Feminism: Gender, Culture, and Social Change.* London: SAGE, 2009.

Miller, Judith G. "Reviewed work(s): *The Theatre of Fernando Arrabal: A Garden of Earthly Delights* by Thomas J. Donahue," *Substance*, 9: 28 (1980), 92.

Mogul, Joey, *et al. Queer (In)justice: The Criminalization of LGBT People in the United States.* Boston: Beacon Press, 2011. Kindle Edition.

Mohanty, Chandra Talpade. "Under Western Eyes: Feminist Scholarship and Colonial Discourse," *boundary 2* 12-13 (1984), 333-358.

Mulvey, Laura. *Visual and Other Pleasures.* 2nd edn. London: Palgrave Macmillan, 2009 (1975).

Olivier, Jean-Jacques. *"Et ils passèrent des menottes aux fleurs*, d'Arrabal," *Combat*, February 10, 1969.

Phelan, Peggy. *Unmarked: The Politics of Performance.* London: Routledge, 1993.

Pizzato, Mark. "Genet's Violent, Subjective Split into the Theatre of Lacan's Three Orders," *Journal of Dramatic Theory and Criticism* 5 (1990), 115-30.

Plunka, Gene A. *The Rites of Passage of Jean Genet: The Arts and Aesthetics of Risk Taking.* Cranbury: Associated University Presses, 1992.

Poggioli, Renato. *The Theory of the Avant-garde.* Cambridge, MA: Harvard University Press, 1968.

Pough, Gwendolyn. "Love Feminist but Where's My Hip Hop?: Shaping a Black Feminist Identity." Ed. Daisy Hernández and Bushra Rehman. *Colonize This! On Today's Feminism.* Berkeley: Seal Press, 2002, 85-98.

Pousseur, Isabelle. "*4.48 Psychose*, Sarah Kane," *Théâtre Océan Nord*, http://www.oceannord.org/4-48-Psychose-55.

Prasso, Sheridan. *The Asian Mystique: Dragon Ladies, Geisha Girls & Our Fantasies of the Exotic Orient.* New York: Perseus Running, 2005.

Pruner, Michel. *Les Théâtres de l'absurde.* Paris: Armand Colin, 2005 (2003).

Puar, Jasbir K., and Rai, Amit S. "Monster, Terrorist, Fag: The War on Terrorism and the Production of Docile Patriots," *Social Text* 72, 20: 3 (Fall 2002), 117-48.

Puar, Jasbir. *Terrorist Assemblages: Homonationalism in Queer Times*. Durham: Duke UP, 2007.

Sandman, Jenny. "*The Blacks: A Clown Show* – A Curtain Up Review," http://www.curtainup.com/blacks.html.

Sartre, Jean-Paul. "Mythe et réalité du théâtre." Ed. M. Contat and M. Rybalka. *Un théâtre de situations*. Paris: Gallimard, 1992 (1973).

Scarlat, Cristina. "Le Spectacle comme forme de résistance: Eugène Ionesco, Jean-Luc Lagarce et *La Cantatrice chauve*," *Philologica Jassyensia*, 14 (2011), 353-361.

Schwenkel, Christina. *The American War in Contemporary Vietnam: Transnational Remembrance and Representation*. Bloomington: Indiana University Press, 2009.

Sedgwick, Eve Kosofsky. *Epistemology of the Closet*. Berkeley: University of California Press, 1990.

Sell, Mike. *The Avant-Garde: Race, Religion, War*. Chicago: University of Chicago Press, 2012.

–. *Avant-Garde Performance and Material Exchange*. Basingstoke: Palgrave, 2011.

–. *Avant-garde Performance and the Limits of Criticism: Approaching The Living Theatre, Happenings/Fluxus, and the Black Arts Movement*. Ann Arbor: University of Michigan Press, 2005.

Serano, Julia. *Excluded: Making Feminist and Queer Movements More Inclusive*. Berkeley: Seal Press, 2013.

Smith, Caleb. *The Prison and the American Imagination*. New Haven: Yale UP, 2009.

Solanas, Valerie. *S.C.U.M. Manifesto*. London: Verso, 2004.

Spade, Dean. *Normal Life: Administrative Violence, Critical Trans Politics, and the Limits of Law*. Durham: Duke UP, 2015.

Swanson, Roy. "Ionesco's Classical Absurdity," in *The Two Faces of Ionesco*. Ed. Rosette Lamont and Melvin Friedman. Troy, N.Y.: Whitston, 1978, 130-136.

Tasker, Yvonne and Negra, Diane (eds.). *Interrogating Postfeminism: Gender and the Politics of Popular Culture*. Durham: Duke University Press, 2007.

Taylor, Valerie. "How You Can Fight Cultural Appropriation," *Eri Dansa in Blog*, April 30, 2017, https://nativeapples.wordpress.com/2017/04/30/how-you-can-fight-cultural-appropriation/.

Thompson, Debby. "'What Exactly Is a Black?': Interrogating the Reality of Race in Jean Genet's *The Blacks*," *Studies in Twentieth Century Literature* 26 (2002), 395-425.

Vanden Heuvel, Michael. *Performing Drama/Dramatizing Performance: Alternative Theatre and the Dramatic Text*. Ann Arbor: University of Michigan Press, 1991.

Waite-Jones, Asher. "Review of *Queer (In)Justice: The Criminalization of LGBT People in the United States* by Joey L. Mogul, Andrea J. Ritchie & Kay Whitlock," *Berkeley Journal Of Gender, Law & Justice*, 30 (2015), 182-197.

Warden, Claire. *British Avant-Garde Theatre*. New York: Palgrave, 2012.

Westheider, James E. *The African American Experience in Vietnam: Brothers in Arms*. Plymouth: Rowman & Littlefield, 2008.

White, Edmund. *Genet*. London: Chatto and Windus, 1993.

Whitelaw, Billie and Ben-Zvi, Linda. "Billie Whitelaw, interviewed by Linda Ben-Zvi." Ed. Linda Ben-Zvi. *Women in Beckett: Performance and Critical Perspective*. Urbana: University of Illinois Press, 1990, 3-10.

Whitelaw, Billie. *Who He? An Autobiography*. London: Hodder & Stoughton, 1995.

Wilkerson, Margaret B. "*Les Blancs*: A Critical Background." Ed. Robert Nemiroff. *Les Blancs: The Collected Last Plays*. New York: Vintage, 1994, 27-36.

Wilson, Ann. "'Her Lips Moving': The Castrated Voice of *Not I*." Ed. Linda Ben-Zvi. *Women in Beckett: Performance and Critical Perspective*. Urbana: University of Illinois Press, 1990, 190-200.

Winfrey Harris, Tamara. "Ain't I a Woman: Making Black Women's Lives Matter," *Fusion*, May 11, 2015, http://fusion.net/story/132822/making-black-womens-lives-matter/.

Worthen, W.B. *Modern Drama: Plays, Criticism, Theory*. Fort Worth: Harcourt Brace College Publishers, 1995.

Wulf, Catharina. *Imperative of Narration: Beckett, Bernhard, Schopenhauer, Lacan*. Brighton: Sussex Academic Press, 1997.

Zinman, Toby Silverman. "Hen in a Foxhouse: The Absurdist Plays of Maria Irene Fornes." Ed. Enoch Brater and Ruby Cohn. *Around the Absurd: Essays on Modern and Postmodern Drama*. Ann Arbor: The University of Michigan Press, 1991, 203-220.

Zupančič, Alenka. *The Odd One In: On Comedy*. Cambridge, MA: MIT, 2008.

—. *The Shortest Shadow: Nietzsche's Philosophy of the Two*. Cambridge, MA: MIT Press, 2003.

Index

DRAMATURGIES

Texts, Cultures and Performances

This series presents innovative research work in the dramaturgies of the twentieth and twenty-first centuries. Its main purpose is to re-assess the complex relationship between textual studies, cultural and/or performance aspects at the dawn of this new multicultural millennium. The series offers discussions of the link between drama and multiculturalism (studies of "minority" playwrights — ethnic, Aboriginal, gay, and lesbian), reconsiderations of established playwrights in the light of contemporary critical theories, studies of the interface between theatre practice and textual analysis, studies of marginalized theatrical practices (circus, vaudeville, etc.), explorations of emerging postcolonial drama, research into new modes of dramatic expressions and comparative or theoretical drama studies.

The Series Editor, **Marc MAUFORT***, is Professor of English literature and drama at the Université Libre de Bruxelles.*

Series Titles

No. 32 – Gerald Gillespie, *Ludwig Tieck's* Puss-in-Boots *and Theater of the Absurd. A Commentated Bilingual Edition*, 2013, ISBN 978-2-87574-026-7

No. 31 – Julie Vatain, *Traduire la lettre vive. Duos anglais sur la scène française*, 2012, ISBN 978-2-87574-012-0

No. 30 – Ève Feuillebois-Pierunek (dir.), *Théâtres d'Asie et d'Orient. Traditions, rencontres, métissages*, 2012, ISBN 978-90-5201-847-8

No. 29 – Thierry Dubost (ed.), *Drama Reinvented. Theatre Adaptation in Ireland (1970-2007)*, 2012, ISBN 978-90-5201-800-3

No. 28 – Dorothy Figueira and Marc Maufort (eds.), with the assistance of Sylvie Vranckx, *Theatres in the Round. Multi-ethnic, Indigenous, and Intertextual Dialogues in Drama*, 2011, ISBN 978-90-5201-690-0

No. 27 – Sébastien Ruffo, *Jeux d'acteurs comparés. Les voix de Belmondo, Depardieu, Lebeau et Nadon en Cyrano de Bergerac*, 2011, ISBN 978-90-5201-657-3

No. 26 – Catherine Bouko, *Théâtre et réception. Le spectateur postdramatique*, 2010, ISBN 978-90-5201-653-5

No. 25 – Marc Maufort, *Labyrinth of Hybridities. Avatars of O'Neillian Realism in Multi-ethnic American Drama (1972-2003)*, 2010, ISBN 978-90-5201-033-5

No. 24 – Marc Maufort & Caroline De Wagter (eds.), *Signatures of the Past. Cultural Memory in Contemporary Anglophone North American Drama*, 2008, ISBN 978-90-5201-454-8

No. 23 – Maya E. Roth & Sara Freeman (eds.), *International Dramaturgy. Translation & Transformations in the Theatre of Timberlake Wertenbaker*, 2008, ISBN 978-90-5201-396-1

No. 22 – Marc Maufort & David O'Donnell (eds.), *Performing Aotearoa. New Zealand Theatre and Drama in an Age of Transition*, 2007, ISBN 978-90-5201-359-6

No. 21 – Johan Callens, *Dis/Figuring Sam Shepard*, 2007, ISBN 978-90-5201-352-7

No. 20 – Gay McAuley (ed.), *Unstable Ground. Performance and the Politics of Place*, 2006 (2e tirage 2008), ISBN 978-90-5201-036-6

No. 19 – Geoffrey V. Davis & Anne Fuchs (eds.), *Staging New Britain. Aspects of Black and South Asian British Theatre Practice*, 2006, ISBN 978-90-5201-042-7

N° 18 – André Helbo, *Signes du spectacle. Des arts vivants aux médias*, 2006, ISBN 978-90-5201-322-0

No. 17 – Barbara Ozieblo & María Dolores Narbona-Carrión (eds.), *Codifying the National Self. Spectators, Actors and the American Dramatic Text*, 2006, ISBN 978-90-5201-028-1

No. 16 – Rachel Fensham, *To Watch Theatre. Essays on Genre and Corporeality*, 2009, ISBN 978-90-5201-027-4

No. 15 – Véronique Lemaire, with the help of/avec la collaboration de René Hainaux, *Theatre and Architecture – Stage Design – Costume. A Bibliographic Guide in Five languages (1970-2000) / Théâtre et Architecture – Scénographie – Costume. Guide bibliographique en cinq langues (1970-2000)*, 2006, ISBN 978-90-5201-281-0

No. 14 – Valérie Bada, *Mnemopoetics. Memory and Slavery in African-American Drama*, 2008, ISBN 978-90-5201-276-6

No. 13 – Johan Callens (ed.), *The Wooster Group and Its Traditions*, 2004, ISBN 978-90-5201-270-4

www.peterlang.com